PET LIBRARY'S

Complete Dog

Guide

PET LIBRARY'S

Complete Dog Guide

by Frances Sefton

England

THE PET LIBRARY LTD

The Pet Library Ltd., Subsidiary of Sternco Industries Inc., 600 South Fourth Street, Harrison, N.J. Exclusive Canadian Distributor: Hartz Mountain Pet Supplies Limited, 1125 Talbot Street, St. Thomas, Ontario, Canada. Exclusive United Kingdom Distributor: The Pet Library (London) Ltd., 30 Borough High Street, London S.E. 1.

Printed in the Netherlands

ISBN 0-87826-445-0

Table of Contents

Index of Dog Breed Pictures

Earl Sherwan

AKE WINTZELL

Affenpinscher

This is a very old European breed. It is also known as the "Monkey Dog" because of its quaint expression. Height at the shoulder: under 10 inches. Registered by the American Kennel Club in the "Toy" group.

I   The History and Origins of the Dog

With Dogs It's Different

Where there are people there are dogs. Whether they are stray dogs roaming the alleys of an eastern town, sheepdogs in mountain pastures, or purebred toy dogs living luxuriously in a modern western city, dogs undoubtedly like to be near people.

People like dogs too. They like them for all sorts of reasons — because they do a good job for them, guarding their homes and property, herding their livestock, keeping down vermin, or hunting and retrieving game. People like a dog because he's fun to be with, a good companion to share a game, a walk, a warm fire, and a friendly creature who thinks his human master is just great.

The bond between man and dog is a unique relationship. There is no other quite the same between man and his other domesticated animals. Man keeps sheep and cattle, ducks and chickens because they are useful in providing food, but the deep friendship, the reliance on one another, is not there. The horse perhaps builds up some relationship with his human master, but with rare exceptions it isn't real friendship — mostly it is based on trainability through physical contact with man, and on the reward of sugar and oats. Horses are basically still wild animals at heart — they don't particularly want a human friend.

Cats come and go in the human home; sometimes they get very fond of their human friends, but however long the cat lives with people, it retains its independence. Its devotion is based mainly on an appreciation of the food and warmth that it gets from man. If they go, so does the cat. It too remains basically a wild animal, but one intelligent enough to appreciate that food and shelter can come the easy way. Nevertheless, if it has to, it is perfectly capable of leading an independent existence.

Children keep hamsters, rabbits, pigeons, rats and mice and even insects as pets — but the devotion is usually more on the human side than the animals'.

With dogs, it's different. The affection between man and dog is mutual. We love 'em as much as they love us.

Yet for all this close companionship, this mutual devotion which has existed for such an incredibly long time, we know very little about the hisory and origins of the dog. To give him a scientific label, the dog is a member of the genus *Canis*.

We know, from fossils mostly, that the dog's immediate ancestors probably existed about half a million years ago.

Early Origins

Nobody really knows for sure, but it is thought that the history of the dog began, in a remote sort of way, as long ago as 40 million years. There was a small family of carnivores (meat-eaters) then called *Miacidae*.

The *Miacidae* family had two descendants, one called *Daphaenus*, which eventually gave rise to the bears. The other was called *Cynodictis,* and was a smaller creature. From this creature there eventually evolved a dog-like animal called *Tomarctus,* which is thought to be the ancestor of dogs, wolves and jackals.

In the past it was often believed that the wolf and the jackal were the ancestors of the dog. All three are scientifically classified as being in the *Canis* family, but is has now been accepted by some authorities, that, though they are related, they are all separate off-shoots of *Tomarctus.* Other authorities hold that our dogs are descendants of the wolf.

Of course it is a long way from *Tomarctus,* the granddaddy of them all, to the modern dog that we know. *Tomarctus* had descendents. They developed differently in different places. Thousands of years went by, and sometime during this period man-like creatures met dog-like creatures.

All of this is unrecorded, and the sparse information available is based mostly on the evidence of geologists and archeologists working from fossilized remains.

They can give an approximate date for a type of prehistoric dog living domestically. It is placed between 6,000 and 3,000 B.C. A portion of the remains of a dog of no specific breed were found buried next to the remains of a woman on the coast of Zeeland.

There have also been archeological discoveries of domesticated dogs in Switzerland and in several other places, all prehistoric.

From this authorities conclude that dogs must have been domesticated in other parts of the world during those periods. As evolution takes such a long time, it is reasonable to suppose dogs must have been living in some kind of association with man many thousands of years before that.

They say that domestication could have taken place any time from 50,000 to 250,000 years ago. This would make the dog a very old friend indeed.

Man and Dog Meet

How did man and dog become associated in the first place?

Since we've agreed it must have happened long before the time of recorded history, we can only guess. Both primitive man and primitive dog were hunters. Their paths must have crossed sometime or another. Perhaps man on one of his hunting expeditions caught a dog and used it for food — and kept on hunting it.

Maybe primitive man came across a female dog with puppies at some time, took them home to his cave or hole and kept them because he found that they could be fattened up for better eating. Perhaps playing outside the cave one day, Junior, primitive man's son and heir, and his baby sisters found that the puppies romped and played rather attractively, and primitive man and his wife watched indulgently.

Somehow, somewhere, perhaps in several places in the world around about the same time, primitive man discovered that the dog was more than just another wild animal to be hunted, killed and eaten.

He discovered that instead of being a rival on the hunt for food, the dog would go along and help. He discovered that the dog would make a noise, giving warning when danger approached. He discovered that the young of dogs were attractive play companions for his own young, that if the puppies grew up in the human encampment they became friendly and affectionate.

The dog too probably discovered that food was easier to come by in the vicinity of humans. The odd bone that primitive man threw over his shoulder when he'd finished with it probably gave primitive dog hours of pleasurable chewing. Perhaps a chance incident like that was the first step ever in animal training — the first time mankind discovered that there were ways other than killing to bring an animal under control.

Why the dog should be willing to stay near man instead of running away as all other animals would do is one of those freaks of nature. It is a freak that has paid good dividends to both.

AKE WINTZELL

Afghan Hound
Originating in the Sinai Penninsula, this regal dog spread throughout the Far East. Used as a guard and hunter, today he is valued as a companion and for show. Height at the shoulder: male 27 to 29 inches—female 24 to 26 inches. Registered by the A.K.C. in the "Hound" group.

How the Breeds Originated

We've already said that either *Tomarctus,* the dog-like animal, or the wolf was probably the ancestor of the true dog, which is known scientifically as *Canis familiaris. Canis familiaris* developed into various forms, and on the chart on page 20 you will see the different types of the dog that scientists have been able to classify. The earliest date that can be put to a specific type is about 4000 B.C., which is the date given to the remains of *Canis familiaris palustris* which were found around the Swiss Lakes.

Any of the various types of *Canis familiaris* could be earlier or later. Nobody knows for certain. Perhaps in the future more archeological searches will turn up new evidence that will tell us more.

Otherwise, the furthest back we can go is to the beginning of recorded history, which is 4000 to 3000 B.C. There is evidence that a greyhound type of dog like the Saluki, and a Mastiff type were in existence then. There are representations of them both on an ancient green slate tablet which was found at Thebes and dates back to 4000 B.C.

On some tombs of ancient Egypt, dating back to 2200 to 2000 B.C., there are depicted hunting hounds of the Saluki type, as well as a heavier, mastiff-like dog, and a hunting dog with prick ears and a tightly curled tail not unlike a bigger, longer bodied Basenji. These tombs also show some dogs shorter in the legs and with thicker coats. There is a dark-coated one with a tassled tail, and another with a spotted pattern marking and a curled tail.

Nature herself must have caused the first variations in dogs to develop.

All dogs started off as hunters, but they would hunt different kinds of prey, depending on where they lived. Where the natural animals of the area were fast moving creatures, then the dog would have to develop the kind of body that would move even faster — like the lean sight hunting breeds of the greyhound type who can spot a moving object a long way away and chase it at terrific speed.

Where the natural animals lived in dense cover, in forests, with plenty of undergrowth, then the hunting dog would need to have a good tracking nose to seek out his food. Where the prey lived in burrows underground, the dog after his dinner would need to have not only a good nose but the instinct to dig down into the ground. Dogs hunting big animals would need to be bigger and fiercer to combat their adversaries.

Airedale Terrier

Often called the "King of the Terriers," he is the largest member of that group. Bred in England as a working and water dog, the Airedale is unsurpassed as a guard and companion. Height at the shoulder: male 23 to 24 inches — female 22 to 23 inches. Registered by the American Kennel Club in the "Terrier" group.

SALLY ANNE THOMPSON

Climate too would make a difference. Dogs living in the cold parts of Northern Europe and North America would need thick, dense coats to survive the icy conditions. Dogs that lived in thick forests and jungles would need to be smooth coated because a long coat would tangle in the undergrowth. Dogs in hot climates would develop short coats for coolness.

Man and dog teamed up, as we have seen, and man found that the dog could be useful. Eventually he would discover that the different kinds of dog could do different jobs. So man started to dabble in the development of the dog. He kept some kinds of dogs for hunting, some for guarding his property.

As man grew more civilized and started to keep animals around his encampment to raise for food instead of having to go out and hunt for meat all the time, he discovered that dogs could be used to guard his livestock, and then to herd them for him.

Gradually, under man's guidance, physical qualities and qualities of temperament and character began to be developed and fixed.

Some of the different breeds were beginning to appear.

Most of these early dogs had a natural length of nose and width of head. Quite early in the history of dogs, however, another kind of dog appeared. This is the dwarf. This does not mean a miniature. The proportions of any miniature are exactly like the bigger version, only the size varies. A true dwarf, however, is quite different. The limbs and body are foreshortened and malformed, giving an abnormal appearance. How these dwarfs first appeared is not known. It was probably by what is called mutation. Mutations are one of the mysteries of nature — they just happen. Very little about how and why they happen naturally is known.

Enough of these dwarfs survived, and produced their own kind, to influence the varieties of dogs. How long it took we do not know, but there are signs of dwarfed ancestry in any breed which has crooked front legs, loosened folds of skin, squashed-up face, and very broad, domed skulls.

Man has of course encouraged some of these features, mostly perhaps because they appealed to him. Man has mixed them up and introduced them in to other breeds. As a result you have such varying kinds of dog as the Bloodhound, the Boxer, the Bulldog, the Basset Hound, the Welsh Corgi, the Pug, the Pekinese, the Japanese Spaniel, and many more, all of which show some signs of having "dwarf" characteristics, perhaps introduced a long, long way back in their ancestry. Small dogs like the Pekingese are the most obvious examples of an almost complete dwarf dog, deliberately bred that way by man.

Dogs like the Chihuahua and the Miniature Pinscher and the Toy

Alaskan Malamute   AKE WINTZELL

The origin of this dog is lost in antiquity. From time immemorial it has been used to draw sleds and as a beast of burden. Dignified in manner, the Malamute is fond of children. Height at the shoulder: male to 25 inches—female smaller. Registered by A.K.C. in the "Working Dog" group.

Poodle are not dwarfs. They are midgets — miniatures — exact replicas of their bigger relatives. Small specimens occur in any living thing, including people. In dogs, man has deliberately encouraged the miniature and "bred down" to it.

As man continued to develop his civilization, he continued to create new breeds of dogs to suit his various needs. Man also moved about the world more easily, and dogs moved with him so that dogs from different kinds of places were interbred. Some kinds of dogs became extinct; new kinds were created. Some kinds of dog remained basically the same for thousands of years.

It is thought that there are at present between 400 and 500 distinct breeds of dog in the world. In another hundred years there might be more or less. Many of them are man-made. The dog has come a long way from old *Cynodictus*. He probably still has a long way to go. In all that changing, one thing has remained unchanged, and that is the strength of the dog's unique relationship with man.

The Dog at Work

We've seen that the earliest work the dog did, some thousands of years ago, was to work alongside primitive man, first in hunting, then as watchdog, guard of his master's property, home and livestock, and later in herding his livestock.

Very early in their history dogs were also a form of food and in some parts of the world they were raised, and still are raised, to provide meat.

Throughout the centuries, the dog's usefulness to man has extended, until today it reaches very sophisticated and advanced forms.

Hunting dogs can be classed among the oldest. In ancient Babylonia, and in the Egypt of the Phahaohs, they were highly valued for this. They include the "sight-hounds" — fast greyhound types; the "scent-hounds" — heavier and slower, and usually hunted in packs or groups. Getting nearer to modern times the short-legged terriers and small breeds like the Dachshund, which go to earth and drive the prey above ground for the scent-hounds to kill; and finally the sporting dogs, the pointers and setters, the retrievers and spaniels, all of whom assist man by finding and retrieving, while their master does the actual killing with his gun.

The guarding dogs are almost as old as the hunters. They defend their master and his property. Mostly they are big breeds, starting

American Water Spaniel
A crossing of the Irish Water Spaniel with the Curly-Coated Retriever. Height at the shoulder: male 15 to 18 inches—female 14 to 16 inches. Registered in the "Sporting Dog" group.

EVELYN M. SHAFER

Australian Terrier
A sturdy little terrier, bred from various crossings of native British terriers brought to Australia by emigrants. His popularity is proliferating as his outstanding qualities as a housedog are increasingly recognized. Height at the shoulder: about 10 inches. Weight: 12 to 14 pounds. Registered by the American Kennel Club in the "Terrier" group.

SALLY ANNE THOMPSON

with the Molossus of olden times, developing into the Mastiff, the massive sheep-guarding kinds like the Komondor, and the heavy coated dogs of the Greek mountains. Many of these dogs that guard sheep from the roving wolves and other predators are white, with coats that resemble a sheep's wool, and are very fierce.

Guard dogs generally, though, are not uncontrollable, vicious animals. To make the best use of them mankind had to temper their fierceness and power with intelligence. Powerful guard dogs have always had the reputation of never attacking on sight, but only when the intruder interferes with their master's property, his master's person, or attacks the dog himself.

The culmination of man's efforts in breeding this kind of dog is seen in the modern guard dog, the wonderfully trainable German Shepherd dog, and the supremely efficient Doberman Pinscher.

In early times, the massive guard breeds were used in actual battle. Big and fierce, they were made even more ferocious looking with spiked collars, and they were protected by special suits of armor. Dogs were used for fighting as late as the 16th and 17th centuries.

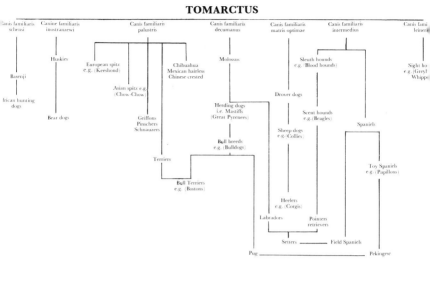

TOMARCTUS

Canis familiaris scheusi · Canine familiaris inostranzewi · Canis familiaris palustris · Canis familiaris decumanus · Canis familiaris matris optimae · Canis familiaris intermedius · Canis familiaris leineri

Huskies · European spitz e.g. (Keeshond) · Chihuahua Mexican hairless Chinese crested · Molossus · Sleuth hounds e.g. (Blood hounds) · Sight hounds e.g. (Greyhounds, Whippets)

Basenji · Asian spitz e.g. (Chow-Chow)

African hunting dogs · Bear dogs · Griffons Pinschers Schnauzers · Herding dogs i.e. Mastiffs (Great Pyrenees) · Drover dogs · Scent hounds e.g. (Beagles) · Spaniels

Bull breeds e.g. (Bulldogs) · Sheep dogs e.g. (Collies)

Terriers · Toy Spaniels e.g. (Papillons)

Bull Terriers e.g. (Bostons)

Heelers e.g. (Corgis)

Labradors · Pointers retrievers

Setters ——— Field Spaniels

Pug ——————————— Pekingese

PRUDENCE WALKER

The relationship and origin of the different breeds.

The modern war dog is a different type — his value lies not just in his size and fierceness but primarily in his intelligence. In World War I, and later with even greater success in World War II and in the Korean War, dogs were trained for sentry duty, for scout work, for messenger duty, for patrol work, and as sled and pack dogs. With their marvelous olfactory abilities they were particularly successful in things like mine detection!

Modern war dogs don't need to be as massive as their ancient Mastiff predecessors. Mostly they have been German Shepherds, Doberman Pinschers, Giant Schnauzers, Airedales, farm Collies, even Dalmatians.

At home, the shepherding and droving dogs did, and still do, provide wonderful service to their masters. There are the Collies of various kinds, the cattle dogs like the Australian Kelpies and the little Welsh Corgi, among others.

Some heavy breeds of dogs can draw light carts, and they were used for this on the continent of Europe a lot at one time, although in recent years that use has declined. The dogs of the Arctic, the sled dogs like the Huskies and Samoyed, still work in harness in snowy wastelands.

Less obvious in its usefulness is the dog's value as a companion. The first men who kept the first dogs probably didn't rate this aspect very high, but certainly from the time history began to be recorded there is evidence that people found joy in the company of a dog.

Cheops, the great Egyptian pyramid builder, left sculptures of his favorite hound, as did other Egyptian Pharaohs. So it went on over the centuries, as many literary works and works of art reveal. In the books and pictures of the famous there often appears a beloved dog. Today newspapers frequently feature heart-rending stories about a boy and his dog, or a picture of the Queen of England or the President of the United States with canine companions.

Perhaps the most selfless and honorable work that the dog has ever done for the human race is the work of the Seeing Eye dogs, as they are called in the U.S.A., or Guide Dogs for the Blind in other parts of the world.

These intelligent and sensitive dogs are virtually the eyes of their blind master or mistress. Using a specially designed harness, they will guide their human charges unerringly and safely through busy streets, heavy traffic and congested sidewalks. They give their master or mistress confidence in strange places and buildings, and they are taught not only to respond to the commands of their masters but also to substitute their own initiative and judgment if necessary to insure the blind person's safe conduct.

Of course a strong bond of affection grows between sighted dog and blind master or mistress, perhaps the closest ever in the associated history of dog and man. It is so strong and devoted, that the only heart-breaking part about it all is when the dog gets too old to carry on.

Using dogs to guide the blind was first begun in earnest by the Germans after World War I. Now it has become world-wide. Guide dogs are usually spayed females, and they must be of impeccable temperament. The breed that was first used was the German Shepherd dog. Labrador and Golden Retrievers and other breeds are now proving increasingly popular.

Basenji
From Central Africa, the Basenji is known as the "barkless dog". A clean-limbed, all-around hunting dog with great courage and a keen sense of smell. Height at the shoulder: male 17 inches—female 16 inches. Registered by the American Kennel Club in the 'Hound" group.

SALLY ANNE THOMPSON

II The Dog — Sacred and Secular

Even in our highly advanced civilization dog owners frequently credit their pet dogs with mysterious powers, "He knows there's a storm coming up; he sits and whines on the porch." Or, "The house would have burned down around us if it hadn't been for that dog. He wouldn't rest, kept trying to make us go out back..."

Such remarks and incidents are not unusual as any random glance at a newspaper or magazine will confirm. The dog's behavior may sometimes seem strange, uncanny, almost mysterious, but with our scientific knowledge and modern studies of animal behavior and physiology, we can readily make a reasonable explanation. Most of the time anyway!

We know, for instance, that two of the dog's senses — in particular, his hearing and his sense of smell — are far more acute and highly developed than the human equivalent, and this may give him prior warning of impending danger. Primitive man did not have the advantage of our greater knowledge, so any odd behavior from his dog that could not be easily explained was regarded with something like awe, perhaps even fear. Each incident would grow in the telling, and, eventually, become a legend, a myth.

It is only a step then to endow the dog with supernatural powers, until he becomes part of an accepted superstition and then of religion.

This did indeed happen right from very early times. In some primitive societies all dogs were regarded as having powers unknown to man, while in others, only certain were so endowed. The more elaborate the civilization, the more complex became the religious trappings of the canine race. As demons and deities, in rites, rituals, sacrifices, and as bearers of good and of evil, dogs were a formidable element in the religious beliefs of the world.

Oddly, apart from a few scattered intervals during thousands of years, only in one important period of history was the dog not given religious significance, and in fact, was barely tolerated in everyday life. This was the time of the three influential religions that began and spread from the Eastern Mediterranean — the religions of the Hebrews, the Mohammedans, and the Christians. The dog was no object of worship, endowed with no supernatural powers, but an "unclean" animal, regarded with contempt and tolerated only for its usefulness. The days of the Old Testament and early Christianity were the days of the dog's deepest degradation, and in the Western world it was only as the centuries passed that his qualities of fidelity and loyalty have raised his status again to something other than a lowly slave.

Still something lingers of the old lowliness, in speech, for instance, when the term "dog" is still used in a derogatory sense. But generally the dog in modern times has found a balanced place in society.

What a contrast to some of the ancient civilizations! The Aztecs and the Mayans made stone idols of dogs, and worshipped them. The ancient Egyptians, too, built graven images to Anubis, the dog-headed god, who was held in great esteem. They named an important star for the dog. The lives of most of the people of Egypt depended on the annual flooding of the river Nile to fertilize vast areas around the river so that they could grow crops and keep their pastures rich. Every year, the impending flood was heralded by the appearance in the sky of a very bright star, and when the peasants saw this star they would move their flocks of sheep and goats to higher ground and wait for the life-giving advancing waters. The star which they watched for so anxiously, they called Sirius, the Dog Star.

So valued was the dog and so much part of Egyptian life that, when dogs died, they were given special ceremonial burials, and were mummified as were their masters.

The esteem with which the Egyptians regarded the dog has proved very useful historically to cynologists, who study the dog. There are many statues, carvings, and other representations of the dog — many of them accurate in detail, dating back five or six thousand years, and these are a valuable record of the types of dogs of that period and the kind of jobs they did. They are a great help in tracing back the origins of the various types and breeds.

The Chinese too, from earliest times, made a great deal of the dog. They believed in dog demons and thought that the thunder and heavenly disturbances, such as comets and meteors, were the signs that the heavenly dogs of *Tien-kow* were coming down to earth.

As the Emperor of China became more and more identified with holiness and godliness, the dogs played an even more important part in Chinese life. The little pet dogs of the Royal Palaces became sacred.

They were regarded as the protectors of the faith and of the Imperial person. The dog was believed to change its form from dog into lion, and this symbolized its powers of protection over the deified Imperial family! The little pet dogs became more and more lion-like in their appearance. Some were treated with such esteem that they were given titles and honors that would have been accorded to very high ranking officials. Only the Imperial Court was allowed to own these dogs, and any person found harming or disposing of a royal dog was instantly punished, sometimes by death.

Equal honor was paid to dogs in Japan too at one time. One of the Emperors, born under the celestial sign of the Dog, passed laws compelling his people to worship dogs, and special temples were built in their honor.

The idea of being descended from the dog is quite a common one. Several tribes of people in different parts of the world had this belief — the aboriginal tribes of southern China, of Formosa, Java, Sumatra, the Pacific Islands, Madagascar, and, of course, the Dog-rib Indians of Alaska.

The legend that explains the dog ancestry of this Alaskan tribe is rather charming. One of the first men on earth, an Indian, found a female dog in pup. When the puppies were born, he looked after them, and tied them in his tent when he went out hunting. Every time he came home he heard the noise of children's laughter, but he could never find any children, only the puppies. One day he pretended to go out, but hid nearby, and as soon as he heard the children laughing and playing, he rushed into the tent. There were dog skins on the floor, and the tent was full of children. He quickly burnt the dog skins, so that the children could not turn back into puppies. They then grew up as humans, and became the ancestors of the Dog-rib tribe.

The very qualities that make the dog such a good worker and companion to man, are the ones that have given rise to his use in religion. With his superior sense of smell and hearing, the dog warns his master of danger, and protects him and his property from harm. Thus the dog becomes a symbol of protection against all kinds of evil. Symbolism is an essential part of any religion. To Christians, for instance, the cross is a symbol of the supreme sacrifice of Jesus Christ, the basis of their faith.

Many primitive peoples, full of fear and ignorance, grasped at some symbol to drive away their fear of evil and bad luck, and chose the dog to protect them against the demons of the unknown. They did not always actually worship the dog or regard him as a god, although this was sometimes the case. Occasionally the dog is considered a sign of ill fortune or devastation, but nearly always as a token or talisman of good.

Just as a black cat has more significance generally than any other color, so color has some importance to the protective qualities of the dog. Nearly always, the most lucky, fortunate or powerful kind of dog is the white one. In China, and Japan too, color was very important. The blood of a white dog smeared around the gates and doors was said to keep away disaster. The Iroquois Indians had a great festival during which a white dog of marvelous temperament and ability was sacrificed to the Great Spirit as a symbol of their Loyalty. In Japan there was a belief that the hair of a white dog could cure illness.

The Chinese, too, always made a great point of the importance of color in a dog. The five-colored dog featured several times in superstition and legend, symbolized powerful qualities. The patterns on the royal dogs had great importance, and if a puppy was born with a white blaze on the forehead this was highly valued, as one of Buddha's thirty-two superior marks. In fact, much of the breeding of the pet dogs of the Imperial court was aimed at including some identifying links such as this with Buddha.

In contrast to the good qualities of the white dog and the sought-after markings on patterned dogs, the black frequently bodes only ill, particularly in European witchcraft. In Wales, the appearance of a black dog near the house of a person who was dying meant that the soul of that person was damned forever, whereas a white dog meant a soul saved. On the other hand, many times in primitive beliefs, a black dog had to be sacrificed to ward off bad luck, such as disease, drought and other disasters. Perhaps this was with the idea that the evil in the black dog had to be offered up before the deity, probably a fearsome one, would be appeased. This is in reverse to the usual practice, in which only the best and finest is considered fit enough to be sacrificed.

Dogs, alas, were often used in ritual sacrifice. The Huron Indians dedicated dogs to the war god so that he would support them in their battles. Other Indian tribes ate dog flesh before going to war, in the belief that the dog's courage would pass into them. Frequently this pre-battle feasting was done with great ritual, in some cases the bones and remains were carefully buried with the proper rites, quite different from the eating of dog flesh as a delicacy, a habit that was, and still is, common practice in many parts of the world.

Parts of the dog — teeth, ears, tails, blood, and so on — were used in religious rituals, or carried as talismans.

The ancient Greeks were among those relatively civilized peoples who believed in magical powers of protection vested in the dog. The idea that illness and disease would be transferred from humans to the dogs was very strong among them.

Because of the dog's special relationship from early times to mankind, it is inevitable that many stories should grow up around this. Man is an inveterate gossip, and he loves a good story. Actions and behavior on the part of his canine companion intrique, delight or puzzle him. He likes to tell his neghbor, sometimes with pride, sometimes with wonder.

Many legends are told of how dog and man first became firm friends. Two are rather charming. The first tells how God made Adam and Eve, but during the night they were eaten by a serpent. So He made them again, but again they were eaten by a serpent. God was extremely angry, so He made Adam and Eve again, and also made a dog to protect them. When the serpent came in the night, the dog ferociously drove the serpent away.

The other story is very ancient. God created the world and

everything in it. Man He made last of all, and He was very pleased with this creation. But man was very bad, and God got very angry with him, so angry that He caused a great rift to open in the earth cutting off man from all other animals. But the dog was so devoted to man that it leaped over the widening gap to join man. And the dog has been man's faithful friend and companion ever since.

The fidelity of dogs is honored in many tales. From the ancient world comes the tale of Ulysses' dog, Argus. When Ulysses went off to travel the world, Argus was left behind. Ulysses did not return for ten years, and when he did he came disguised as a beggar. Only one friend recognized him instantly — his old dog Argus. Argus was old and very weak, and almost dying, but managed to crawl toward his long-lost master. Trying to lick his hand, he died.

Even more touching is the legend of the Welsh Wolfhound, Gelert. This story reflects poorly on the untrusting soul of man. The story, like most legends, is based on fact, and the celebrated account of it is in a ballad by W. R. Spencer. The ballad relates how Llewelyn the Great, Prince of Wales, was presented with a magnificent hound by King John of England. Gelert, the hound, became a great favorite with the Prince, and always went with him on the hunt. One morning the hound refused to leave the castle, where the Prince's infant son was left alone. After a successful hunt, the Prince returned home, to be met at the castle door by Gelert, whose mouth and muzzle were covered with blood. The baby's bed was overturned. In a fury, believing that the wolfhound must have mauled or killed his son, Prince Llewelyn slew the dog — only to find the dead body of a huge wolf lying near where the boy, who was alive and well, had played.

Marie Antoinette's small pet dog followed its mistress when she was taken to prison. It waited faithfully for several outside, but its ultimate fate is not known. Nor is the fate known of the toy spaniel belonging to Mary Queen of Scots. When she went to her execution, her pet dog is reputed to have been hidden under her long skirts.

In the war in 1860 between China and the Western Powers, when the French and British marched on Peking and sacked the Summer Palace of the Imperial family, five small "lion dogs" were found guarding the body of the Emperor's aunt, who had committed suicide. Such fidelity to their mistress obviously attracted the foreign invaders and perhaps their ferocity too — for the little dogs looted from the Palace were the first members of the breed that we now know as the Pekingese in the Western world.

From the nineteenth century also comes the story of the little terrier that went climbing in the English Lake district with her master. The climber fell to his death, but the terrier stayed by the body for three months, living somehow, and giving birth to puppies during that time. She was eventually found by a shepherd.

A faithful dog of more modern times was the old Italian dog called Fido. Rain or shine, he would go at the same time every day to a bus stop and wait for the bus to arrive. He would sit patiently and watch all the passengers get off, and when his master did not come, would dejectedly go home. He didn'n know that his master would never return, that years before he had been killed in a wartime bombing raid. Fido's fidelity became well-known through television, and he was much loved. Even the Italian government acknowledged it with a special award.

The story of the dog that much later recognized and identified attackers who had harmed its master crops up over and over again.

One story dating back a couple of hundred years B.C., tells of a slave who was attacked and killed by some attackers, despite the efforts of his dog to protect him. The king of the country discovered the dog guarding the body, and took the animal back to his palace, and made quite a favorite of him. Some time later, when the king was parading his army, the dog suddenly attacked two soldiers. They confessed that they were guilty of the crime.

A similar story comes from the England of the seventeenth century. A dog was noticed regularly swimming to and from a small island in the River Thames. A local man followed the dog to the island one day, and was led to the body of a man who had obviously been murdered. After some months, the dog, now adopted by the man, was with his new master on the wharf when a strange boatman pulled in. You've guessed it — it was the man who had killed the man on the island, as the dog made clear! This story is factual. There are records of the man's trial, conviction and hanging for the crime.

The modern purveyors of dog stories are the movies and the television screen. Rin Tin Tin was but the first of many great dogs that became world-wide heroes through the movie screen. Many movies and television films tell real life stories of dogs and their courage, and their fidelity to man — some of the true stories being even more fantastic than the fictional ones.

Basset Hound

The name "Basset" comes from the French word *Bas*, meaning "low," but the only thing low about the Basset is his height. Originally bred to meet the need for less speedy hounds which could be followed on foot, the Basset today has made himself a place in the home because of his charm and good nature.

TOM CARAVAGLIA

Beagle

This merry little hound is noted for his ability to hunt rabbits. In fact, he is at times called the "rabbit hound". At ease whether in the field or in the home, this is one of the most popular breeds in America. The American Kennel Club recognizes two varieties: 13 inch for hounds not exceeding 13 inches in height, and 15 inch for hounds over 13 but not exceeding 15 inches in height. Registered by the American Kennel Club in the "Hound" group.

AKE WINTZELL

Bearded Collie

A working sheepherder from the Scottish-English border, it was near extinction until revived in the mid-50's. Height at the shoulder: male 20 to 24 inches—female 18 to 22 inches. Not registered by the American Kennel Club. Registered by the English Kennel Club. Affectionately known as the "Beardie."

Bedlington Terrier
The sheep-like appearance, enhanced by the typical clip, belie the innate toughness of fiber which characterizes this dog. Originally bred in England for ratting and vermin killing as well as for dog racing and dog fighting, his stylish appearance and assertive manner have won him a host of admirers.

AKE WINTZELL

III These are the Breeds

In the pages that follow, we give a brief written description and commentary on most of the dogs recognized by the American Kennel Club grouped according to the Club's six classifications. Only a few, the less common ones, are omitted. You will find pictures of all of these in this book. We have also included pictures of those breeds not described in the text as well as pictures of a number of breeds which have not as yet been granted registration privileges by the AKC.

Sporting Dogs

Brittany Spaniel

This is a European breed, recently introduced. A good all-around sporting dog, popular for hunting and field trials. Tail usually docked, but oddly, many Brittany Spaniels are born without tails! A rugged, strong dog, reaching up to 45 pounds and about 20 inches at the shoulder. Despite his strength and working ability, he is a sensitive dog, often highly prized as a family pet and requiring careful handling. He is at his best as the close companion of a hunter, or one person who will work him regularly.

Chesapeake Bay Retriever

The very name of the Chesapeake Bay Retriever has a historical ring about it. The story has it that the breed originated with two puppies rescued from a British brig which sank off Chesapeake Bay in the very early 1800's. The puppies grew up to be good retrievers and were bred with local Maryland dogs. They are a distinctive breed, fearless and hard-working, and superb in the water in all weathers. If you own one and have young children, you'll probably never lose a child in the water! The Chesapeake's coat is almost completely waterproof, as anyone who has ever had need to bathe one will vouch, and it protects them from icy water and brushwood. They have web-like feet and strange orange eyes. A very strong, active dog, usual retriever size — about 70 pounds.

Cocker Spaniel

The merry Cocker is one of the most attractive dogs there is. This, alas, has almost led to its ruination. Once one of the greatest of bird dogs, beloved by sportsmen to flush and retrieve, it was taken up in a big way on the show bench and as a popular pet. Consequently commercialization took over and injured the breed. Only now, when other breeds have passed it in the registration stakes, has the Cocker started to regain something of its former temperament.

Like all good gun dogs, the Cocker should have an easygoing disposition. Find one like that — and you're more likely to find it among those bred to work and not just for their looks — and you will have a most attractive, delightful companion dog.

The American Cocker is smaller than the English, up to about 28 pounds as against 35. The American is more "spanielly," the English more like a small Springer.

Cockers are active dogs. Without enough exercise and bathing they can get fat and smelly, especially as they grow older. As he is a natural retriever, it is easy to teach him to return a ball. Ten or fifteen minutes a day of this will keep him in fine shape. The coat needs regular clipping and grooming and the dead hair should be stripped.

Don't keep a Cocker or any bird dog alongside pigeons or doves, or the birds will never get any rest!

English Setter

An attractively coated dog — white with colored flecks — the

Belgian Sheepdog
These dogs have been used for sheeperding, in the European equivalent of our K-9 Corps and in police work. They are courageous and devoted companions. Height at the shoulder: male 24 to 26 inches—female 22 to 24 inches. Registered by the A.K.C. in the "Working Dog" group.

AKE WINTZELL

English Setter is one of the basic bird dogs. He is such a well-balanced dog in looks, ability and temperament that in years past he was bred into many of the British and North American bird dogs to improve their qualities. The English Setter is not as well known as the Irish, being appreciated mainly by sportsmen, yet as a companion dog he can be strongly recommended. His character is friendly and quiet, his silky coat is easily kept in trim – no complicated clipping is required, only simple stripping and occasional combing. He is an alert, intelligent, readily trained and well-mannered dog — a real gentleman of the canine world. The dog weighs about 60 pounds and stands about 25 inches in height.

English Springer Spaniel

Bigger than a Cocker — at 35 to 50 pounds — it is a bird dog that is becoming increasingly popular among sportsmen. It gets the springer part of its name from its habit of "springing" the gamebird — that is, flushing the bird out so that it rises into the air, ready for its master's gun. It will then retrieve the fallen bird. The Springer will work in water as happily as in its natural rough briar and undergrowth. Like all gun dogs, it needs a fair bit of exercising, and gets bored without work to do.

German Shorthaired Pointer

This dog combines both retrieving and pointing abilities. He is named "short-haired" to distinguish him from his lesser known cousin, the German Wirehaired Pointer. The country of origin is obvious. His great attraction for sportsmen is his versatility, because while he isn't a fast dog in the field, he is very workmanlike. The German Shorthaired Pointer is a good example of a dog created deliberately by man for a specific purpose. It is said that first the old Spanish Pointer was crossed with the Bloodhound to improve the scenting and trailing ability. Then a dash of Foxhound added some speed, but by this time the pointing ability needed a boost, so the English Pointer was bred in. After several generations of carefully selective breeding the dog was up to 70 pounds and 25 inches in height — a mild-mannered, efficient animal. His color is always liver, or liver combined with white, and his tail is docked.

Golden Retriever

The uninitiated might regard the Golden Retriever as a longer-coated relative of the Labrador. They have little in common in their ancestry, however, although both are retrieving dogs, and what is said later on for the "Lab" applies equally to the Golden, which has the edge on him for glamor, and comes in a rich variety of golden tones. A good one has the even temperament that all gun dogs should have and is easily trained. It weighs about 70 pounds. The coat needs regular grooming.

Irish Setter

Perhaps the most beautiful of all gun dogs. The glorious red color of his coat is almost indescribable. They come in two strains — those bred by people for the show bench. The specimens which are not up to show standard are sold as pets. The working strains have the best temperaments. He's bird dog so never forget that all flying things interest the Irish Setter. A dog of racy appearance, he is about 25 inches high and weighs about 60 pounds.

Bernese Mountain Dog
Fairly large, he is a guard and companion. Originally bred to assist with cattle drives; also used to draw carts. Very trainable. Height at the shoulder: male 23 to 27 inches—female 22 to 25 inches. Registered by the A.K.C. in the "Working Dog" group.

AKE WINTZELL

Black and Tan Coonhound.
A "bred-in-America" hound, he combines a mixture of Bloodhound and Foxhound. Extremely keen scented, he is valuable for working any animal customarily hunted by following a ground trail. Height at the shoulder: male 25 to 27 inches—female 23 to 25 inches. Registered by the American Kennel Club in the "Hound" group.

R. W. TAUSKEY

Labrador Retriever

One of the all-time best all-round dogs — he is a fine gun dog, perhaps not only the finest of retrievers, but a great companion too. His popularity is well deserved. He'll work in water or on dry land, he can stand any amount of hard going, and yet he'll settle on the rug or roll about with the kids with equal enjoyment. The "Lab" is alert, so he makes a good housedog; he responds superbly to all kinds of training, so you'll see him as guard dog, police dog, seeing eye dog, and obedience trial champion. But even if you don't want to work him you'll find him an easygoing obedient house and companion dog. Most owners love their "Lab" so dearly they keep him in the house despite his size — all 70 pounds of him. His only drawback is that being a working dog he needs a good bit of hard exercise. If you haven't the temperament to join him in it, then don't buy a "Lab"; it's unkind to allow him to get fat and lazy. "Labs" come in black or yellow. The blacks, with a fine sheen on their short, dense, water-repellent coats, are probably the flashiest.

Pointer

Let's say it from the start that Pointers, as a rule, are better as workers than as pets. They like to "point", that is, line up nose and body in a straight line in the direction of the game bird. Their tails are carried straight up. And a very impressive, exciting sight it is too. Perhaps it is as well that this breed has been encouraged mostly by sportsmen, or they might have lost the distinctive habit in the coziness of fireside domestication. Pointers are a smooth-coated breed, in lemon, orange, liver or black, all with white. They are supposed to have originated in Spain. They weigh 60 or more pounds.

Weimaraner

The "gray ghost" from Germany is a sporting dog which has a unique steel gray coat and gray or yellow ghost eyes. Bred and disciplined, so we are told, by the autocrats of the Weimar province in Germany some hundred years ago, the Weimaraner is a superb example of a breed in which only the best was considered good enough. At one time it was hard to get because enthusiasts guarded their breed's reputation zealously, but is now plentiful.

The Weimaraner may become one of the outstanding bird-hunting breeds. It is a fair pointer and retriever and it has impeccable manners — fairly easy to discipline and to train for obedience trials. It usually weighs 60 to 80 pounds and stands 25 inches at the shoulder.

Hounds

Afghan

The Afghan is a powerful, fast hound, very beautiful, with a long silky coat and an incurable desire to hunt. Give him an open space and he is off. He is one of the greyhound family, and as a breed type dates back some 4,000 years. He originates from the Northwest frontier area of India and the Afghanistan area. He is bold and courageous, but he is a one-man dog, and suspicious of strangers.

He is a big dog — about 60 pounds and 28 inches at the shoulder — needing plenty of exercise, with a glorious coat that needs grooming.

Think twice before you indulge in one if you live near other people's livestock, or in suburbia and can't give him the freedom he should have. But if you have the will to give him the exercise he needs, you couldn't ask for a more attractive companion.

American Foxhound

As old as the nation itself, the American Foxhound has always had highly placed sponsors. George Washington himself was a fox

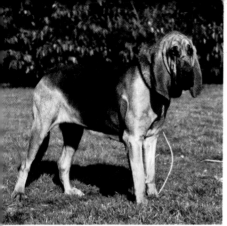

Bloodhound
His scenting ability so far surpasses that of all other breeds there can be no comparison. At heart, he is a gentle beast, friendly, wanting only to be loved. He is so reliable that his evidence is accepted in a court of law.

AKE WINTZELL

hunter. Packs of Foxhounds came to America in the 17th century, and since then have been bred by loving owners into several strains — Walker, Trigg, July, Birdsong and many more.

In 1966 the American Kennel Club placed the American Foxhound in 96th place in registrations. This is not a true indication of its popularity, however, as there are several other organizations which register hunting dogs so the actual number are immense. Several magazines are devoted to their welfare.

The Foxhound, whichever strain, is a handsome fellow. His big disadvantage as a companion dog is that he loves to hunt. Unlike Beagles and Bassets, they have not been exploited as a popular show bench and companion dog, and people who breed them aim to maintain their hunting instincts rather than improve their pet qualities. However, if you can accept and control this instinct, a Foxhound with his reliable temperament can make a fine companion.

Basenji

Everybody knows this one as the "barkless" dog. Actually, the noise he makes is a sort of chuckle. He can on occasion, when hurt, let out a piercing shriek. The natives fitted him out with thigh bells so that they could locate him as he trailed the prey. He's a hunting dog, and a very good one, from Africa, and his type can be seen on ancient Egyptian rock carvings from five thousand years ago.

His quietness and his cleanliness — Basenjis wash themselves like a cat does — make him a good choice as a companion dog. He is not large — about 30 ponuds of active, intelligent, easy to train, short-coated dog. His temperament is perhaps a little too alert for small children who've never had a dog before.

Border Collie

His intelligence and responsiveness must be seen to be appreciated. Height at the shoulder: male about 19 1/2 inches—female about 17 1/2 inches. The International Sheepdog Society in Australia and the North American Sheepdog Society in Wooster, Ohio, register these dogs.

Border Terrier

As his name implies, this doughty little terrier comes from the area of the Cheviot Hills, which form the border between England and Scotland. A hunting terrier, he was used for bolting the fox. Intelligent and obedient, he makes a fine housedog. Males weigh from 13 to 15 1/2 pounds, females 11 1/2 to 14 pounds. Registered by the American Kennel Club in the "Terrier" group.

AKE WINTZELL

SALLY ANNE THOMPSON

Borzoi

In Russia a dog must show his hunting ability before he can attain the title of Champion. Also known as the "Russian Wolfhound." Height at the shoulder: male 28 to 31 inches—female 26 to 29 inches. Registered by the American Kennel Club in the "Hound" group.

Basset Hound

This doleful looking hound makes a good house pet, though it must be remembered that a special characteristic of the breed is the voice, which is deep and resonant. He is a European hound and if you think that the ears and head, the voice and his exceptional scenting ability suggest he stems from the same ancestry as the Bloodhound, you are right.

A large dog, averaging 45 to 50 pounds, the Basset come is in tricolor (black, white and tan) and red and white. Occasionally one sees a blue tri color or a lemon and white. He is a slow but excellent hunter, docile and dignified by nature. In spite of his awkward appearance, he needs a lot of exercise. So bear this in mind if you're thinking of having one as a pet.

Dachshund

There's at least one "Dachsie" in every neighborhood. A cheerful busy personality, often laughed at for his odd, long-bodied, short-legged, low to the ground appearance, the Dachshund ranks among the first dozen of America's most popular dogs.

Did you know that there are at least six different varieties? There are smooth coated, all glossy and shining; the roughcoated with bearded chin; and the elegant longhaired, whose silky hair when red in color reminds one of the Irish Setter coat.

Then there are miniature versions — under nine pounds and preferably about six pounds — of all three coats, perhaps not so well-known in this country as in Europe. Germany also recognizes a toy variety — under six pounds. Though usually black and tan or red, occasionally one sees a dapple Dachshund. This is a basic blue with darker markings.

The AKC classification of the Dachshund as a sporting dog is incorrect; he is really a terrier. He should not be classified as a hound. *Hund* is German for dog and *Dachs* means Badger. This is the work he was originally bred for in Germany; to go into a burrow and "draw" the Badger — that's why he's the long low shape that he is. The miniature was bred for use in the burrows of smaller game.

But those folk who value him as a house dog and companion do well in their choice for he is an intelligent and playful fellow, and though he tends to fix his affections mostly on one person, he is loyal and protective to the whole family.

Boston Terrier

One of the few breeds developed in America, the name is derived from the area in which it originated. Smart, clean-limbed, alert and lively, there are few dogs which can equal the Boston as a gentleman and housedog. Males may weigh up to 25 pounds, females somewhat less. Registered in the "Non-Sporting Dog" group.

Bouvier des Flandres

A large, powerful dog from flanders and France, the Bouvier was developed to guard and drive cattle. He has seen duty with the army, the police and as an all-around utility dog. Height at the shoulder: male 27 1/2 inches—female somewhat less. Registered by the American Kennel Club in the "Working Dog" group.

AKE WINTZELL

Borzoi

Here is an aristocrat of great beaty, the Borzoi or Russian Wolfhound. The Borzoi represents all the elegance and ruthlessness of the Czarist Courts of long ago. The Russian royal family bred them specially for the hunting of wolves. The dogs, which are of the greyhound family, usually worked in couples, and a matched pair of these graceful long-coated dogs in full pursuit of their quarry must have been a sight to see. Dog shows in Russia even today require that the Borzoi show his ability to hunt.

The Borzoi's hunting ability is often matched against the coyote in the West, but nowadays he is much more appreciated for his beauty. Borzois are a favorite prop of photographers and many

Boxer

It is common practice in Germany and America to crop a Boxer's ears as a puppy. This practice has been made illegal in England, Holland, as well as in a number of other countries and is practiced less and less even where it is legal. The Boxer, as shown here with a natural ear, is one of the most picturesque of dogs.

Brabançon Griffon

One of the toy Griffon group which includes the more familiar Brussels Griffon. Unfortunately, not well-known in this country, the Brabançon is valued in Europe for his bouncing gaiety and good humor. Weighs under 10 pounds. Not registered by the American Kennel Club.

Briard

A powerful and vigorous herding dog from France. Originally known as "Sheepdogs of Brie" they are used, not only for herding sheep, but as police, war and guard dogs. Height at the shoulder: male 23 to 27 inches—female 22 to 25 1/2 inches.

branches of "showbiz". And they maintain their appeal as a glamorous companion dog and show bench star. They are usually thirty inches high and up to 100 pounds of elegant canine.

Bloodhound

With his extraordinary scenting ability and his use over the centuries as a man-tracking dog, plus his impressive appearance, the Bloodhound has earned an often exaggerated, almost supernatural, reputation.

His ancestral type dates back at least two thousand years, and hounds like him have served usefully all this time.

The Bloodhound is a gentle, affectionate creature and needs to be treated as such by his master. The word "blood" in his name does not refer to any propensity for seeking blood, but refers to the old English word "blooded", meaning pure bred. He does not deserve the fearsome reputation he has earned. However, that repuation can be used to advantage by anyone who wants a house dog whose very appearance will act as a deterrent to intruders. Provided one can accomodate 100 pounds of large dog, he makes a most loving companion and is ideal for a spacious surburban home because he is gentle with children and civilized in his behavior to other dogs.

Beagle

The merry little Beagle is an attractive dog, a favorite in many homes as a companion and pet. But he is not merely ornamental for he has a keen nose that puts him in the first rank as a hunting dog. He is primarily a rabbit dog, but he'll take on any upland game, squirrel or bird.

He is a tough dog and yet handy in size. Officially he is recognized in two distinct sizes: 14 to 15 inches at the shoulder and weighing about 25 to 30 pounds; 11 to 13 inches at the shoulder and weighing about 14 to 22 pounds. Unofficially there is a third size, under 11 inches or the "pocket Beagle." At 8 to 10 inches measured at the shoulder, this little fellow can weigh as little as 12 pounds. The smaller rabbit hound can be traced back to Tudor England — these are supposed to have been taken to the fields for a day's hunting in the panniers of horses' saddles.

Greyhound

Dogs of the greyhound type are represented among the earliest of all breeds. Originally a fast hunting dog prized in ancient Egypt five thousand years ago, it was bred for speed and keen sighting ability and is nowadays used primarily for coursing and racing. But its type, seen on ancient pottery, tomb carvings and decorative work, is unmistakable. The basic Greyhound has probably changed the least of any breed.

It comes in almost any color. The dog bred for the show bench is heavier — up to 70 pounds in weight — than the coursing and racing dog. It stands about 26 to 27 inches at the shoulder.

Irish Wolfhound

Probably the largest of all breeds — standing on his hind legs, this harsh-coated hound will dwarf a six foot man. Owning a pair of these would "Out Jones" any Joneses — providing one had the mansion, the estate, and the pocketbook to accomodate them.

The Irish Wolfhound, *Canis graius Hibernicus,* has a romantic history, replete with legend and fable. Royal dogs, used by the Irish kings to hunt elk and wolf, they became gift material to be exchanged between royal households, including the Court of the Czars.

You are perhaps more likely to see them in the show ring unless you live in timber wolf or coyote country, where they are used for serious hunting. They have the strength and courage to tackle big game, and like all good sporting dogs, have an even temperament despite their impressive looks.

The ideal dog should average 32 to 34 inches at the shoulder and weigh around 125 pounds. Usually grey, it can also be brindle, fawn, red, black or cream. One of the greyhound family, his closest relative is the smaller Scottish Deerhound.

Norwegian Elkhound

A breed from Scandanavia where it is known as the *grahund* (grey dog). It is a good all-round farm dog, used for hunting as well as herding. Elkhound is really a misnomer. The correct name is *Elghund. Hund* means dog and *Elg* means bear — the bear referring to the dog's appearance, not its prey.

Brittany Spaniel

Originally bred in France, the Brittany has ,sometimes been called the "Pointing Spaniel". A gentle breed, he is as much at home with the family as in the field. Height at the shouldder—male 17 1/2 to 20 1/2 inches—female somewhat smaller, Registered by the American Kennel Club in the "Sporting Dog" group.

The Elkhound is a strong, hardy dog, bold and energetic in temperament. He can gallop tirelessly for hours and miles. Aan alert dog, the ideal companion for an active owner living close to the wide open spaces, hills and beaches. About 20 to 21 inches at the shoulder, and up to 50 pounds in weight. A solid dog in varying shades of grey, with thick coat, pricked ears and a tail that curls tightly above his back. His temperament is gentle and kindly but fearless.

Saluki

Old in civilization, the Saluki is considered to be the originator of the Gaze Hounds. Its representation is found in ancient Persian art, and recorded in ancient Egypt at Hierakonpolis dating back to 3600 BC. A most elegant dog with long ear-fringes and feathered

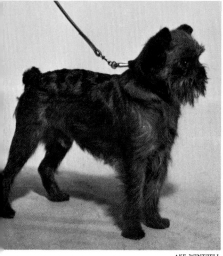
AKE WINTZELL

Brussels Griffon

The Griffons which were developed in Belgium and the surrounding area were based on the Dutch and German Affenpinscher, to which was added the Pug, the Belgian Streetdog and the Ruby Spaniel. In spite of their small size, they are sturdy dogs and cheerful companions, although slow to take to strangers. Weight: under 10 pounds.

tail, streamlined body and swift movement. Salukis are probably more ancient than recorded history can tell, for they are reputed to have reached the civilized Persian and Egyptian empires from the vast reaches of the Arabian desert, where the Arabs prized them for their speed and grace, and their ability to hunt the swift gazelle. Among Mohammedans the dog is considered an unclean animal, the one exception being the Saluki. He is the only dog permitted to enter the tent of the Sheik.

Salukis were first taken to Europe by the Crusaders. The American Kennel Club recognized them as a pure breed in 1927!

A Saluki dog can be anywhere from 23 to 28 inches at the shoulder and weigh up to 60 pounds. The females are smaller. The coat is silky and the most frequent colors are white, cream, fawn, golden, red — though tricolor and black and tan also appear.

Whippet

A product of necessity, a greyhound in miniature, he was bred by English miners who wanted a small racing dog. They combined small Greyhounds, toy Italian greyhounds, and added a dash of terrier — some say Manchester, some Bedlington, and some of the now extinct English White.

As a breed it is about one hundred years old. Whippets look like delicate cretures but they are not. Their extremely powerful jaws earned them the name of "Snap Dog" at one time. They have a fantastic turn of speed over sprint distances — up to 35 miles an hour. Friendly and affectionate in temperament, quiet by nature, Whippets make excellent housedogs. They range in weight from 10 to 28 pounds, and are about 18¹/₂ inches in height.

Working Dogs

Alaskan Malamute

One of the Spitz type dogs of the Arctic regions, the Alaskan Malamute developed as a distinctive type among Eskimos living on the Pacific coast of Alaska. The Malamute people were "high type" and their dogs equally so.

The Alaskan Malamute is an exceptional sled dog, and his strength, skill and stamina have often been proved under real conditions with Arctic expeditions and sled dog racing competition.

Like all Spitz dogs, he has a proud carriage, heavy doublecoat, prick ears and tail carried over the back. He is a big dog — weighing up to 80 pounds, and standing 25 inches at the shoulder. Usually black, wolfish grey, with white, the Alaskan Malamute has distinctive, attractive face markings.

Boxer

Everybody knows the Boxer — he's an outstanding guard dog, and popular family dog. At least he should be. Unfortunately, many people who buy a Boxer puppy don't realize that this clownish puppy will grow up into a powerful dog.

Boxers are by nature bumptious and bounding, and they are big dogs — up to 75 pounds when full grown. An animal this size that has never been taught any control is downright dangerous. Fortunately, the Boxer responds readily to training. His strong guarding instincts, together with his capacity for devotion, his courage and energy can be channeled to make him unsurpassed as a family and household dog. Anyone investing in a Boxer pup would do well to take himself and the pup to a local dog training class and learn together.

He is sleek and flashy, partly because the American Kennel

Club Standards allow no more than 25% white markings. Fawn or brindle are the only background colors permitted. In the U.S. and his native country of Germany, the ears are cropped to keep them erect. Ear cropping is not permitted in the United Kingdom.

Bullmastiff

Originally created by crossing the Mastiff and the Bulldog in order to combine the size and power of the former with the courage of the latter. He is big — up to 100 pounds — and all muscle. Like all big dogs of the working-guarding variety, Bullmastiffs should be tamed and under control right from puppyhood. But like all big dogs, too, once well-trained the Bullmastiff is as gentle and docile as a lamb. The Bullmastiff, believe it or not, was bred to guard the big estates in England from poachers. They were the gamekeeper's dog, and were trained to attack on command.

Collie

The Collie is a quick moving sheepdog of elegance and high intelligence.

This kind of sheepdog probably originated many centuries ago when man began to need not only a guard for his livestock but an agile herder to bring them in from wherever they had wandered.

The name Collie covers several types. The best known is probably the Scottish Collie, the graceful, showy "Lassie" type, made internationally famous by the movies and television. The glamor of this long-coated Collie has been appreciated for many years by show bench enthusiasts. The smooth-coated Collie is similar except in coat — perhaps it is the lack of this glamorous finish that makes it less popular. Both these types are large — averaging 60 to 75 pounds.

There is also a smaller Collie from Britain, about 30 to 50 pounds, known by the name, Working Border Collie. Selectively bred for its working ability, not looks, this may be short or roughhaired; it may have a variation of markings in the combination of black and white. It has always been selectively bred for its brains, not its beauty, and the result is a black and white sheepdog that takes top place anywhere in the world. You won't find this dog among the AKC registered breeds, or even in the English Kennel Club register.

Bulldog

Originally bred to "bait the bull," the Bulldog's pushed-in nose enabled him to breathe while hanging on with his famous "Bulldog grip." Since the sport was outlawed, the Bulldog has been out of work but his sturdy self-reliance, loyal and loving nature, unique appearance make him known and welcomed in households all over the world. Weight: male about 50 pounds; female about 40 pounds. Registered by the A.K.C. in the "Non-Sporting Dog" group.

SALLY ANNE THOMPSON

But you will find him handling as many as 1000 sheep all on his own in North America, Britain, New Zealand — any sheep country. You'll find him winning at International Sheepdog Trials and at the obedience trials of the great Cruft's Show in London, England. You'll even find him working turkeys, cattle, horses and hogs on high ground or low, in cramped pens or enclosures, or in wide open spaces.

Alert, agile, sensitive, intelligent, possessed of remarkable stamina, the Working Border Collie is so good at his job that he hardly needs a master to tell him how!

A similar working Collie is one of the most important dogs on American farms. It is known variously as the American Farm Shepherd or the Collie-shepherd. Like the English Border Collie, it is a dog of top intelligence — a perfect companion or worker.

Doberman Pinscher

This is a dog and a half. The supreme guard dog when well-trained. Superb in war, and yet he is gentle enough to succeed as a guide dog for the blind. Owners who neglect to teach their Dobe good manners, are thoroughly disliked by real Dobe people.

The Doberman Pinscher is a muscular powerful dog of great nobility. He was created initially around 1890 by a German, Herr Louis Dobermann. Herr Dobermann wanted a powerful large terrier type with a sharp temperament. He started by crossing the black and tan German Pinscher and native Alsatian strains. Rottweillers were used to bring in great power, and later the English Manchester Terrier brought in alertness, refinement and some gentling of the original "sharp" temperament.

Dobermanns average 65 to 75 pounds. Their ears are naturally of the drop shape, but are cropped to an erect shape in most countries, Great Britain being the chief exception.

German Shepherd Dog

The German Shepard Dog is the American name for the European Alsatian Wolf dog. Because of movies, television and the Seeing Eye, he is, today, right up at the top for popularity. Known as a worker and companion the world over, the German Shepherd Dog fully deserves much of its fame and success.

Although considered basically a guard dog, the German Shepherd is usually found as a companion, or doing other types of work. He is most successful as a guide for the blind, as a guard dog and as a military dog, and he is among the leaders in obedience trial competition.

The German Shepherd Dog has had ups and downs in his popularity over the years. At one time he was given the label "wolf dog", probably because of a passing resemblance to a wolf. The German Shepherd Dog has no wolf in his ancestry however; he is a purely man-made breed. He was created in Germany in the late part of the 19th and the early 20th centuries. He was carefully and selectively bred by German fanciers who wanted to fix type and improve on their native working dog, but who chiefly wanted a guard and attack dog.

The German Shepherd is a big active dog, 80 to 100 pounds, with a sensitive response to his master. He is a dog that needs to be well trained with a job to do if he is to be fully happy.

In England he is commonly known as an "Alsatian." In the United States, he is popularly although incorrectly called "Police Dog."

Great Dane

The Great Dane is one of the really big breeds, statuesque in appearance rather than heavily massive. He can be anywhere from 100 to 150 pounds in weight, and he should be at least 30 inches at the shoulder. The type probably dates back at least to the Colossus dogs of ancient Greece and Rome, although the Dane, as we know it, was perfected in the 1800's. Despite the name, the modern Dane is not Danish but German in origin.

In the past it was used a lot for boar hunting in Europe, and certainly also as a guard dog. Until the last fifty years it had the reputation of being a ferocious, aggressive animal. Modern breeders have managed to inject majesty and gentility into the breed. Like all big dogs, Danes should be trained from puppyhood in good behavior, and should be chosen with care. Any pup showing either timidity or over-aggressiveness should be rejected. A nervous Dane is virtually untrainable and is, therefore, a potential danger. The Dane tends to be a one-man dog and responds best to training by one person. They are not long-lived — about nine years in the average.

Danes come in solid colors, brindle and attractive broken patterns called Harlequins. The ears are often trimmed.

Great Pyrenees

Another big breed which is gentle by nature, the Great Pyrenees is an excellent family dog. Basically a pastoral dog, he seems to regard his human family as his flock, placed in his care to be protected. He has earned a well deserved reputation of complete trustworthiness with children.

The Great Pyrenees is an immense dog, up to 125 pounds in weight and with a magnificent thick white coat. He is highly intelligent, easily trained, quiet and serious in work and play, and if you have the space for him you won't find a better, more devoted friend of the family.

Bullmastiff
The Bullmastiff was developed to be small enough to be agile, large enough to handle any prowler, and courageous enough to fight the devil. Today his noble appearance and dignified manner make him welcome in large homes and estates.

Bull Terrier

Originally bred as a fighting dog. In an age when courage was valued above all, he reigned supreme. No longer used for fighting, the breed has been refined into a lovable, tractable, utterly reliable family dog. Dignified and reserved, yet quite capable of looking after his family. Pound for pound, he is probably the strongest breed of dog ever developed. Weight: male about 50 pounds—female about 40 pounds. Registered by the American Kennel Club in the "Terrier" group.

Mastiff

The name "Mastiff" was originally a general term used to describe very large dogs of the Molossian type. It is considered to be one of the basic kinds of dog, constantly cropping up in history. The modern Mastiff as seen in the show ring, is developed from the English line of massive dogs. Several times it has almost disappeared as a breed type, but has been saved by ardent bands of enthusiasts. Looked at from any angle, the Mastiff is vast. He's 150 pounds and he looks every ounce of it. And that's the trouble.

Because they are so big and heavy, the breed has a tendency to limb and joint troubles. They eat a lot of food and take up a lot of space. Few people these days can accomodate them. But if you can and if you like your dogs imperial size, you'll find him a giant of good nature and docility.

Newfoundland

Big, black and long-coated, the Newfoundland is a magnificent 140 pounder. Sometimes he comes in black and white, and then he's called a Landseer Newfoundland after a famous painting by the English artist, Sir Edwin Landseer. It's questionable whether the Newfoundland originated in Newfoundland, but people who believe he did have books of tales to prove it. Wherever he came from, there are two facts undisputed — his sweetness of character and his love of water. The first makes him a wonderful companion of children. The second rates him a stay-at-home when a swimming party is on, unless you want to spend the day being hauled from the water. The Newfoundland is the best lifesaver in the business!

Old English Sheepdog

Here's a dog with audience appeal. On television shows, in the show ring, and in advertising, he generates instant attraction. To the initiated, the Old English Sheepdog's peculiar ambling gait reveals its sheep droving ancestry; to the merely amused onlooker it resembles the shuffle of a teddy bear; an impression which the full heavy coat does nothing to dispel. That thick coat needs a great deal of attention if the dog is not to look a mess. The heavy covering over his eyes and head restricts his vision, but his hearing is very acute, and so is his sense of smell. He is big dog (around 60 pounds) but of amiable, quiet disposition. Sometimes he is called Bobtail for his lack of tail. Occasionally, the puppies are born without tails, but usually the tail has to be docked. He's a homebody, not given to roaming, so he makes a good family dog for the suburbanite.

Rottweiler

This powerful dog gets his name from the Southern German town of Rottweil, but his breed type is older than the town. His ancestors are reputed to have been brought to the area two thousand years ago by the Romans who used them to guard their camps and to drive the livestock they took along to feed their armies. The Rottweiler's more recent claim to fame is the influence he had in the creation of the Doberman Pinscher. His cattle droving days are almost over now, and the Rottweiler is more frequently used as a police dog —

a role he fulfills very well — and as a guard dog. He is more dignified in disposition than his more volatile companions in this work, the German Shepherd and the Doberman, and perhaps is the better choice for anyone with little experience in dog training. A big fellow, 26 inches at the shoulder and heavy, he has a close, flat coat which is easy to keep.

St. Bernard

Everybody knows St. Bernards. They roam about the Swiss Alps with a barrel of brandy around their necks and rescue people lost in snowdrifts. It is a lovely story but, alas, owes much of its origin to the great English painter, Sir Edwin Landseer, who tended to get sentimental about large dogs. There is a Hospice at the St. Bernard Pass in the Swiss Alps where there are St. Bernard dogs. Undoubtedly they have contributed to the rescue of travellers in the difficult region of the pass, but mostly they are used as guides.

The St. Bernard is an enormous dog; he can be as much as 180 to 200 pounds in weight. This weight brings its problems in faulty hindquarters and, like many large breeds, St. Bernards are not long-lived. They have equable temperaments and docile manners that make them good companions for children. The are either rough or short coated; the smooth variety is seldom seen today.

Samoyed

The beautiful Samoyed is one of the most glamorous of dogs, with his outstanding white coat, pricked ears and curled tail. He is a member of the Spitz family from Northern Siberia, and takes his name from the nomadic Samoyede people. He is naturally a hardy dog, and excels in cold climates but is at home anywhere. Intelligent, alert, be is, like all the Spitz, capable of strong affection towards the master. This last characteristic is so strongly marked in the Samoyed that he tends to attach himself to one person. Don't get me wrong; the Samoyed isn't unfriendly — just exclusive.

Shetland Sheepdog

The Shetland Islanders off the coast of Scotland breed small sheep and cattle and diminutive ponies, and the dog that bears their name is tiny too. Weighing about 15 pounds and standing 10 to 12 inches high, he is dainty and beautifully proportioned, and is frequently called a "Miniature Collie". Actually he is not, as so many toy dogs are, a bred down version but he is a distinct, independently evolved breed.

His working ability finds him a place in sheep growing areas of America, and he is also frequently seen in obedience trials where he does exceedingly well. Shelties have a full coat like the bigger Collie, with an abundant frill and mane. They have the same glorious colorings of sable, black and tan or merle, all with white. Their charming appearance and affectionate natures have made them a popular choice as a companion dog, but they are active little dogs and enjoy a busy life.

Siberian Husky

The Siberian Husky is an Arctic sled dog, more refined in build than the Alaskan Malamute, less glamorous than the Samoyed, but as hardy and tough a worker as either, perhaps more so. He has a wide reputation for gentleness with human beings, but is less

Cairn Terrier

The smallest of the terrier breeds, yet all dog, with a great heart far out of proportion to his small body. Alert, intelligent and eager, he is small enough to be at home in a crowded household and sturdy enough to hold his own with a vigorous youngster. Height at the shoulder: male 10 inches—female 9 1/2 inches. Weight: male 14 pounds—female 13 pounds. Registered by the American Kennel Club in the "Terrier" group. TOM CARAVAGLIA

Canaan

An ancient breed from Israel, this breed goes back to biblical days. They have been used for hunting, herding, and during the recent war in Israel as sentries and for mine detection work. Not registered by the American Kennel Club. Registered by the Israeli Kennel Club and the *Federation Cynologique Internationale.*

reliable with other dogs. He needs, therefore, to be chosen carefully and kept under control from an early age. Average weight is 50 to 60 pounds, and the most attractive of a wide range of colors are the silver grays, and light sables. Sometimes you'll find one with a "cap" and "spectacles" of darker color, which gives an intriguing and unique appearance.

Welsh Corgi

The Welsh Corgi is the most popular and best known of all the Welsh breeds. It appears in two types, the Pembroke and the Cardigan. The first is the better known, though the Cardigan is probably the older. The Pembroke has a "foxy" head and is usually of a reddish color, with a stump tail. The Cardigan comes in a wider choice of colors, has a long tail, and something of a short-legged Collie look about it. The name Corgi is said by some to mean "dwarf dog" and by others to mean "cur dog"!

Both types of Corgi were bred as cattle dogs and it is only in recent years they have become common as pets. Corgis were deliberately bred short legged so that they could easily duck under the backward kick of a cow. The Pembroke, being the more popular of the two, has been bred on a grand scale commercially. If you want a Corgi as a pet and housedog, you can't go wrong if you choose a Cardigan — there is little chance of getting a doubtful temperament; or take your time and find the right Pembroke. They are small — about 12 inches at the shoulder and up to 25 pounds in weight — and their coats are easily groomed.

Terriers

Airedale

The largest of the terrier breeds, 60 pounds in weight and 24 inches at the shoulder, the Airedale is the most adaptable of them all. Not only does he excel in the true terrier quality of seeking out and dispatching vermin, he is superb at other jobs too. Airedales have done good work as police and war dogs, and are readily trained as guard dogs. Their indomitable courage makes them fearsome defenders of property. They have a good nose, almost as good as a scent hound's with the possible exception of the Bloodhound and Basset. In addition, the Airedale has a big heart and usually becomes exceptionally devoted to his owner. For the farmer or the homesteader who wants a companion dog that will earn his keep, an Airedale can't be bettered. He has to be controlled around working livestock because in America he has killed a lot of sheep — but any breed of dog would be hard-pressed to beat the Airedale at keeping down the vermin around the barns and buildings. It is said that an Airedale can do anything any other dog can do and then beat the other dog. The Airedale's wiry coat needs regular attention — mostly plucking or stripping. About 24 inches at the shoulder, the Airedale comes in black and tan only.

Australian Terrier

This very small terrier — 10 inches high and about 10 to 12 pounds — is not an old breed; he probably derived from a blend of several of the older British terriers. He is an alert, self-confident fellow, possessed of a highly developed temperament. He was bred to be versatile and suited to the demands of the Australian outback. He's a hunter, house and man guard, sheep tender — anything that a working dog needs to be. In addition, he is of quiet disposition and very affectionate, all of which, with his small size, makes him well suited to apartment living or small houses. His harsh coat sheds little.

Bedlington Terrier

This terrier looks like a lamb, and nowadays he is often as shy. The trouble with the Bedlington is that he's too glamorous, and people have tended to breed for unique looks without regard to temperament. Visit the place where your prospective purchase was raised, and see as many of his immediate ancestors as possible. That way you're more likely to get one of the temperamentally sounder kind. The Bedlington was originally a terrier that would hunt and kill any vermin, from rats to badger and foxes. Not that one has so many rats, badgers and foxes around the house, but some of the old spirit makes for a better dog. This powerful little dog was also used as a pit or fighting dog, so don't let that lamb-like look mislead you. He has an unusual topknot and long ears, his waterproof coat needs regular trimming. The shades of blue and sandy are most attractive. They are about Miniature Poodle size — 22 pounds in weight and 15 inches in height. Chosen with care in respect of temperament, the Bedlington should appeal to people who like the looks of poodles but want something a little different.

Border Terrier

The Border in the name Border Terrier refers to the border between England and Scotland. From that kind of country — hilly terrain, sparse grazing for sheep — came the several tough terrier breeds that specialize in going in after the big hill foxes. The Border Terrier is one of the great working terriers of that type. He looks a real "scamp" '— very workmanlike and weighing 15 pounds. He's not glamorous enough to have ever been really "taken up" in the show ring, and has remained basically a working dog of great stamina and unlimited courage.

Bull Terrier

Except for the Pit Bull Dog used in dog fighting, there's more power and strength packed into 50 or 60 pounds of Bull Terrier than in any other dog of equal size. He is ferocious to the extreme when aroused, but luckily this doesn't happen too often. The fighting spirit is combined with a remarkably docile disposition and an incredible reliability with people, especially children. This may seem a contradiction, but it isn't. Bull Terriers do not seem to feel pain the way other breeds do, and they are not likely to snap when hurt by a child. The Bull Terrier with the eggshaped head, also known as "down face," and his relative, the Staffordshire Terrier, were bred originally solely for the so-called "sport" of dog fighting — to the

AKE WINTZELL

Cavalier King Charles Spaniel

This elegant little spaniel is becoming quite popular as a house pet and companion in England, the country where it was developed. It is somewhat similar to, but lighter in build and larger than the English Toy Spaniel. The color type pictured here is called the Blenheim. Weight: 10 to 18 pounds. Not registered by the American Kennel Club. Registered in the "Toy" group by the English Kennel Club.

death if necessary. Their sponsors, however, needed a dog that would respond instantly to human control, otherwise the fighting contests would get out of hand. So they bred in the quality of responsiveness. As a result Bull Terriers are remarkably sensitive to human beings, and actually *need* devotion and attention from their masters. The fighting instinct is far more marked in kennel-raised dogs than in those that grow up in a family setting. Anyone wanting a Bull Terrier must be prepared to treat it as a constant and close companion, and will be repaid with complete loyalty and protectiveness toward the family. The females are usually more affectionate and docile than the males, and thus easier to control. When buying a male, it's wise to be even more careful about inquiring into the family history. Bull Terriers may be either all white, or for those who don't like the "pink-eyed" look, some are parti-colored, usually black or brindle on the white. According to the Standard, even all-whites are permitted patches of color on the head. The whites are sometimes born deaf, owing to a genetic

Chesapeake Bay Retriever
A large, powerful dog, the Chesapeake, the only retriever developed in America, is noted for his stamina and courage. He is strong enough to retrieve in the roughest of waters, while his courage also makes him valuable as a guardian for the home.

make-up. Staffordshires are either red, fawn or brindle. There is also, in England, a miniature variety, weighing not more than 20 pounds.

Cairn Terrier

The Cairn is an active, short-legged terrier reputed to be old in the history of the Western Highlands of Scotland. Although only about 15 pounds in weight and about nine or ten inches high, he has a formidable reputation as a hunter of vermin. He makes a good, lively companion dog, but any would-be Cairn owner must remember that he is a little fellow with a lot of energy which he needs to work off. Color can be, except for white, any, including brindle and grizzle. Cairns often have dark muzzles and ears which are rather attractive.

Dandie Dinmont

An unusual looking dog, the little Dandie Dinmont terrier is distinctive with his silky topknot, long, flexible body with slightly arched loin, short legs and gaily carried tail. He comes in unusual colorings best described by the standard of points names: Pepper and Mustard. The Dandie's character is as individual as his looks.

People who know him consider the Dandie Dinmont to be the most courageous dog of all. He is self-possessed, probably the most level-headed of all the terriers. He goes about his daily business purposefully and without fuss. He makes a good house and apartment dog, especially for people with temperaments like his own. The Dandie Dinmont got his name in an unusual manner befitting such an individual dog. Up until the early 1800's, Dandies were called a variety of names in their native Scotland. Then Sir Walter Scott published his novel, "Guy Mannering," which featured a farmer called Dandie Dinmont and his wise little Mustard and Pepper terriers. Soon after that, the little terriers acquired his name, and it has stuck ever since.

Fox Terrier

Most popular and best known of all the terriers, the Fox Terrier is a smart, plucky little fellow weighing about 16 pounds. He comes in three varieties, wirehaired, smoothcoated, and a toy — less set in type perhaps, but similar to the smooth variety. The wirehaired kind needs to have his coat stripped regularly or it will get clumped and shapeless. These terriers are very popular in the show ring, and some of the record prices for purebred dogs have been paid for top winning Fox Terriers. When buying a Fox Terrier as a companion dog, look for one slightly broader in the head and without the spindly straight hind legs so beloved by some show judges.

The smaller variety is not registered by the AKC, but is far more prevalent in America. Its nose is more pointed and head wider than its English cousin and its coat smoother than the so-called smooth type.

Irish Terrier

Red as the Irish Setter, and full of its charm, the Irish Terrier is less well-known as a family dog than he deserves to be. He is lively, loves to play, and is a fine guard of children and household. Like all lively dogs, he needs a firm hand and some basic training early, or his enthusiasm will get the best of him. As a working dog he's very versatile and can do practically anything he's called on to do. In size he runs op to about 30 pounds, a little bigger than most terriers.

Chihuahua

The Chihuahua is the smallest breed of dog and is available in both the longcoat and shortcoat varieties. Photographers delight in snapping the Chihuahua alongside a Great Dane or a Saint Bernard to emphasize the contrast in size. A lot of dog in a very small frame. Weight: 1 to 6 pounds, with 2 to 4 pounds preferred. Registered by the American Kennel Club in the "Toy" group.

Kerry Blue Terrier

The Kerry Blue Terrier comes from Ireland, from County Kerry — and he's a real character. The color is the Kerry's most obvious distinction, a gray-blue tone like no other. The pups are not born that way, however, and up to about 12 months of age you can expect them to stay black. In the following months, all shades of dark blue, brown, and gray appear, until with full maturity — sometime around 18 months of age — the gray-blue color settles in. So, if you want the true Kerry color, make sure you see as many adult ancestors of your pup as possible before buying. The Kerry is a most versatile dog. It averages about 35 pounds in weight and 18 inches in height. It is a sheep and cattle dog, guard dog, and will even hunt and retrieve small game. It makes a most efficient farm dog, and a worthwhile companion worker for any man. BUT, the Kerry needs a master he can respect to keep that Irish temperament in control. The Kerry is one of the few rough-coated terriers that can be kept "in the rough." The Irish don't permit the coat to be trimmed for showing; the American and English Kennel Clubs are still insistent on some trimming. A regular brush and groom to keep down dead hair, and a general scissoring to tidy up the coat will suffice for the companion dog.

Lakeland Terrier

A trim little terrier — weight about 16 to 17 pounds — from the Lake district of England. He comes in the blue, tan, black, grizzle and wheaten shades, but no white. Lakelands traditionally hunt the fox with the hounds, going into the lair to flush them out, or even to kill. They are exceptionally narrow chested, deliberately so, to enable them to get into and through the rocky crevices that abound in that part of England. This terrier is particularly tough.

Manchester Terrier

Way back in the 16th century, a famous dog expert called Dr. Caius published in England an encyclopedia on dogs. Among the breeds he described was a Black and Tan Terrier that has since become one of the ancestors of most of the terrier types, big and small. The nearest modern version of this black and tan you'll see is the Manchester — a finer, trimmer version. It is said that some Whippet was bred into the original terrier, to produce a keen dog with not only ratting ability but enough speed for rabbit coursing as long as he can see one. A medium sized version was known in America as the "Rat Terrier" due to its rat killing abilities.

Nowadays, the Manchester is a favorite house dog and pet, and quite justifiably, because he is a smart, clean, handy little fellow, and his sleek coat is easy to groom. You can have him in two sizes: the standard original, 12 to 20 pounds size, or the toy version, which weighs from 3 to 10 pounds. No cropping of the ears is permitted in the toy, which has naturally erect ears. The bigger version can have erect or button ears, and may be cropped. The Toy Manchester, incidentally, has existed for over one hundred years, and has had its problems. Like most miniature breeds when they reach high popularity, soundness and temperament deteriorated, but nowadays, thanks to some hard work on the part of keen devotees of the breed, the Toy Manchester can be numbered among the soundest and best balanced of the tiny breeds. May it long remain so.

Miniature Schnauzer

Although classed as a terrier, the Miniature Schnauzer has no common ancestry with the other terriers, which are British in origin. The Schnauzer in its miniature version is related to the Giant and Standard Schnauzers which are basically German cattle and guard dogs. All three have similar distinctive hair coloring, giving a salt and pepper appearance, although they all also come in black. This 12 to 15 pound breed has gone up remarkably in popularity in recent years, and is now numbered eighth in the American Kennel Club registrations. No wonder, because Miniature Schnauzers are hardy, intelligent, excellent with children, not given to wandering, and are very adaptable. They are small enough to live in a city or town (provided there is a nearby park in which they can let off steam occasionally), and active enough to live and work usefully in the country. They can work — they are excellent ratters and, in fact, were once kept as a yard and stable dog. It is an excellent little dog to have around the farm, and can be well recommended to the farm wife wanting a pet dog that can also make itself useful. In the U.S. and Germany, the ears are trimmed although not in England. The tail is docked.

Scottish Terrier

Like all the terriers from the Highlands of Scotland, the Scottish Terrier seems to have all the Scottish characteristics of temperament deeply inbred, and like all good Scotsmen he retains them no matter how long his ancestors have been in exile. The Scottie is renowned for his tenacity, his individualism, his obstinacy and his courage. He is a real character among dogs. He is a one man dog, and to his master he will give his all in loyalty and devotion. He comes in a variety of workmanlike shades, from jet black to sandy grizzle, to steel grey, and he weighs about 20 pounds. A word of warning: never leave the painters, the plumber or the man who has come to fix the gas leak in the house alone with the Scottie while you pop down to the supermarket to pick up the groceries. The Scottie will never let him out of the house in one piece, and your repair man will blacklist you forever after.

Sealyham

Even among terriers, which are a tough lot on the whole, the Sealyham has a reputation for gameness. He is said to have been originated by an eccentric Welshman, Captain John Edwardes, who was dissatisfied with all the existing terriers. The result is a small dog — 10½ inches at the shoulder and 20 to 22 pounds in weight — that will take on and beat any vermin, including the skunk. Sealyhams are a reserved race, not gregarious by nature, but their enthusiasts will have no other. The name, incidentally, comes from the Captain's estate.

Skye Terrier

Queen Victoria of England liked this terrier, and her interest gave the oddly picturesque breed a run of popularity in the 19th century. Originally, probably about four centuries ago, the Skye was bred for fox and badger hunting. Nowadays he mostly appears on the show bench and as a pet. He came, of course, from the isle of Skye near Scotland. The famous Greyfriars' Bobby was believed to be a Skye. The long, flowing coat is a great feature, and the breed needs regular brushing. Only 10 inches in height, the Skye weighs 25 to 30 pounds.

Welsh Terrier

The Welsh Terrier is supposed to be the most ancient of British Terriers, and the original owner of the wire coat so common in the terrier breeds. Or that's what the Welsh fanciers say. At first glance, the dog could be mistaken for a small Airedale. Black and tan, with a close wiry coat and about 20 pounds in weight, he is virile in

Chow-Chow
The Chow Chow is quiet, clean and absolutely fearless. One unique characteristic is a black tongue and mouth. Height at the shoulder: at least 18 inches. Registered by the A.K.C. in the "Non-Sporting Dog" group.

AKE WINTZELL

Clumber Spaniel
The thick legs and heavy body of the Clumber are propably due to an infusion of Basset Hound blood. A slow but steady worker, and an excellent retriever as well as being a very attractive dog. Weight: male 55 to 70 pounds— female 45 to 60 pounds. Registered by the American Kennel Club in the "Sporting Dog" group.

temperament, vigorous in his activity and stamina. Although the Welsh Terrier was one of the earliest classified on the show bench, is has never become a commercial breed, and has remained relatively unspoiled. The head, although long, is broader than that of a Fox Terrier, and the expression is quite unique and unmistakable, possibly because the eyes are set a little more apart than usual in a terrier.

West Highland White Terrier

Derived from the Cairn Terrier, the dog is allowed only in the one color that the Cairn isn't — white. The Westie is even more of a goer than his cousin, if that is possible. Lots of people keep them in city apartments because they are cute and clean looking with a cocky air. But these 15 pounders need to be occupied all day. Give them an interesting patch to work on, several sessions of serious play in the parks or woods, and they'll be happy. Don't expect them to live like lap dogs, because they aren't. There is a lot of dog in that small body.

Toys

Chihuahua

The little Chihuahua has gone up rapidly in popularity and gone down just as rapidly in size in the last few years. Unfortunately, the smaller the dog, the more trouble there may be with general soundness. Chihuahuas are basically tougher dogs than they are given credit for, with a somewhat terrier-like disposition. They make excellent housedogs and can be trained to quite an advanced obedience trial standard. They are popularly thought to be originally a Mexican and Central American dog, but research in recent years tends to establish that they were probably brought into Central America via the trade routes of the Spanish from China and the Orient where tiny dogs have always been popular. Chihuahuas can have either a close smooth coat, or a soft feathered longer coat which many people consider more graceful and attractive. Show judges and popular choice favor a two pound weight; veterinarians would rather this were six pounds at least, particularly for breeding.

English Toy Spaniel

These little dogs are known in England as King Charles Spaniels. There is also an allied type, slightly larger, called Cavalier King Charles. But whatever they are called, they make an excellent companion dog. In disposition they are like a Cocker Spaniel, dependable and affectionate. They are capable of, and enjoy, an outdoor life, and are a particularly suitable choice for an active suburban family dog. The only chore involved is grooming; this should be done regularly and thoroughly once a week. The Toy weighs in at 10 pounds and is under 10 inches in height. If you found a Cavalier King Charles, it would be 12 inches high and about 20 pounds, with a more natural nose and head. Supporters of the bigger one claim theirs as the original favorite of the kingly Court of Charles.

Italian Greyhound

Classed as a toy but really the tiniest of the greyhound family. For centuries this dainty miniature has been a darling with the wealthy. From Renaissance times onward, every royal court in Europe counted an Italian Greyhound or two among its favorite dogs.

They are perfect for apartment living, being tiny, weighing on average 6 to 12 pounds, and exceptionally clean in coat. They look very fragile, but in fact they are not. However, having slender bones they are not the pet for a family of boisterous children. Reactions to chills, sudden changes to damp cold temperatures, and drafts are probably their only real weak points.

Japanese Spaniel

The Japanese Spaniel, or "Chin" as it is sometimes called, is another small Asian breed that was living as a valued pet in wealthy households while Europe was still overrun by barbarians, and America was populated by buffalo. Ideally bred to be around 7 pounds in weight, the Japanese Chin has a flat face similar to the Pekingese, but is higher on the leg. It dances through life with a lively, dainty temperament, and is an alert, excellent housedog. It is reputed to have a remarkable memory. Sensitive and independent, it tends to be a one-man dog.

Maltese

Small, but strong, intelligent and high-spirited, the little Maltese is an attractive toy dog that becomes utterly devoted to its owner. With its long, white silky hair, dark eyes and black nose, the Maltese retains puppy charm into old age. Reputed to be an ancient breed. Whether it actually originated in the island of Malta as some believe isn't certain, and its ancient background remains a puzzle. Preference — and high prices — are given to the very tiny two pounders. The pet buyer is better advised to look for one somewhat bigger, say about 6 pounds.

Miniature Pinscher

If you always fancied a Doberman Pinscher, but haven't the room for one, here is a miniature which resembles him. In German, *Pinscher* means terrier. Doberman Pinscher means Doberman Terrier. Thus our Miniature Pinscher is not a bred down Doberman, but a distinct breed several hundred years older than the Doberman. The resemblance is little more than accidental. The "Minpin", however, is as exact a replica as any miniature can be, and it has its cousin's intelligence, lively temperament, style and watchful instincts. It is an ideal small apartment dog, alert and bold in temperament, affectionate and protective of home, master and family, and has a smart clean appearance, with a slick coat that requires the minimum of attention. You'll find them in a really rich red, in sleek black with tan markings (a throw-back to the ubiquitous Manchester Terrier in the ancestry) or in a deep brown shade. They are about 11 inches at the shoulder and weigh between 6 and 10 pounds. They are tiny dogs with big hearts.

Papillon

Because of its upstanding prettily fringed ears, the Papillon is often called the Butterfly Dog. It is a very decorative, dainty, little thing, but despite its small size — twelve pounds and twelve inches high — it is still all dog. Papillons are bright eyed and lively, make excellent apartment dogs and fit very happily into city life. One of the toy spaniel group, it comes in spaniel colors.

Pekingese

Surrounding the Pekingese is an aura of romance and legend. Pekingese puppies are probably he most attractive of all, the adult

Cocker Spaniel (American)

One of the most beautiful breeds ever developed, the American Cocker Spaniel is worthy of his popularity. Number one in American Kennel Club registrations for more years than any other breed, the silky ears and large, liquid eyes endear them to everyone. While seldom used in the field today, their cheerful manner and engaging ways make them a most desirable companion dog. Height at the shoulder: 15 to 16 inches: Weight: 22 to 26 pounds. Registered by the American Kennel Club in the "Sporting Dog" group.

Peke has more courage and dignity per pound of weight than any other dog. Strong men confess a weakness for Pekes; "big dog" people have a sneaking admiration for them and old ladies are their adoring slaves. Most other dogs regard them with respect. There is just no other member of the canine family quite like the Peke. It arrived in the Western world from behind the restricted walls of the Imperial Courts of China at the end of the 19th century, and it climbed rapidly to the top in the popularity stakes. The Poodle and the German Shepherd may have passed it numerically, but nothing can quite equal the Peke's appeal hold on the hearts of dog lovers of the Western world. What is his secret? No dog could be more unnatural physically. The squashed-in face almost demands breathing and dentition troubles, the protuberant eye invites damage, the heavy coat if neglected leads to skin troubles, the large head seems certain to give cause for worry in breeding. Yet the Pekingese survives. It can all be summed up in one word: temperament. The Chinese, for centuries, bred Pekes tough. Consequently he is full of pluck, courage and the basic vigor for survival. He is indestructible because he will never, ever, give up. The American Kennel Club Standard calls for a weight under 14 pounds. Today, many miniatures of 6 to 8 pounds are being bred.

Pomeranian

The modern Pomeranian is a miniature version of the Spitz types, probably bred down from the Lapland and Iceland sled dogs. However, little dogs of the Pomeranian type were the earliest ones referred to as "Melitae," or Maltese, dating back to 800 BC. They are depicted on ancient Greek vases dated 500 BC — not quite so showily coated, but unmistakably Pomeranian. The dog we know, however, derives from more modern times. Just over a hundred years ago they weighed 30 pounds. Nowadays a show specimen is more often around 5 pounds. The fact that Queen Victoria of England had a kennel of Poms gave them a burst of popularity which lasted on and off until the "Roaring Twenties." Pomeranians are alert, lively little housedogs.

Pug

"Mops," the Victorian English — with whom he was a favorite

family dog — used to call him, and the name somehow suits the affable Pug·dog, with his funny face, eager way of living and complete amiability. His squashed-up face sometimes leads to breathing and dentition problems, and the globular eyes have a tendency to get damaged easily, but basically the Pug is a hardy, long-lived dog.

He's another of the tough housedogs that came to the West from ancient China. It's thought that the Dutch, via the Dutch East India Trading Company, which did a good business with China, introduced it to Europe. Like all Chinese breeds, the Pug is essentially resilient, and makes a fine family dog, absolutely reliable with children.

It is thought that the Pug derives originally from the Mastiff, being a miniaturized version. He is certainly a compact, square dog with large round head, heavy for his size. He is 12 inches in height and 14 to 18 pounds in weight.

Silky Terrier

A product of that "down under" country, Australia, the Silky Terrier is a dog of fairly recent manufacture. It was produced by crossing Yorkshire Terriers with Australian Terriers, and is the only Australian breed which isn't regarded chiefly as a worker. It is a true terrier type and is perfectly capable of controlling vermin as well as any other of his kind, but in his homeland he is appreciated chiefly as a pet and housedog. His small size — 8 to 10 pounds — and his intelligent, knowledgeable air and friendly manner make him a delightful family dog. The silky coat of blue and tan is less long and easier to keep than the Yorkie's.

Yorkshire Terrier

He is classified as a toy now, but originally in Yorkshire, England he was bred to be a game rat–catching terrier. Nowadays,the smaller Yorkies come, the more they cost, and in those bred for minuteness only — down to two pounds in weight — you may find that the tough terrier temperament verges on snappiness. So if you want a tiny, choose with care. Find one that is too big for the expensive lap dog market, nearer the ten pound mark, and you'll have an attractive small dog of spirit, even if he'll never be a show champion. Yorkies have a long silky coat that requires a lot of attention.

Puppies are born a dark sable and black color; the distinctive steel blue shade develops as they mature.

Non-Sporting Dogs

Boston Terrier

The Boston Terrier is one of the few all-American breeds that is internationally known. He was created from a combination of the English Bulldog and the English Terrier. Formerly called the American Bull Terrier, this name was eventually changed. The Boston became "official" in 1893 when the American Kennel Club accepted registrations. He is as smart as paint, and the pattern of the markings of white on the brindle or black of his coat are very important. He is compact and stylish, and should give the impression of strength and determination wrapped up in a small package. He usually weighs between 15 and 25 pounds. Like all the the bull terrier breeds, he craves a close and affectionate relationship with people.

He is great all-around pet and companion. In spite of his size he is a tough little fellow, and larger dogs who snarl at him had best look out for this little fellow doesn't back off.

Bulldog

The English Bulldog isn't what it once was. The dog that was used for bull baiting, and later dog fighting, some hundreds of years back must have been far more agile, higher on the leg, and longer in the muzzle than the present day heavyweight. The tenacity remains, however, and it is the most endearing feature of the breed; so much so that the word, Bulldog, has passed into common usage as a synonym for perseverence. English Bulls may be slow and docile and ultra-affectionate nowadays, but when they want to they can be very stubborn and determined. They have become so exaggerated in appearance that they have a great number of health problems. Not only are there the usual dentition and breathing difficulties of all the short-faced breeds but they frequently run into breeding trouble as well. Caesarian section is very common — too much so. Bulldogs come in almost all colors. A male Bulldog can weigh 50 pounds or more when fully mature. They are not generally as long lived as are some of the other breeds.

Cocker Spaniel (English)
One of the finest breeds of dog ever developed. A great sportsman and a fine companion, his gentle ways and engaging manner make him a favorite. Height at the shoulder: male 16 to 17 inches—female 15 to 16 inches. Weight: male 28 to 34 pounds—female 26 to 32 pounds. Registered by the A.K.C. in the "Sporting Dog" group.

AKE WINTZELL

Still, in spite of it all, the Bulldog retains his popularity and always will. "Old Sour Mug" has a bizarre sense of humor which endears him to all. He has tremendous powerful jaws with which he can quell an intruder or play ball gently with the smallest child. Did you ever see a dog smile? Well, watch a Bulldog when children pay attention to him. It's the ugliest beautiful thing you ever saw.

Chow-Chow

Aloof as only an Asiatic can be, the Chinese Chow-Chow has a truly disdainful air. Of course, if you'd been valued for your edibility for centuries you'd be somewhat suspicious in your approach to human beings too! Chow-Chow fix their affections on one person, and distrust the rest of the world. This makes them unsuitable as family pets, when there are a lot of people coming and going, but ideal for the human personality that fits in with theirs. They are gorgeous creatures; the most often seen long-coated variety has an off-standing coat usually in glorious red, dark blue or deep, rich black. They are powerful and compact dogs, weighing about 50 pounds. Their independent temperament is shown in their lordly expression. Chow-Chows are the unique possessors of a blue-black tongue and roof mouth. The characteristics of the Chow-Chow are its quiet nature — they are not yappers — its great courage and fighting ability, and a dainty cleanliness which makes it one of the easiest dogs to housebreak. Their stiff hair resists tangling and for some unfathomable reason, they are seldom bothered by fleas.

Dalmatian

Spotted dogs have always had an appeal. Way back in ancient Egypt their oddity value was appreciated, judging by the number of times spotted and quaintly marked dogs appear on decorative panels and sculptured plinths. The modern Dalmatian seems to have originated in the part of Europe that is now Yugoslavia, but his type was probably fairly common around the Mediterranean area for centuries. He can turn to almost any kind of work — hunting, retrieving, herding, guarding and sentry duty. He has also competed successfully in obedience trials. Like many an all-rounder the Dalmatian is perhaps not as good at any of these as the best specialist, but there is one field in which he does excel. That is as a "coach dog." In the days of coaching, the Dalmatian made a superb escort, a vigilant guard against marauders, and a faithful follower for miles upon miles. His easy stride and muscular body gave him great endurance. There aren't any coaches to follow now, but the Dalmatian will still accompany horses with great delight.

He is a medium sized dog and very active. Because of this, Dalmatians are happier as country dogs. Their protective anti-stranger instincts make them good guards. They have very little "doggy" odor, are easily groomed and kept clean, so this makes them very suitable for living in the house. Dalmatian puppies are born white. The spots develop later.

French Bulldog

A dog of intriguing appearance, due chiefly to the unique bat-like ears, the French Bulldog is primarily a companion and housedog. It is thought to have originated from a toy version of the English Bulldog. It weighs about 25 pounds, and is a compact, strongly built dog. It has the Bulldog temperament without the veterinary problems of that breed. The "Frenchie" makes an excellent dog for a small house or apartment because its smooth coat is easy to care for; it is protectively alert and affectionate and yet not a noisy, yappy dog.

Keeshond

The Keeshond is one of the Spitz family, and comes from Holland. There it has been used for centuries as a watchdog in the house, and

Dogs' tails come in various sizes, shapes and positions, and there is a name for each.

These are the names given to the various ear shapes found in different breeds of dogs.

also on the barges which ply up and down the River Rhine. It has more working ability than is usually exploited, but the fact that it has been used for so many years as a companion dog has encouraged its housedog qualities. The Keeshond is inclined to be sentitive and needs kind handling; it responds better to a small family than a large boisterous one. It weighs about 40 pounds and stands 18 inches in height. The main feature of the breed is its coat, which is full, outstanding, and waterproof and which despite its denseness and length, rarely mats.

Lhasa Apso

The Lhasa Apso is an exotic and unusual little dog. He originated in Tibet, the land of Mount Everest, where he lived as a companion and indoor "alarm" dog. His chief feature is his heavy coat, which grows long enough to trail the floor. The Lhasa Apso needs to be a hardy little dog, for Tibet has a cruel climate.

After many centuries of close association with people, the Lhasa Apso has developed a remarkable sensitivity to human wants and a high degree of intelligence. For anyone prepared to spend the necessary time on grooming the long coat, the Lhasa Apso makes a sturdy, charming companion and takes up little room, being only 10 inches in height and weighing ideally an average of 12 to 14 pounds.

Since Tibet has been overrun by the Chinese, it is difficult to

SALLY ANNE THOMPSON

Collie
Queen Victoria's sponsorship of this breed insured its meteoric rise to popularity, a popularity which has never waned. Careful breeding has refined a once small-sized sheep herding breed of medium-length coat, into the magnificent specimen we know today. Majestic in appearance and with a nature to match.

predict whether the breed will survive in its country of origin. Luckily, it is well established in America and in Europe.

Poodle

The Poodle is the most popular dog there has ever been. In numbers it has far outclassed any other breed. This has not been an entirely good thing. A good Poodle, whether it is the big Standard, the smaller Miniature or the little Toy, is a truly great dog. It has the glamor, the intelligence, the adaptability, the temperament, the style, and the all around appeal to satisfy the most demanding of dog owners. It is only sad that commercialism and human greed have produced a number of poor specimens. You must buy your Poodle with care and without haste and from someone who really cares about the breed; and don't expect to get a "bargain." The big Standard Poodle has probably been the least affected by commercialism; the tiny Toy, the most.

Basically the only difference between the three types should be in size. The Standard is 15 inches or more in height, the Toy is under 10 inches, and the Miniature is in between. The Poodle is supposed to have been originally a water bird retriever from Germany, but nowadays is universally accepted as a companion dog. This role it fills very well. The Poodle coat needs regular clipping to keep it trim. This is because the Poodle does not shed; the hair just keeps growing longer and longer. For this reason, many people who are allergic to other dogs are not bothered by the presence of a Poodle.

Schipperke

The Schipperke is a perky little dog from Belgium. He has the pet name of "Little Skipper," and this is very appropriate because he has long been the favorite guard dog for the barges on the Belgian waterways. He is very alert little watchdog despite his small size — 10 to 20 pounds. He makes an excellent housedog and, having been bred for life in a restricted space, is perfect for a small apartment. The Schipperke has a lively, questioning personality — it is a personality rather than a temperament; he is always busy and occupied, and is very protective of his home and family. He deserves to be better known than he is.

Curly-Coated Retriever

It is primarily in Australia and New Zealand that this breed has attained the popularity it deserves. A large, powerful dog, sweet natured and trainable. In field trials open to all breeds of retrievers, the Curly-Coat has acquitted himself with distinction. Height at the shoulder: male about 26 inches—female about 24 inches. Registered by the American Kennel Club in the "Sporting Dog" group.

IV Which Breed to Choose

Let's assume that, having read this far, you like dogs; that, in fact, you'd like to own one and join the long line of people in the history of mankind who have had a dog in their family.

Maybe you want a dog to do a job — there are many jobs at which the dog excels, and can even do better than you. This was how man and dog got together in the first place. It didn't take primitive man long to discover that the dog could do a lot of the "leg work"! Just think how silly a man would look dashing around a herd of sheep; and how inefficient he'd be at finding and retrieving the game bird, slashing and searching futilely in the undergrowth.

Every potential thief will be wary of the savage teeth, the snarling threats and the game courage of a dog protecting his patch. Not for the dog any thoughts of, "Am I going to get hurt if I attack," nor any hesitation about what to do. The dog reacts instinctively to the intrusion; his first thought is to threaten, and then, if that is not effective, to attack purposefully and drive away the trespasser.

Perhaps you don't want a dog for a particular job, but just to love and be your friend, to be a pal to the kids, a companion on walks, or company around the house when you get lonesome. There are few living creatures who can do this as well as a dog. He never questions or argues as even the nicest of human friends do. For every bit of love you give him he will return it doubled. You are, without any doubt, God as far as your dog is concerned.

The dog, by just being dog, can bring out the best in the human, and can often unleash the love and affection that many people find so hard to express. Human beings do need to love someone or something and be loved in return, for this helps to strengthen their faith in life and keep a warm sense of security alive when things get tough.

This ability of the dog to be man's faithful companion, as well as his workmate, is probably the most important aspect of the dog/man relationship.

The working dogs give loyalty as well as service to their masters, and between man and dog a bond of respect and understanding is built as they work together. If the job is a lonely one — shepherding, guarding, some kinds of hunting — the companionship each gives the other is comforting.

Some kinds of dogs are more pets and companions than workers — the little lapdogs and toys; but they have other uses too, for they are usually good housedogs. Though their looks may not scare away intruders, their alertness and shrill barkings give a warning. So even the most cynical observer cannot say that any dog is completely useless.

Which Dog?

Choosing a dog to do a job of work is often a simple matter — you select from the dogs specially bred to do best that particular job, and buy from a kennel or a shop with a good reputation.

It is when you want a dog simply as a companion that most difficulties of choice arise. Despite the fact that dogs generally are loving and giving in their affections, different dogs fit different circumstances. Choosing the dog that is going to be yours and your family's companion for maybe the next twelve years is not something to be done lightly and without a deal of thought.

The worst way to choose your canine companion is on a whim; because the kids like that "doggie in the window," or because when you were a youngster you always fancied having, say, a Bull Terrier and never got one.

Maybe now that you're grown up and have a couple of youngsters of your own, you live in suburbia, with no fences to your yard, and everybody in the neighborhood has dogs — or cats. Unless you know a lot about Bull Terriers, it could be that your pet dog is going to have a whale of a time chasing the neighborhood Poodles and

Dachshund

The friendly little figure of the smooth-coated Dachshund is so familiar that many people are unaware that Dachshunds are also available in both the wire-haired and long-haired format. While most Dachshunds are either a solid red or a black and tan, there is also a dappled variety as well as a striped. The miniature variety is 9 pounds or under, while the standard Dachshund may weigh up to 25 pounds. Most popular in America is the so-called "small Standard" which matures at about 12 pounds. Registered by the American Kennel Club in the "Hound" group.

SALLY ANNE THOMPSON

Yorkshire Terriers. Whisper it, he might even kill one in his enthusiasm.

Not that there is anything wrong with Bull Terriers. They are very amiable characters — to human beings; very obedient to their masters; very reliable with children. But they were bred to fight other dogs. The master may be at the office all day, and the Bull Terrier may not feel that he should take orders from the lady of the house, particularly if he has been dying for weeks to get at that Beagle across the street and today the kids left the house door open . . . . .

A Greyhound in a similar environment might be a mistake, too. All the Greyhound types are bred to chase — and catch — anything that moves, especially anything about the size of a hare. And suburbia abounds with active toy dogs, and with cats.

More obvious, perhaps, is the unsuitability of a St. Bernard in a two room city apartment, or a heavy coated Husky living in the Nevada desert area with or without airconditioning, even if you are prepared to keep his coat sheared.

Are these exaggerations? Perhaps. But these are the kind of things that happen and, as a result, an otherwise good companion gets labeled a misfit; everybody is unhappy, including the dog, and he winds up being given away to the first home that's offered or taking a one way trip to the veterinarian. Which all seems a sad waste.

So what kind of dog should it be?

Consider first your needs, your likes and dislikes, including any ideas you might have had about your ideal dog. Do you hate small dogs, or love dogs with long hair? Are you besotted by the sad looking dogs? Does the very tiny dog make you feel protective and strong?

Consider, second, the way you live, whether you have a small apartment, a house and yard, or a farm. Do you live near a park, near woods or acres of open space, or miles of open beach? Do you have children and do all your neighbors have children? Are there lots of other dogs and pets nearby, or livestock such as sheep and cattle and chickens? Do you live on Main Street or near a busy road, and can't build a fence around your property perhaps because of zoning restrictions?

Then, thirdly, consider the characteristics of the 150 or so recognized breeds, and see if you can find your ideal dog, the one that most fits not only your likes, but also your needs and circumstances.

Dalmatian

A breed of dog that is entitled to be called "all around" is that sparkling gentleman, the Dalmatian. He has been used for hunting upland game, trailing, retrieving, in packs for hunting large animals, a circus performer, a coach dog and a fire dog.

Look at Size

Dogs come in assorted sizes and weights; from Chihuahuas weighing less than one pound, to St. Bernards weighing close to two hundred. The size of the dog you choose depends on several things: how much *space* you have, for instance; is the dog going to fill your rooms and be always in the way; is there enough space for it to stretch its legs to get some exercise? Obviously a St. Bernard needs a larger backyard than a Chihuahua; but, contrary to what you might think, a St. Bernard, though bigger, doesn't need as much wide open space for exercise as a medium sized, more active dog such as one of the sight hunting hounds or a shepherd dog. A house in the suburbs with a good sized back yard and nearby streets for a sedate walk, or even a large roomed city apartment with a handy park are big enough for a dog of the massive breeds.

Size has a bearing on things other than space: is a big dog going to be too much for you to handle? If you are inclined to be easygoing and casual in temperament, maybe you'd be better off with one of the smaller breeds. At least you can pick up — and thus keep under control — a smaller dog if it starts to get uppity. A really powerful sixty pound lively Boxer, for instance, takes some handling.

How Far to Walk?

If you go everywhere by automobile, or never get far on your own two legs, from either choice or necessity, obviously an active dog needing a three mile walk every day to keep happy and healthy is not for you. Most of the working and hunting dogs fall into this category. On the other hand, very big dogs require only brief walking, as do Bulldogs and other heavy slow moving breeds. Some of the tiny toy lap dogs do not object if they don't get much walking. Then there are one or two breeds that, if all else suits, are ideal for the lazy; for instance, the little known Shih Tzu (a long-haired Chinese dog, related to the Lhasa Apso and the Pekingese) can be very content with the idle life. Also the Schipperke, the dog of the Belgian taxicabs and barges, is almost self exercising — just trotting busily about the house and yard keeps him happy.

Good Mixers — and Loners

The right temperament is vital for the companion dog. In a family, the ideal is the dog whose temperament is even, but who is alert, friendly, and not too lethargic. The family dog has to adapt to the maulings of children, the helter-skelter of the household, the comings and going of friends, the mailman, the meter reader, the delivery boys. He must be obedient to normal discipline and sufficiently devoid of wanderlust to stay in his own yard even when the door or gate is left open.

Some dogs require training and discipline to fit into the hurly-burly of family life. Several of the sheepherding dogs, who are upset by even an imagined reproof, can be numbered among these; so can the overprotective dogs, like the one man Chow-Chow, or the little Pekingese who jealously guards every inch of his territory against man and beast.

These dogs, however, simply because of the qualities that make them less suitable for families, may be just the companions for the sensitive, introspective person who lives alone; or for the older, perhaps deaf, "senior citizen" who would appreciate the protective, warning qualities of the lion hearted little Peke.

Avid flower and vegetable growers should think twice before choosing the digging kind of dog — mostly to be found in the terrier family — to whom digging is second nature. Terriers are high keyed dogs; some might call them quarrelsome, so a well disciplined household is their best environment.

Dandie Dinmont Terrier

There is something almost comical, and yet very appealing, about the bushy dome of the Dandie. But don't let appearances fool you—this dog was bred in the border area between England and Scotland to hunt vermin, a job requiring courage and at which he excels. His fondness for children make him a preferred housedog. Height at the shoulder: 8 to 11 inches. Weight: 18 to 24 pounds. Registered by the American Kennel Club in the "Terrier" group.

To Bark or Not

Many a dog becomes a nuisance when he barks incessantly and annoys the neighbors night and day. It is natural for any dog to bark when he hears an unusual sound or senses the approach of a stranger. Some breeds have this instinct more than other breeds. Small dogs are usually very alert, and quickly announce vocally anything unusual.

But the barking should be reasonable, not uncontrolled. Good "warning" instincts can go over the top, and the so-called housedog becomes a house nuisance with its hysterical yapping at every imagined sound and at every person, friend or foe. So make sure when buying one of the kinds of dog renowned as housedogs that it has an even temperament and is not high strung or excitable.

The bigger dog usually gives warning first by growling, not by barking, and only barks when his first signal is ignored. When looking at the larger breeds, don't even consider the puppy or youngster that goes off his head with barking when you approach. He'll be a nuisance in the neighborhood for sure.

If your neighbors are anti-dog, or if the landlord is very touchy, the answer may be a Basenji. This African hunting dog is the ultimate — normally he has no bark at all, just a small voice. Or, one of the Bulldogs is less likely to yap.

A few other things to remember: some hounds bay when excited, the Bloodhound in particular. Some toy dogs have been the pets of mankind for so long they consider it their right to go everywhere with their owner; never leave a Pug at home alone unless you warn the neighbors first, otherwise they'll think you've shut up a baby in the house! Some Poodle owners have the same problem!

CHART OF CANINE CHARACTERISTICS

An attempt to compartmentalize dogs into a limited number of categories, such as we try to do in our chart on page 86, requires a certain flexibility. However, a dog chart is valuable because by its very nature it compresses a great deal of information into a limited space. Its weakness is that many dogs have characteristics which fall half-way between the various categories, and no matter on which side of the line they are placed someone is sure to be unhappy. In addition, many of the evaluations are subjective, depending in large part upon those specimens of the breed which the compiler of the chart has encountered. This is less true when discussing temperament. For a fuller discussion of any particular breed, one of The Pet Library's books on that breed should be consulted.

How to Make the Most of the Chart

Size: This section is divided into three columns, S, M and L, indicating respectively small, medium and large.

Dogs range in size from the tiny Chihuahua, which may mature at less than two pounds, to the giant St. Bernard, that may well weigh over two hundred. Within those extremes there is ample room for variation. Some dogs, such as the Basset Hound and English Bulldog, are very heavily built, and while they weigh as much as some of the so-called larger breeds, they occupy much less space. Dogs such as these have been categorized as "medium." Others, such as the Saluki, are long-legged, light-framed and, while not too heavy, are considered for our purposes as large dogs. In general,

Doberman Pinscher

This breed was developed by Herr Louis Dobermann, a dog warden in Thuringia, Germany, according to a preconceived plan, thus making him one of the few "made to order" dogs. The Doberman has an extensive and honorable record of service with various police departments and armed forces units throughout the world and is the breed chosen for service with the United States Marines. Height at the shoulder: male 26 to 28 inches—female 24 to 26 inches. Registered by the American Kennel Club in the "Working Dog" group.

then, any dog from approximately Miniature Poodle size down would be placed under "S," any dog about the size of a Dalmatian or English Setter and up would be classified as "L" or large, while dogs falling between those two categories would be "M" or medium.

Temperament: Here we are involved in a controversial subject, embodying as it does those traits which distinguish the breeds. Again, it must be stressed that these are subjective opinions. For example, under the heading "Tr" we include those dogs which by general consensus are considered the most easily trained. This does not mean that every dog of a breed not so listed is untrainable, or is not, perhaps, every bit as trainable as an individual in the Tr column. Nor, conversely, does it mean that every dog of every breed indicated as trainable will turn out to be a Rin Tin Tin or a Lassie.

Always remember that these are the characteristics of the breed in general, and that individual members of that breed can move from category to category:

Tr   indicates those breeds considered readily trainable. You will see representatives of this group on movie and television screens, in circuses and dog acts.

H   These dogs, because of their size and docile disposition, adapt themselves readily to confinement in limited quarters. This does not mean that they are hothouse flowers requiring protection. Many of them can be, and are, kenneled outdoors where they will prove to be as tough and hardy as their larger brethren.

Ex+ These are considered vigorous dogs that should be exercised regularly.

Ex— These dogs are not considered extremely active and will thrive on a minimum of exercise.

Fam All-weather dogs, these will adapt readily to outdoor kenneling. Of course, any dog, no matter how hardy, does require adequate draft-free, waterproof shelter.

OM Some breeds of dogs are considered more gregarions than others. They love the world and everyone in it. Other breeds tend to form close attachments to an individual or to a family, regarding strangers with caution. Almost any breed of dog, provided it has the physical ability, can be trained to act as a watchdog or guard. However, you are more likely to find dogs with a highly developed protective instinct in the group indicated under OM.

Coat Characteristics: These are divided into three categories: Sh (shorthaired), Lo (long-haired), and C/S (needs clipping or stripping). The first category is, of course, self-explanatory. We have placed in the second (Lo) those dogs which do not ordinarily require intensive clipping or stripping. Almost any long-haired dog will benefit from a light trimming from time to time, while it is a practice of some people to clip down all long-haired dogs, regardless of the style, during the warm weather. Most long-haired dogs will require a small amount of clipping or stripping to tidy up their outlines, and improve their appearances for show purposes. However, we have reserved the category C/S for those dogs whose coat does require regular barbering, and whose kennel club Standard calls for the dog to be shown trimmed.

	Size			Temperament						Coat		
	S	M	L	Tr	H	Ext	Ex-	Fam	OM	Sh	Lo	C/S
Afghan Hound			x			x		x	x		x	
Alaskan Malamute			x			x		x	x		x	
Airedale Terrier			x	x	x	x		x				x
American Foxhound		x				x		x	x	x		
Australian Terrier	x			x	x		x				x	
Basenji	x			x	x	x				x		
Basset Hound		x		x	x		x			x		
Beagle	x			x	x	x		x		x		
Bedlington Terrier	x			x	x	x		x	x			x
Bloodhound			x	x			x	x		x		
Border Terrier	x				x	x		x			x	
Borzoi			x			x		x	x	x		
Boston Terrier	x			x	x		x			x		
Boxer			x	x	x	x		x		x		
Brittany Spaniel		x		x		x		x			x	
Brussels Griffon	x			x	x		x					x
Bulldog		x			x		x			x		
Bullmastiff			x	x		x		x	x	x		
Bull Terrier		x		x	x		x	x		x		
Cairn Terrier	x			x	x		x	x			x	
Chesapeake Bay Retriever			x	x		x		x	x		x	
Chihuahua	x			x	x		x			x	x	
Chow-Chow		x			x		x	x	x		x	
Cocker Spaniel, Am.		x		x	x		x	x				x
Cocker Spaniel, Engl.		x·		x	x		x	x				x
Collie			x	x		x		x		x	x	
Dachshund	x			x	x		x			x	x	x
Dalmatian			x	x	x	x		x		x		
Dandie Dinmont		x			x		x	x	x			x
Doberman Pinscher			x	x		x		x	x	x		
English Setter			x	x		x		x			x	
English Springer Span.		x		x		x		x			x	
English Toy Spaniel	x			x	x		x				x	
Fox Terrier		x		x	x		x	x		x		x
French Bulldog	x			x	x		x			x		

	Size			Temperament						Coat		
	S	M	L	Tr	H	Ext	Ex-	Fam	OM	Sh	Lo	C/S
German Shepherd Dog			x	x	x	x		x	x		x	
German Shorthaired Pointer			x	x		x		x		x		
Golden Retriever			x	x		x		x			x	
Great Dane			x	x		x		x		x		
Great Pyrenees			x	x		x		x			x	
Greyhound			x			x		x	x	x		
Irish Setter			x	x		x		x			x	
Irish Terrier		x			x	x		x				x
Irish Wolfhound			x	x		x		x				x
Italian Greyhound	x				x		x			x		
Japanese Spaniel	x			x	x		x				x	
Keeshond		x		x	x	x		x			x	
Kerry Blue Terrier		x			x	x		x	x			x
Labrador Retriever			x	x	x	x		x		x		
Lakeland Terrier		x			x		x	x				x
Lhasa Apso	x				x		x	x			x	
Maltese	x			x	x		x				x	
Manchester Terrier	x	x		x	x		x			x		
Manchester, Toy	x			x	x		x			x		
Mastiff			x	x	x		x	x	x	x		
Miniature Pinscher	x			x	x		x		x	x		
Newfoundland			x	x			x	x			x	
Norwegian Elkhound		x		x		x		x	x		x	
Old English Sheepdog			x	x		x		x			x	
Papillon	x			x	x		x				x	
Pekingese	x				x		x		x		x	
Pointer			x			x		x	x	x		
Pomeranian	x			x	x		x		x		x	
Poodle, Toy, Miniature	x	x		x	x		x	x				x
Poodle, Standard		x	x	x	x	x		x				x
Pug	x			x	x		x			x		
Rottweiler			x	x		x		x	x	x		
St. Bernard			x				x	x	x	x	x	
Saluki			x			x		x	x		x	
Samoyed			x	x		x		x	x		x	

	Size			Temperament						Coat		
	S	M	L	Tr	H	Ext	Ex-	Fam	OM	Sh	Lo	C/S
Schipperke	x			x	x		x	x	x		x	
Schnauzer, Miniature	x			x	x		x					x
Schnauzer, Standard		x		x	x		x	x				x
Schnauzer, Giant			x	x		x		x	x			x
Scottish Terrier		x			x		x	x	x			x
Sealyham Terrier		x			x		x	x	x			x
Shetland Sheepdog		x		x	x		x	x			x	
Shih Tzu	x				x		x				x	
Siberian Husky			x			x		x			x	
Silky Terrier	x			x	x		x				x	
Skye Terrier		x			x		x	x			x	
Staffordshire Terrier		x		x	x		x	x		x		
Weimaraner			x	x		x		x	x	x		
Welsh Corgi, Cardigan and Pembroke		x		x	x	x		x	x	x	x	
Welsh Terrier		x		x	x		x	x				x
West Highland White Terrier	x			x	x		x	x				x
Whippet		x		x	x	x		x	x	x		
Yorkshire Terrier	x			x	x		x				x	

Crossbreeds

There is one other kind of dog to be considered. He isn't included in anybody's classification, or on anybody's register. He's the mongrel, mutt or crossbreed — call him what you will.

Mongrels make good family pets for lots of people. They come in all shapes and sizes, with all kinds of coats, and all kinds of instincts. But they have just as much puppy appeal as any purebred dog. And usually they cost only a few dollars.

Contrary to popular opinion, they are not more intelligent or more healthy than purebred dogs. It is just that the rules of natural — and unnatural — selection operate far more ruthlessly on them. Because it has little dollar value, the mongrel puppy is not tended and guarded so fiercely as the expensive purebred. It is more readily passed on or left to wander at the mercy of strangers.

The mongrel failures are soon forgotten. Those who survive represent the temperamentally sound, the healthiest, and the most intelligent specimens. It it a simple matter of the survival of the fittest.

The real problem when buying a mongrel puppy, however attractive, is that you cannot predict with any certainty how it is going to turn out. How big will it grow? What sort of dogs are in its ancestry? Were they hunters, herders, terriers, fighting dogs, or toy purebreds that got out of somebody's garden gate and went astray? Were all the dogs in its ancestry of reliable temperament, or were there some vicious ones among them?

Acquiring a mongrel puppy is always a gamble. But if you are the kind who would love your dog anyway, no matter how he turned out, and to whom price is an important consideration, then among the mongrel population you may find the dog that is right for you.

Choosing the ideal dog is a gamble anyway. The most careful assessment of all the characteristics of the canine race will still not

English Setter
The physical beauty of this dog is matched only by its sweetness of disposition. Thus both its appearance and character have endeared it to sportsmen and dog lovers for at least 400 years since its development in England.

English Toy Spaniel
A charming little dog which is becoming increasingly popular in the United States. An ancient breed, its origin is obscure although there is evidence to indicate that the breed was originally developed in Japan.

insure the perfect match. In the end, a companion dog must be chosen with love as well as common sense.

Inherited Traits

Recent genetic studies emphasize the importance of heredity in the development of dog behavior. Heredity has an important effect on almost every trait tested. So concluded Dr. J. P. Scott and Dr. John L. Fuller working at the Jackson Laboratory, Bar Harbor, Maine. They worked with five breeds of dogs representing the major groups: Wirehair Fox Terrier, American Cocker Spaniel, African Basenji, Shetland Sheepdog and the Beagle.

Among other things, they found that sex does have definite effects upon the aggressive tendencies of dogs and upon the dominance order, but not upon their trainability and ability to solve problems. This means then that the male is more dominant (the pack leader) and aggressive, but that the female is his equal when it comes to training and intelligence.

Inherited emotional traits profoundly influence performance. Although the various breeds differed widely in emotional and motivational characteristics, no one breed was superior to any other in solving problems. Detailed statistical analyses indicate that there is a highly complex relationship between the basic genetic inheritance and its final effect upon behavior.

Perhaps the most important of their findings so far as the pet owner is concerned, is that there is a critical period in the puppy's life which exerts a lasting influence upon its adult behavior and ability to adjust to human relationships. A puppy removed from its mother and littermates at the age of six to eight weeks, and brought into a home and family environment, where it is handled and petted, has a far better chance of becoming a well-adjusted dog in its relationships with both people and other dogs than the one left behind in the kennel where, although it is adequately fed and housed, it is not given the advantage of human handling. For a puppy to turn out well then, it should be brought into the home as early as possible (before it is eight weeks old) and certainly not after 13 weeks if it has never known the human touch. Let it be emphasized that this contact with humans need not necessarily be extensive. Even picking a dog up gently once a day is sufficient to establish the proper rapport.

Entlebuch Sennenhund
"Sennenhund" means mountain dog, and there are a number of varieties in Switzerland, all descendants of cattle dogs left behind by the Romans. The Entlebuch, like the others, is named after the Swiss Canton where it is best known. Height at the shoulder: 16 to 20 inches. Registered by the Swiss Kennel Club.

AKE WINTZELL

V The Puppy For You

You've decided which breed you want; now to find the right puppy.

Should it be a male or female? This depends on several things. Do you want puppies at a future date? If so, obviously you must choose a female. If you do, she should be the best possible example of her breed you can find and afford — a show dog, in fact.

Maybe, though, you just want a pet, a dog to live with the family and be part of the household. Does it matter then, which sex it is?

More people probably favor the male dog. The male doesn't have the inconvenient habit of coming "in season" twice a year, wandering and attracting all the dogs in the neighborhood to his door. Other people argue: Ah, but the female is only interested in the opposite sex twice a year, while the male dog is always out on the town looking for a girl friend!

These days, though, with modern veterinary science to come to our aid, the major disadvantage of the female no longer really matters. If you really prefer a "her" to a "him," there is no need to worry about the twice yearly "season." A bitch can have a relatively minor operation, called spaying, which will prevent her from having puppies, and even from being interested in a suitor.

This operation is usually performed when she is about six months of age, just about maturity. Your veterinarian will be glad to explain what is involved.

Don't be fooled, incidentally, into buying a young female only a few weeks old, which, you are told, has had this operation. A female spayed too early in life usually grows to look as much like a male as a female.

Of course, if there is the slightest chance that later you might want your female to have puppies, she should not be spayed.

Females, especially if they have been spayed, are usually quieter in temperament than males and generally more affectionate. Males are usually bigger and more boisterous.

As for the idea that the male will always be wandering, the dog that leads a full and happy life as the pet of the family, and has never caught on to the idea that there are girl dogs, won't worry about it. Dogs are not like people — they don't sit and yearn, they just enjoy every day as it comes. Kept in sweet innocence, they have no problem.

So, male or female, there is really nothing in it apart from your own personal preference.

Puppies in pet shops come in appealing tumbling groups. They come in bouncing mobs in spruce runs at kennels. They come in special departments, all efficient and hygienic, in large sized department stores. They come, by way of advertisements, from private breeders.

They are also kept in over-crowded, dirty, underfed conditions by puppy-factory breeders or "quick-buck" dog dealers. If the conditions in such places are bad enough to make you shudder or raise your hands in horror, don't linger long enough to lose your heart to one of these little mites, because you will only be buying a load of trouble and veterinary bills. Heartless as it may seem, you must resist the tender feelings that rise in you at the sight of such puppies, and *not buy*. It is only when people refuse to buy these dogs that "quick-buck" dealers will mend their ways.

Buy only from the best places. Buy with care and a guarantee. Remember that you are buying a companion who will be with you for the next ten, twelve, or even fifteen years.

Pet shops, most big kennels, and department stores are the most professional sellers of puppies. Good ones have their reputations to consider, and they will want you, the customer, to be satisfied with your purchase. So they will welcome your questions and the care you take in choosing your dog.

Look around and see that the place is clean and the puppies kept in decent surroundings, whether in an indoor run, cage or outdoor kennels. See that all the puppies appear in lively good health, bouncing and playing about, not huddled miserably in

Field Spaniel

The modern Field Spaniel is an American creation, based largely on crossings of the Cocker and Sussex Spaniels with the original English Field Spaniel. It is a thorough but somewhat slow worker, with a fine disposition. Height at shoulder: about 18 inches. Registered by the AKC in the "Sporting Dog" group.

R. W. TAUSKEY

Finnish Spitz.

Unlike most European Spitz which are primarily pet and guard dogs, the Finnish Spitz, a native to Finland for hundreds of years, is utilized extensively when hunting birds. They are also locally popular as a home guardian and pet. Height at the shoulder: male 17 to 20 inches— female 15 to 18 inches. Not registered by the American Kennel Club.

AKE WINTZELL

AKE WINTZELL

Flat Coated Retriever

It is unfortunate that this fine field dog is not better known in the United States. A cheerful, steady worker, it is equally good when water retrieving or working upland game birds. Height at the shoulder: about 23 inches. Registered by the American Kennel Club in the "Sporting Dog" group.

93

R. W. TAUSKEY

corners with a limp lethargic look about them.

Ask the owner about guarantees and whether you can have the puppy you choose examined by a veterinarian. Anyone selling good stock certainly will not object.

The Papers

When you buy a purebred puppy, the so-called papers are an essential part of the purchase. These are *not* the dog license, the vaccination certificate, and the details of the pedigree with all the names of the dog's ancestors on it, important as they may be.

The vital papers, your documentary proof that the puppy you are buying is a purebred specimen of the breed, is the Registration.

There are several registration associations, some of them specializing in sporting and working dogs; but the association your pup is more likely to be registered with is the American Kennel Club, which is the overlord of most of the big dog shows. Unless a dog is properly registered with the AKC, it cannot be entered in a show licensed by the AKC. Should you ever have puppies from your dog, they cannot be registered unless the parents were.

So you can see how important registration papers are when you

Foxhound (American)

Foxhounds probably first arrived in this country with the Spanish Conquistadors. However, it was the hard-riding, fox hunting gentlemen of the South who deserve the most credit for the early importations of the English Foxhound, the foundation of our American Foxhound. Today, Foxhounds are used in field trials, as trail or drag hounds, for hunting with a gunner and their best-known use, that of fox hunting as a pack followed by riders in formal attire. Height at the shoulder: male 22 to 25 inches—female 21 to 24 inches. Registered by the American Kennel Club in the "Hound" group.

buy a purebred puppy. Never even consider buying a puppy if the seller says you can have it cheaper "without papers." If someone is selling you a guaranteed purebred puppy, the registration papers are part of that purchase.

When a puppy is AKC registered, it means that his ancestry — that is, his pedigree — is recorded with the AKC. You can always get details of your puppy's pedigree from the AKC once you have his registration details.

If the puppy is already individually registered, the seller will give you a purple bordered white certificate of registration, on the back of which he will fill in your name and sign it. This you must send to the registration society, so that you are on record as the puppy's owner. Puppies individually registered will already have an official name and a registration number.

If the puppy has been registered only as one of a litter, the seller will give you a different registration application form. The breeder is issued these application forms, one for each puppy, by the AKC when the birth of the litter is registered. When a puppy is sold, the sex and color of the puppy, and the name of the purchaser, must be filled in correctly, and the seller must sign the form.

You, as the purchaser, fill in the name you have chosen for the puppy, sign your name in the proper place, and send the form with the correct fee to the AKC. The puppy is then individually registered and your name goes down on record as the lawful owner.

It may be that neither an application form nor a transfer form is available; perhaps because the breeder has not yet registered the litter, or the necessary forms have not yet been issued by the AKC. Then you should have, as a minimum, a written guarantee that you will be given the necessary papers, and also, as part of that guarantee, the name and registration number of the sire and dam, the date of birth, and the name of the breeder. It is most important that the sire and the dam should already be registered, because unless they both are, the puppy cannot be registered.

A dog's *pedigree* is only a record of his ancestry; the names of the parents, grandparents and great grandparents. It isn't a guarantee that he is purebred; if someone took the trouble to write down the names of the ancestors of any dog, he would have a "pedigree" even if the ancestors were of several different breeds.

The pedigree of a purebred dog is one in which all the registered names are the names of dogs of the same breed. Your guarantee of pure breeding is that each of those dogs, for several generations back, is a dog *registered* as being of the same breed.

So beware of anyone who wants to sell you a "purebred" puppy with only a "pedigree," and no sign or guarantee of registration papers.

Homecoming

The moment you take your chosen puppy in your arms and carry him to your car to take him home is an exciting one. A new kind of life is beginning for him — and for you.

What you do in the next few days is important as it will set the pattern of your life together. Right from the start, your puppy should be one of the family, and treated as such, but first of all he will need a little extra special care and attention.

He is bound to feel a little strange and confused, a bit scared perhaps. If he's very young, he's probably never been in a car before, so he might feel nauseated by its motion. Be prepared for this and make sure you have a box to put him in so that he can rest quietly.

If it's a long journey, arm yourself with plenty of newspapers and some kind of toweling or clean rags as well. One woman I know, who raised four children and lots of puppies too, used to swear by the old-fashioned baby's cotton diaper. She never took a puppy anywhere without a bundle of the last baby's castoff diapers in the car!

As the puppy grows a little older, and gets more used to car travel, he'll grow out of any tendency to travel sickness. Most dogs just love to travel by car, often sensing when you are headed for the garage or carport so that before you've even had time to put the key in the car door they are there waiting, tails waving expectantly, all ready for the travel treat.

Your new young pup is also going to be confused by the strange person he's been handed over to — meaning you. So make him feel secure, and ease his anxiety by handling him gently. Ask the children to resist their perfectly natural desire to cuddle and fondle him at first, until he feels that you are okay and *his* people.

Teach them, too, the right way to pick up a puppy. This is *not* by the scruff of the neck, letting legs and body dangle. That's the wrong way. I know that you've probably seen female dogs and cats pick up their young this way, but they don't do it when their offspring get older and heavier.

You must always pick up a puppy — and an older dog for that matter — by supporting the whole body. Do this by sliding one hand under the chest, the other hand picking him up and supporting the hind quarters, so that his body is resting on your hands and arm, and against your body. No part of the puppy's body should carry the weight of any other part. If you have to carry a puppy one handed, use the whole of your forearm and the side of your body as well as your hand to support the body.

Foxhound (English)

The poet, Canon Kingsley, wrote, "Next to an old Greek statue, there are few such combinations of grace and strength as in a fine Foxhound." He is an intelligent dog, and, given the opportunity, excels at other tasks. Height at the shoulder: about 23 inches. Registered by the American Kennel Club in the "Hound" group.

Fox Terrier (Smooth)
A smooth-coated version of the Wire Hair, the two varieties have the same characteristics. Originally, these dogs were bred to be carried in the fox hunter's saddle bag. When the fox went "to ground," the Fox Terrier was used to bolt him. Height at the shoulder: male just under 15 inches, female somewhat lower.

AKE WINTZELL

Fox Terrier (Wire Hair)
One of the most popular dogs in America, this English breed is noted for its vivacity, showmanship and jolly character. Alert and lively, he will play with the kids all day and guard the house all night. Fox Terriers have made an enviable record in obedience competition.

Teach the children right from the start to handle the puppy gently and correctly. Guard against their tendency to pick it up out of balance, so that the puppy slips from their arms head (the heaviest part) first. A young puppy can be badly hurt if it falls heavily on its head. Dogs don't have the quick recovery of equilibrium that cats do.

Part and parcel of making the pup feel at home is to give him a name, preferably a short one syllable name that he can readily understand. Hearing his name should bring an instant response. It should alert him, so that when you add a command, his attention is already focused on you. Always use his name in a pleasant tone, never a scolding one. Keep the scolding tone for the reprimand that is to follow once you have alerted him to the fact that you are talking to him.

Have a special place ready for your puppy at home. Dogs like to feel they have their own bed, and their own place in the house. Most people put the puppy bed in the kitchen, and this is a good idea, provided the kitchen is big enough for the bed not to be in everybody's way.

If the kitchen isn't suitable, then the living room is a good place, or in milder climates, on a draft free porch.

An enclosed porch off the kitchen, or one which is an extension of the living room, is actually a very good place for a dog to have his own special "home", provided it is free of drafts, and has some kind of air conditioning to keep a constant, comfortable temperature. If it is a sunny porch, the dog's bed should be in the shade — he'll find the sun to lie in when he wants to — and there should be plenty of ventilation so that the temperature can be kept to a comfortable level.

If a porch is used, it is easier to fence off a small pen when the puppy first arrives. This is good because it helps with the task of housebreaking. A puppy coming straight from the litter is probably only, at most, paper trained. He won't as yet have the idea not to relieve himself on the living room carpet. This is something you are going to have to teach him; it may take a few weeks for him to learn it well enough so that he can be trusted not to disgrace himself.

When he first arrives, he'll need to settle in before you can expect him to do any real learning, and this is why restricting his movements at first will be a help.

Put his bed in the chosen place and then fence off an area around it. If you are keeping him in the kitchen and have an old-fashioned kitchen table, put some wire mesh around the legs (that means, of course, that your puppy's "own place" is always going to be under the kitchen table). In the living room you might make use of a child's castoff playpen, putting wire mesh around its outside.

With a restricted area, you will have somewhere to put the puppy when he wants to nap undisturbed and where he can sleep at night. Moreover, he can be confined there if you have to leave him home alone; you can then come back to a house that is not all messed up.

Or even when you're at home working around the house, a pen is a good place to keep the puppy, not only to prevent him from getting under foot but so that he gets used to the idea of being left alone.

Your puppy's bed can be a smart red dog bed from the pet store or a basket. Perhaps a wooden bed, made by Dad or one of the children. Even a not too big drawer from an old chest can be easily adapted. Or the pup's bed can be a strong cardboard box. Whatever it is, is should be raised a few inches from the floor to keep out drafts. Line it with some kind of mat; a piece of rug is excellent, being tough enough to resist chewing, or several layers of blanket can be used.

Spread the area around the bed with layers of newspaper, in case of accidents, and to encourage the beginnings of housebreaking. A puppy that has already been paper trained will know what the newspaper is for.

Don't line his bed with newspaper, for the obvious reason that dogs don't usually soil their beds. If yours does, the habit can be quickly broken by giving him his meals on his bed.

When you get your puppy home, everybody will want to make a fuss over him, especially the children. Explain to them that he will want to have a look round first.

Let him wander about, sniffing everywhere and exploring. Start to use his name, and let the children call him and talk to him, and try to encourage him to follow them. A little dog kibble, or a special toy, will probably interest him and get him used to the idea that all the strange people he is meeting are his family and friends. Let everybody be gentle and friendly.

Assign someone to keep an eye on him during this time because sooner or later he will want to relieve himself. When he shows the first signs, you can begin the initial lesson in housebreaking. If you've spread some sheets of paper on the floor he may use them. If he does, then he deserves some words of praise. Tell him he's a good boy (or girl), and give him a special dog treat.

If he doesn't head for the paper, but is obviously about to squat, pick him up without fuss and pop him on the paper. If this proves successful, praise him well and reward him. If it does not, or if you weren't quick enough, get to him while he is still aware of what he has done, tell him "No, no" in a gently scolding tone, and take him right away to the paper and, as you do, talk encouragingly to him. It is possible to get a preparation from the pet shops which acts as a housebreaking aid. It can be sprayed onto the paper or whatever spot you want the puppy to use, to attract the puppy.

Any mistake the puppy makes should be scrubbed up immediately with a mild disinfectant and soapy water, and the spot mopped or sprayed with a special deodorizing preparation which you can also buy from your pet store.

In the Doghouse

It may be that you want your puppy to live out-of-doors — many owners who have one of the medium to large breeds prefer this.

Obviously, it involves a little more thought for the welfare of the puppy. A very young pup coming from warm conditions must not be put outside to sleep during the coldest part of the 24 hours at night. He may have been kept under an infra-red lamp, or in a heated puppy room with the temperature kept up to 75 degrees. So he must first become accustomed to colder conditions by being kept outside only during the warmer hours of the day; gradually allow him to stay out longer and longer as the days go by.

It is, nevertheless, better for puppies who have been accustomed to it and who are going to sleep outside the house, perhaps in a kennel or in an outbuilding, to be taken to their new places straight away, and not kept indoors, even for the initial few days. If you bring them home and keep them indoors during the introductory period, you will find them very unsettled when they are put ouside — thoroughly resentful, in fact. They will demonstrate this by constantly whining and howling all night long.

This means that you must not buy too young a puppy — ten or twelve weeks in young enough. A puppy this age will be more or less adjusted to independent living, and be stronger in his development to face the rigors of outdoor life.

Secondly, choose your breed with the outdoor kennel in mind — obviously you wouldn't expect one of the toy or lap dogs to live in an outside kennel (nor would the toy dog want to — your bed is more his ideal!). The working breeds, and the tough medium sized heavier coated breeds are more suitable for this.

Thirdly, don't buy your puppy in the fall or the winter. Wait until spring or early summer so that he has the warmest months of the year to become accustomed to outdoor living.

Of course, you must make sure that the yard or area that the dog will be occupying is fenced in or enclosed, so that he won't wander off. It isn't advisable to secure a dog by confining him on a short chain. Close chaining can sometimes make a dog vicious and unfriendly.

If your newly bought puppy is not to fall victim to the automobile, the city authorities or the farmer's gun because he roams too freely, he should have a well fenced yard to call his own; or a wire stretched between two posts (or the house and a post) to which the dog's leash can be attached so that it slides freely back and forth.

An outdoor kennel should be weatherproofed — insulated to keep out the cold, without cracks or crevices so that it it free of drafts, and leakproof to keep out the rain. You can buy a commercially produced dog house, or you can adapt a crate or even an old-fashioned barrel. Some kind of a door is useful — one of those handy "pop" doors that the dog can operate himself, in or out. Most pet stores keep them, sized for cats and small dogs. For the bigger dog, a piece of canvas will serve as a door.

When painting the doghouse, remember that tests have proven that a house painted white is cooler than one painted black. So if you live in a warm area, paint your pet's house a light color, in cold areas, dark.

An outside kennel or doghouse should be located so that it gets some sun all through the year; it should face east or south or at least have its back to the prevailing wind. Naturally, it should be aired and cleaned frequently. Bedding too should be changed or washed often. This applies to *all* dog bedding, whether for housedogs or yard dogs. Many people clear the insect pests from the dog itself with powders, baths and sprays but forget the bedding, which is always a fertile breeding ground for parasites.

For bedding, a rug can be used. More sanitary is clean, dry straw, or the special wood shavings produced for dog bedding. Both of these must be changed frequently, but neither are really suitable for long-haired dogs. Shredded newspaper is better for the heavier-coated breeds; it doesn't tangle in the coat.

What about size of dog or doghouse? In the enclosed roofed kind, there should be room for the dog to stand up. In all types there should be space enough for the dog to stretch comfortably. Although too large is better than too small, dogs don't like much wide-open space around their beds — they like to feel cozy. Moreover, their body heat keeps them warmer in a more confined area.

Never, incidentally, put a dog to bed, or leave him alone, wearing his collar. Many dogs, particularly puppies, have been known to hang themselves by jumping about and getting the collar caught on a nail or similar protrusion. Equal care must be taken when tying a dog up on a lead; they will frequently twist themselves around objects so that the lead is shortened and shortened, until the slightest pull makes them choke.

The First Few Days

Now that your puppy is home and his bed organized he should quickly get settled. He may be restless and cry a lot the first night, missing his brothers and sisters, and be a little disturbed by a strange place. A warm hot water bottle under his bedding will comfort him, and con him into the idea that he has company. You can continue this for a few nights until he has decided that this bed really is his own.

You must ignore any crying the first night. Harden your heart, and perhaps put up with a sleepless night, for if you weaken and take him to your bedroom, or allow one of the children to do so, you may never again be able to convince him that that isn't his place for always!

You'll ask when you buy your puppy whether he has been wormed. If not, ask your veterinarian to prescribe the right medication. This should take priority. Worming is usually done in two doses, at two week intervals, and it should be repeated if necessary at the age of 6 months.

Next in importance are the puppy's inoculations. Some kennels and pet stores give a very early "stop gap" inoculation. If this has been done, the permanent inoculations will be needed at 10 weeks or so of age, followed by the normal booster shot every year. If your puppy has not been inoculated your veterinarian will advise the course. Don't forget that the puppy must not go out of your house and yard until his inoculations have been completed.

You'll find information on worming and inoculations, and why they are so important, in the chapter on Health.

Housebreaking and Training

Every puppy should be carefully housetrained, both to be clean and mannerly. This will take a little time and attention, but it is worth it if your canine companion is going to be a well-mannered, civilized member of the family.

Puppies usually learn very easily, but they are only babies, and at times a little patience is needed. All the members of the family can cooperate, and once the children understand the routine they can help too.

As you've already read, you can start to encourage the pup to be clean in the house the moment you bring him home. Carry on from this elementary beginning. First thing in the morning, as soon as he wakes, your puppy should go outside, for his instinct as he gets out of his bed will be to relieve himself. Go outside with him, and as soon as he has evacuated praise him and tell him how good he is. Bring him straight back indoors. This is important, because you want him to associate the going outdoors with relieving himself rather than with play.

When he comes in, give him his breakfast. Keep an eye on him after he has eaten it, and about ten minutes later, take him outdoors again, so that he can complete his duties.

You will be feeding him on a time schedule, and this always fits in very well with the housebreaking routine. He should be taken outside always after feeding, always when he awakens from sleep, and the last thing before he is settled for the night. You'll find that until they are about nine months old puppies will need to go outside from four to six times a day. Grown dogs can make do with about three times, usually defecating only once.

It often helps to associate a word with these frequent duty trips. "Out" is a simple one. You can include it in a sentence like "outside and be good," as long as you put the emphasis on the word "out." Alternatively, you could tell him to "Be good in the yard" or "garden." Use the same emphasis and tone every time, and don't forget to praise him when he performs well.

The paper you are spreading around his bed to prevent accidents can be reduced little by little. If you cannot take the puppy out-of-doors every time — perhaps you live in an apartment — you will, of course, need to continue with paper training for much longer than if the pup can have the freedom of a yard. Remove soiled paper, always replacing it with clean, but leave one piece of somer-that soiled paper behind. This will "mark" the permitted spot.

You can use the paper habit to encourage eventual complete

cleanliness. Move the newspaper gradually nearer the door, then under the door so that only a corner is showing, then eventually outside completely — always making use of a little soiled piece that bears the familiar scent to mark it as okay. This method is particularly useful with a puppy who finds it difficult to understand that he should gradually learn to use the out-of-doors.

As has been said before, don't smack the puppy when he makes a mistake; simply make it clear by the tone of your voice that you aren't pleased, as you show him the right place to go. If the mistake was made when you weren't there to see it happen, just scrub up with a deodorizing disinfectant. A young puppy can't connect a scolding with an error made even a few minutes before.

Puppies, and grown dogs for that matter, usually want to please you, and this is a most valuable aid when training a dog. Far better results are gained by using your voice and a few well chosen words than by corporal punishment. But more about that later.

Manners Maketh the Dog

Part and parcel of teaching a dog to live with the family is to teach him good manners. This is his behavior toward people and to things. Let's face it — puppies usually learn a lot quicker than children do! Maybe teaching the pup how to be civilized will rub off a bit on the kids! The kids will certainly have fun joining in.

SALLY ANNE THOMPSON

French Bulldog
Refined in France from under-sized English Bulldogs which were sent to that country in the mid and late 1800's, the "Frenchie," as he is affectionately known, is one of the finest apartment dogs ever developed. Short-haired and clean, he is bright, alert, lovable and sweet natured.

Getting on Chairs and Beds

Maybe you don't want the pup to be always climbing over the chairs. You can make it easy for yourself by spraying chairs and bedcovers with a commercial preparation that smells horrid to him, but is quite odorless to you, and is harmless to fabrics if directions are followed. Right from the start, make it a rule that dogs are forbidden on chairs and beds. The first time the puppy climbs up, pick him off and say "No" firmly. Do this every time he misbehaves, and get the rest of the family to do it too. If he persists, roll up a newspaper, bring it down with a thump on the chair beside him, pick him off and say "No" loudly and firmly. He'll soon catch on.

Hanging Around the Table

It's cute when the dog is small, but it becomes a nuisance later. Every mealtime, there's the dog, begging from everybody; you can't sit down with a sandwich without the dog hanging around, climbing all over you after a bite. If he does it to your guests too, they may not be so tolerant of the habit.

Besides, he doesn't need these tidbits if he is being properly fed; they'll just tend to make him fat, which isn't good for his health. Treats and tidbits should be restricted to professionally prepared dog "candy" or tasty vitamin tablets given when you choose to give

them. You can establish a regular habit, and give them every morning or every evening, but at mealtimes — never.

Use the training word, "No" said quite loudly and firmly, and push the dog down. Persist in this and make it understood that nobody in the family breaks the rule. If you do, you won't have to resort to the ultimate cure — banning him at mealtimes.

Of course, it's a bit hard on him if he's hungry and unfed at the time you are eating. You can resolve this by feeding him first, or at least by making his mealtimes regular so that he knows he is going to get his dinner as soon as you've had yours. Dogs are creatures of habit and they've a very good sense of time.

Jumping Up in Greeting

This is not too bad with a little dog, but it can be downright painful with a dog as hefty as a Boxer or a Labrador. Visiting children get bowled over, houseguests get their clothes dabbed with dirty paws, and grandmother gets to wonder why she ever came on a visit.

Don't be tolerant about this. "No — back!" said loudly along with pushing the dog away every time it happens is the method to use. Don't use the word "Down," because that is used in obedience training, which you may want to take up later and, if learned now, would only confuse the dog.

If the tone of voice and the words don't seem to have any effect, step on the dog's hind feet, and tell the others to do this too. It is shocking, maybe, but is saves a lot of trouble later on. This is a trick, incidentally, which the children can learn to use on strange dogs who jump up on them. If your neighbor has a dog with this bad habit, warn him what your children are doing, or you may upset neighborly relations and have your children labeled monsters, unkind to animals.

German Short-Haired Pointer
A mixture of the old Spanish Pointer, the English Foxhound and the Bloodhound, developed in Germany and refined in Great Britain and the United States, this dog has been acclaimed (and with a great deal of justice) the "all around " hunting dog. He can be taught to point, ground trail, and retrieve both on land and water. In addition, he is handsome and makes a fine family dog. Height at the shoulder: male 23 to 25 inches — female 21 to 23 inches. Registered by the American Kennel Club in the "Sporting Dog" group.

German Wire-Haired Pointer
This is not just a long-coated version of the German Short-Haired Pointer, but a distinctly different breed with a different heritage. While there is some German Short-Hair in the background, there is also Poodle, English Pointer, Griffon, and German Rough-Haired Pointer. The most popular gun dog in Germany, he will both point and retrieve.

AKE WINTZELL

Chewing Slippers and Other Belongings

All young puppies need to chew; it helps them to cut their teeth. They especially like to chew things that smell of you, and this is why slippers are such a favorite. Don't give the pup an old slipper and say that is okay, and then get mad when he chews up your new ones. He can't be expected to distinguish between the two.

A sharp "No!" accompanied by the snap of a rolled up newspaper, or the toss of a book at his feet, will stop him in mid-action. Give him a good marrow bone, and some special toys to chew on instead. You can buy toys from any pet store. A solid rubber ball, or a solid rubber ring, or some such toy made in the shape of a bone works fine. Make sure they are solid and won't disintegrate and stick in his throat if he swallows bits, or else get ones made of a special hide that is chewable and edible.

A marrow bone is excellent. Keep it sweet by scrubbing it occasionally, but use only plain water for this.

Encourage the puppy to take his chewing toys into his bed. His playthings are his, and his bed is his — they kind of go together. Besides, when he has to be left at home, he won't mind so much if he is already used to spending the odd hour or so in bed pleasantly chewing.

Of course, you'll make sure that when you do leave him alone there is nothing in the room for him to chew on. It would be foolish, for instance, to leave your slippers, or Junior's new toy within easy reach of a dog who's going to be looking for something with which to occupy himself while you're gone.

Dangers While Driving

No, this has nothing to do with dogs darting into the road. They are a danger, of course, and one hopes your puppy will never become one of them; if he does his life will be a short one, alas.

Dogs can be a danger to a car driver in other ways. If you use your car a lot for family outings, you are sometimes going to want to take the puppy along. In fact, it is sensible to get the little fellow used to traveling. If, at first, he has a tendency to car sickness, you'll want to get him over it; taking him on short car trips, a little farther each time, should do it. Maybe you'll have to help him along with some travel sickness pills. Your veterinarian will supply these for you — and do get expert advice on using them because the dosage depends on the type and weight of the dog. Never feed a dog before a journey, even if he doesn't usually get sick.

Most dogs, however, like to travel, especially by car. And there's the rub! They love it so much that they can't keep still, but have to be constantly back and forth in the car, looking out the window, trying to stick their heads out. A pup can't understand that if he jumps on your knee while you're at the wheel, or gets around the pedals at your feet, he's likely to cause an accident.

Right from the start teach the dog to stay on the back seat of the car, or if he doesn't particularly care about looking at the passing scene, on the floor between the seats.

If you've a station wagon, you can have a wire grid put up behind the back seat, so that the dog can have the whole of the baggage section to himself. Many of the bigger breeds prefer this, and they find it more relaxing. A rug fastened on the floor will make it quite comfortable and skidproof.

Never let a dog stick his head out of an open window. He can easily get grit or small flies in his eyes' which can cause a lot of pain and may damage his sight.

Train your pup to wait quietly in the car while you are visiting — provided the weather isn't too hot. Never park the car in the sun, and remember to leave a window open a little for ventilation whatever the weather, but not wide enough for the pup to jump out, of course.

Your pup will learn to regard the car as an extension of his territory, and will guard it zealously for you.

Up the Garden Path

Until your puppy is over four months of age, he probably won't be going out of his house and yard much. Eventually, however, he'll need to wear a collar and leash and be taken into the street. This is going to be a big event for him, and a bit frightening too.

You should anticipate this by getting him used to the feel of a collar and leash while he is still quite young. Try him first with a collar. Watch him rush around and try to rub it off. Then he'll scratch and scratch at his neck. Eventually, other things will distract him, and he'll forget about it.

Put on the collar gradually for a longer period every day. At the end of a few days he'll pay no further attention to it. That's the time to try the leash. First, attach it to the collar and let the puppy drag it around on the ground. Watch him all the time, of course, so he won't get tangled up.

The next step is to pick up the leash and let the puppy feel the pull of it on his collar. He will not like the restriction. He will pull, shake his head, and rub at his neck with his paws. Then he'll jump up and down, and twist and squirm, probably whining and squealing all the time. Finally he will sit on his little rear end and refuse to move.

Don't hurry him. If you can persuade him to walk a few steps, all well and good. Tempt him forward with a dog treat if you like, giving it to him as a reward when he walks correctly. Give him a few minutes every day with praise and reward whenever he walks a few yards.

Within a week you will probably be able to lead him up and down the garden path with no bother at all. Don't allow him to strain and pull forward after the first lesson or two. Gently but firmly pull him back to your side, at the same time saying "Heel." If he keeps on tugging forward, gently tap him on the nose with our old friend, the rolled up newspaper, saying "Heel" at the same moment.

Always end lessons on a happy note. Stop after he's done well enough for you to praise and reward him, not when he's fed up and confused. Better to start afresh another day and repeat the lesson than to get the pup hating his training sessions.

He will by now have had a few weeks to settle in his new home, to get used to it, and to love his new family. He's had his inoculations, and he's learned some of the things he can and cannot do. He's ready to go out into the world. In the next chapter you can learn how to build on the basic training you've already given him, and to teach him how to behave in public.

Golden Retriever
Many hunting dogs are specialists, preferring the field to the hearth. This is not true of the Golden Retriever whose intelligence and mild disposition make him welcome in the home, while his undoubted scenting and retrieving ability place him high in field competition. The history of his development in England is well documented.

Gordon Setter
A slow but steady worker, the Gordon (named after Scotland's Duke of Gordon) is noted for his perseverance and excellent scenting ability. To the uninitiated, his work is not particularly flashy, but at the end of the day it is more likely the Gordon that brings back the game.

111

Great Dane
This dog is known in Germany, its country of origin, as the "Deutsche Dogge," or "German Mastiff." Descending from crosses of the English Mastiff and Irish Wolfhound with various native German breeds, he was originally bred for hunting large game. At ease anywhere, this is the tallest breed of dog, although not the heaviest.

SALLY ANNE THOMPSON

VI   Learning and Training

Training

After you've had your puppy a few weeks, you'll find he's learned a lot of things. He's learned who is boss, and his own place in the household. He'll be completely, or almost, housebroken, and he will know the rudiments of civilized behavior. He will be walking nicely on the leash. He'll know a lot of words, too — his name, "No!", "Come," "Good" Boy (or Girl)," "Out," and "Heel!".

Now it's time for him to learn more. He is going to meet all kinds of new situations, as he grows up, and you must make sure that whatever happens he is going to respond to your commands.

Maybe he will prove so good at learning that you'll want to teach him more later on, do tricks, or obedience work. But more about that later.

Now we'll talk about some of the things that every dog should know. Before we start, though, there is an item of training equipment you should know about since it is going to make things easier for you and the pup. This is a training collar, sometimes called a chain slip collar, sometimes called a "choke" chain. It is usually a metal chain, with a ring at each end. When placed around the dog's neck correctly it will tighten up when pulled and slacken when relaxed. If you use this properly, the dog quickly learns that discomfort comes when he pulls and tugs and comfort comes with easing back and not straining.

It makes it easier on you too, because it is obviously doing some of the work of controlling the pup for you!

"Choke" chain training collars come in different sizes. Take your dog along when you buy one, to make sure you get it right, and ask someone at the pet store to show you the right way to put it on as it should be worn correctly for optimum results.

Let's take your pup on his first outing now, on the leash, to a busy main street. If you've been practicing in the yard, your pup should know what you expect of him. Now he is to be put to the test under more frightening and distracting conditions.

When you first take him out into the roads and streets, he will be nervous and perhaps scared of the noise and traffic. His instinctive reaction will be to run. He'll pull back sharply or dive sideways in alarm as the first noisy truck rattles by. You've got to send some confidence and a feeling of security down that leash. He is going to have to *trust* you.

So from the first minute you get out on the street, use exactly the same tone of voice and the same tactics that you used in the garden.

Keep the pup on your left but place yourself between him and the street, and keep him on a short leash so that he cannot dash off the sidewalk. Keep him at your side and say firmly, "Heel," just as you did in his initial leash training. When a big truck or fast car is about to rumble by, talk to him quietly and pat him if he seems really upset. This will help to reassure him.

Make it short and don't try to teach him anything new this first outing. Walk a little farther every day and, within a few days, he will ignore the traffic noises completely.

When a puppy starts to go out on leash, sooner or later he will have to relieve himself; for the city dwelling dog it is usually the only place he can. You must be sure that he does not foul the sidewalks or the front of shops and stores, so train him to use the gutter. Most pups going out in the streets are post-inoculation age and are therefore old enough to have developed some kind of control of their muscles and bodily functions, so you are likely to get some warning of what he is about to do.

As soon as you are aware that the pup wants to relieve himself, get him swiftly into the gutter, and keep him there until he does.

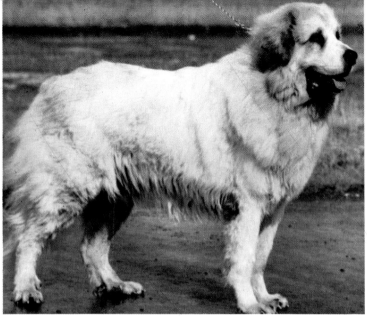

Great Pyrenees

In Europe he is known as the "Pyreneen Mountain Dog" and was developed in the Pyrenees by Spanish and French farmers and shepherds. This large dog is an excellent and reliable guard and companion. Height at the shoulder: male 27 to 32 inches—female 25 to 29 inches. Registered by the American Kennel Club in the "Working Dog" group.

Praise him highly when he uses the right place. If he's a dog who readily catches on to words (and some dogs are undoubtedly quicker at this than others), you could use a special word, such as "Road," or "Gutter."

A Taste of Freedom

You've taught your puppy to walk on leash, to ignore noise and traffic. At home he behaves reasonably well, and whenever you call him he comes. But will he come to you when you call him if he is unleashed in the park or in the countryside? Sudden freedom from the restrictions of the leash will go to any puppy's head. Well, it's fine to give him a real romp in the wide open spaces. He lets off steam — and a growing youngster has plenty of that.

On the other hand, no dog should be allowed to rush about completely uncontrolled, particularly in a park where there are other dogs and children. The unleashed dog should return to his master the instant he is called.

For his own sake it is best to begin this lesson in a fairly secluded spot where there is no danger. An empty beach, secluded woods, or the park early in the morning before too many people are about, is the kind of place you should use.

It is no good trying this exercise at home in a familiar yard. What you are after is the atmosphere of freedom, the fresh distracting smells of a new place. Your pup knows his yard is fenced, and he knows the aroma of every inch of it; he'll be far more interested in the prospect of something new, and be more willing to come when he is called. So get him away from it all.

Arm yourself with a long length of light but strong cord — about twenty feet of it with a snap at the end — and some tasty tidbits, some dog treats or pieces of cooked liver. Take pup on his normal leash to your chosen spot — somewhere with plenty of space but plenty of distractions, too — trees, posts, interesting smells and so on.

Fix the end of the long cord to his collar, and hold the excess and the other end in your hand. Remove the dog's leash. Once he realizes he is free of it, he'll probably dash off. Just before he reaches the end of your twenty foot line, alert him by calling his name, and then command "Come," loudly and clearly. If he carriers on unheedingly, hang on to your end of the cord, so that when he reaches his end he will be caught up short. Call "Come" again in your clearest, most inviting tones. If he is slow in responding, don't get mad at him and just drag him to you, or scold him when he does eventually come back. You can make him come more quickly by turning your back and walking *away* from him, telling him all the time that you are really not going to waste your time chasing him, and you'll go home and take your tidbits with you. You probably won't go many steps before he follows you, but don't drag him.

When he is slow in responding to your call, never scold him. This is important. A puppy should associate coming to you, with pleasant things. Never let him think he is getting punished because he *has* come to you. Be very careful about this. Whether it takes him five seconds or five minutes to respond, when he comes give him a tidbit. Make the giving fairly rapid, so that he will associate his response with the reward.

Every day, go out to the same spot and practice this lesson. When you are fairly certain that it isn't the long cord that is keeping him around, try him without it. Maybe he will go dashing off but if he does, don't panic; just try the walking away and "I'm going home" tactic. It is difficult to make yourself do this, I know, but if you have chosen your spot well, away from traffic and livestock, the dog can come to no harm — and it really does work; the dog will come back when he finds you are not chasing him. Because if you chase him he will think it a game — and a real fun one, too!

If you live near livestock it is as well to extend these lessons a bit further, and teach the dog that he must not chase sheep, cattle and poultry. Once you've got him responding to your call, get out the long line again and take the puppy where there are some farm animals; better ask the owner's permission first. Take off the dog's leash (keeping him on the cord), and he'll probably head straight for the nearest sheep. Pull him back sharply as he does so, shout "No" loudly, and bring him back to you. When you get him back, don't scold him or reward him; simply let him go, apparently free but still on his line. As soon as he shows signs of wanting to chase again, pull him back and go through the discouragement routine once more.

If he turns out to be a inherent chaser, he may find the temptation too strong — young sheepdogs and hunting breeds usually figure in this category. If so, you'll have to resort to the rolled newspaper. If he keeps trying to rush off sheepward, as you pull him up and shout "No," bring the newspaper down with a thwack on his

SALLY ANNE THOMPSON

Greyhound
Five thousand years ago, the Egyptians were carving representations in their tombs of a dog which was astonishingly like the modern Greyhound. Known and appreciated universally for his speed, good manners and hunting ability, the Greyhound is probably the ancestor of most of the sight hounds we know today.

haunches. It won't do him any damage, but it will certainly startle him and make quite clear your displeasure.

Sooner or later — sooner with some breeds than others — he will pause and turn around and look at you in mid-chase when you pull him up on his long line. As soon as he does, call him to you, and if he comes right away, reward him.

If you keep up this practice every day, your pup will finally learn not to chase other animals, and you'll be able to walk him in the vicinity of livestock without his even thinking of chasing them.

Don't ever think you can trust him on his own, though. What he does when you are around, and what he might do if he has the opportunity to roam loose, are two different things, particularly with the herding or hunting breeds of dog.

Further Education

All these things can be taught by the time the pup is eight or nine months old — certainly before he's a year old. Some breeds, and certainly some individual dogs, learn more rapidly than others.

As I've mentioned, you may find the herding or hunting breeds difficult to distract from chasing livestock. On the other hand, shepherding and retrieving dogs respond more readily to obedience training, chiefly because it is part of their breed characteristic to work with, and at, the command of their masters. They are bred for responsiveness.

Poodles, Papillons, and American Toy Fox Terriers among others, learn tricks easier than many other breeds. Several of the Asiatic toy breeds are more difficult to train for obedience work, not because they are less intelligent but because stubbornness and independence are part of their character.

As your puppy grows older you will soon discover how far you and he are prepared to go in training.

There are so many things a dog can learn to do, and enjoy doing, and it can be a hobby for you, to learn and to do them together. Competitive obedience work is becoming more and more popular; it involves some fantastic demonstrations of obedience on the part of the canine competitors. There are sheepdog trials and field trials for sporting dogs. There is competition on the show bench for the dog that excels in beauty, and this involves a specialized form of ring training. Then there are the parlor tricks — the begging, the

Hanoverian Schweisshund
This is the German equivalent of the well-known Bloodhound. Used in conjunction with faster hounds, the Schweisshund is brought up to recover the scent when the pack has difficulty! Like the Bloodhound, he is hunted on a leash. Height at the shoulder: male 20 to 23 inches—female 16 to 20 inches. Not registered by the A.K.C.

Harrier
Somewhat intermediate in size between the large Beagle and the Foxhound, the Harrier is used for hunting the hare in packs, his slower pace enabling the footman to follow. Height at the shoulder: 19 to 20 inches. Registered by the American Kennel Club in the "Hound" group.

Iceland Spitz Dog
One of the oldest breeds in Iceland, he is a fine watchdog and, in addition, an excellent hunter, used for trailing. Height at the shoulder: 12 to 16 inches. Not registered by the American Kennel Club. Registered by the Danish Hunt Society.

dancing on hind legs that you see circus dogs do — which are well within the ability of a bright pup.

Maybe you'll discover that you like working with your dog, getting to know him better. Once he has learned simple good behavior and is eager to learn more, you can, if you wish, take him to obedience school. Or, you can give him advanced training yourself. There are several excellent dog training books available. "Know Obedience and Show Training" covers the formal rules for show competition. "Pet Library's Dog Training Guide" explains how to teach your dog all sorts of tricks, many useful and all of them interesting.

Obedience Training

Many communities have a dog training or obedience school. These are frequently sponsored by the local A.S.P.C.A. or humane society. With the rising popularity of obedience trials, their training sessions never lack enthusiasm. In the basic training section, any dog, purebred or crossbred, and his owner, can learn many things they will find useful in everyday life.

If you've come along this far, your dog has already learned to walk at heel. Perhaps you've even tried heeling him off leash. At school you'll learn to put a bit of polish on his action, and then move on to the next command: "Sit."

In learning to "Heel" the dog has already become accustomed to walking at your left side. Hold the leash in your right hand and control the slack with your left. When you stop walking, the most natural action for the dog is to sit, so encourage him in this. As you stop, keep the dog close at your side, and gently push him down into a sitting position with your left hand; at the same time keep the leash short enough with your right hand to prevent him from rolling over on his back, or jumping up on you. While doing this, give the command, "Sit."

Don't keep him sitting more than a second or two. Start walking again, keep him at heel for a few steps then stop and push him down again, saying "Sit" as you do so.

Repeat this a few times and you'll find he will start to lower his rear to the ground as you stop. When he does, praise and reward him. Once he gets the idea, it is plain sailing, and merely a matter of teaching the dog to sit neatly and squarely at your side.

The fun comes when you want him to sit still while you move away. The ideal is for the dog to remain sitting even while his master goes out of sight, and stay there until given permission to move. It is spectacular and very useful, because there will be many times in the dog's life when you will want him to do just that.

The word used to command the dog to remain where he is seated is "Stay." This is usually taught by holding the hand up, palm facing the dog, and repeating it to him. When he moves to get up and follow, the check is to say "Sit" firmly, and pushing him

Irish Setter
At one time the Irish Setter was an outstanding hunting dog. Today, his great beauty has made him so widely accepted as a pet and companion that he is probably kept more frequently for this purpose than for the original one. A native Irish breed, his solid coat and noble air provide universal recognition. Height at the shoulder: male 27 inches—female 25 inches. Registered by the American Kennel Club in the "Sporting Dog" group.

back into position, command him to "Stay". Move backward a pace or two, then circle round the dog. As he learns to obey, gradually move farther and farther away from him while he remains at "Sit."

The next command is "Down." This is taught after the dog has learned to "Sit." It is simply a command to the dog to sink down on all fours. The trainer assists him into the "Down" position by holding the head low with the lead, easing his front legs out from under him, and pushing his body down to the ground.

A further extension is to teach your dog to sit or stay down while you move right away or go out of sight. This is used in "Long Sit" and "Long Down" exercise. Get him on a leash and into position, either "Sit" or "Down." Tell him to "Stay," and then turn away. If he has learned the earlier "Sit" he will stay there, but should he get up to follow then get him back instantly to the same place and say "Stay" loudly.

Once he is settled again, walk round him a couple of times, keeping him in position, and then start to move backwards slowly, to the length of the leash. Don't let him get up at all. This is important. As the lessons progress and the dog shows more understanding of what you want, gradually extend the time and distance — by using a long cord attached to the leash — until you can move yards and yards away from him without his moving. Also circle around behind and admonish him should he twist around to keep his eye on you. Finally, you can try moving right out of sight.

Don't try to hurry this one, and don't start too young a pup on it. The dog should also understand and obey the simpler commands too, before he starts learning this.

All this is basic elementary training, which many owners teach their dogs simply so that they can have a well-mannered and tractable dog around them. Perhaps it will whet your appetite to taking your dog further in training, to improving his action and response, even competing against other dogs. Most dogs are indeed capable of far more than these elementaries, as a visit to any Obedience Trial will show.

Obedience Trials

Obedience trials are becoming more and more popular every year, and undoubtedly are having the most rapid rise of any competitive dog sport.

Their appeal is to both the public generally and to the dog lovers. Everyone likes to see and admire the proof of complete understanding that exists between dog and handler, and the remarkable results that can be achieved by good training.

It is most unnatural for a dog to lie down in an open ring with several other completely strange dogs, surrounded by a lot of completely strange people, while his owner goes away for several long minutes. Yet dogs do just this, and many other things too.

They are not special dogs, as those at field trials where you expect to see sporting dogs, or at sheepdog trials where you expect to see Border Collies and Farm Shepherds. The dogs that compete and succeed in obedience trials are of all breeds, breeds as diverse as Chihuahuas, Papillons, Pugs, Boston Terriers, Fox Terriers, Bulldogs, St. Bernards. Certain breeds, perhaps more frequently, go on to the highest degrees of obedience work. These include the German Shepherd, Doberman Pinscher, Collie, Cocker Spaniel, Shetland Sheepdog, Golden Retriever, Labrador Retriever, Belgian Sheepdog, Pomeranian, Dalmatian, Weimaraner, English Springer, and of course, the Poodle.

Obedience trials really began in America in the 1930's, although they had been established in England as a popular feature of the dog fancy for some years. Pioneer in the thirties for obedience trials was Mrs. Whitehouse Walker of New York State, who owned and bred Poodles. She studied the English scene and the English methods — where, incidentally, Poodles at that time were also doing well. What she saw and learned convinced her that competitive obedience work had a future back home. The American Kennel Club was far-sighted enough to sanction two trials in 1934, if somewhat cautiously. By the 1940's, obedience trials were well and truly established.

The trials are usually held either along with an all-breed or one-breed bench show, or as a separate event. Five classes are usually scheduled, divided into three sections. These sections are the Novice, which can earn the Companion Dog degree, entitling the dog to the initials C.D. after his name; the Open which carries the Companion Dog Excellent (C.D.X.) title; and the Utility for the Utility Dog (U.D.) title. There are also two awards for tracking, Tracking Dog (T.D.) and the highest of all, Utility Dog Tracker (U.D.T.).

The dogs in each class compete for first, second, third and fourth placings, and at the same time aim to build up scores of sufficient points towards their titles. Each complete set of exercises in the

Irish Terrier

Many superlatives have been applied to the Irish Terrier, among them "daredevil" and "the D'Artagnan of the show ring." A typical Irishman, he works hard and plays hard. Originally developed for vermin hunting, he is at home everywhere and may be taught to retrieve as well as hunt.

AKE WINTZELL

Irish Water Spaniel

Originally a blend of the Setter and Spaniel, there is probably an infusion of Poodle blood as indicated by its curly coat. The tallest, although not the heaviest, of the Spaniels, he is a natural water dog and an energetic hunter. Height at the shoulder: male 21 to 23 inches—female 20 to 22 inches. Registered in the "Sporting Dog" group.

AKE WINTZELL

AKE WINTZELL

Irish Wolfhound

One of the noblest breeds of dog ever developed, this "rough-coated Greyhound" was for all practical purposes extinct by the 1800's. He was recreated by Captain G. A. Graham, a Scottish officer serving in the British Army. Today he is seldom used for hunting.

123

class carries a maximum possible score total of 200 points. These are apportioned to each exercise, based on how difficult and how important the exercise is. At least half the points for each exercise, and a total of 170 out of the possible 200, must be scored to pass. For the points won to be counted towards each title, there must be a minimum number of dogs competing — six in Novice or Open classes, and three in Utility. To win a title, the dog has to have three lots of qualifying pass scores, and they must be under different judges.

Novice and Open classes are of two types, labeled A and B. Both are for dogs of any breed and of either sex, but the A classes are strictly amateur, the dogs being handled by the owner or his family. In B classes, either amateur or professional owners and handlers may compete.

In Novice classes, the dog must first "Heel on leash." The only commands permitted are the word, "Heel," and the dog's name, and the dog must be on a loose leash — always on the left side of the handler, which is the normal position for obedience work, even off the leash. For this first exercise, on the judge's command, handler and dog walk forward, halt, turn right, left, about turn, walk slowly, walk fast, make a figure eight usually around the ring stewards. The judge does not necessarily give the commands in any set order. When the judge says, "Exercise finished," the handler stops and the dog should go to heel position on the left of the handler. This is the practice at the finish of every exercise. Only then is the handler permitted to praise, pet or address other than commands to the dog.

The next exercise is "Stand for examination." The handler stands the dog in front of him at the end of the leash. The judge examines the dog, and the handler must then walk around the dog back to its side.

"Heel free" involves the same work as for "Heel on leash," but without the figure eight in the Novice section.

Next comes "Recall," during which the handler sits the dog where he is told and moves away. On command from the judge, the handler has to call his dog, either by word or signal, and the dog has to come to the handler and sit right in front of him, and, when told to by the judge, move round to the heel position.

"Long sit" requires the dog to sit for one minute, and "Long down" to be down for three minutes, and both these exercises are done with the handler at the other side of the ring. The judge is looking for steadiness and clean action in these exercises, with no fidgeting. Throughout the class he will also note the confidence and lack of nervousness with which the dog does each exercise, and the neatness of the finish at "Heel" position.

The Open classes, also, start with "Heel on leash" and "Heel free" exercises. Then comes "Drop on recall," in which the dog is at one end of the ring, the handler at the other. On the judge's command, the handler recalls the dog, and when told to do so signals the dog to drop. He then calls the dog to "Sit" directly in front of him, and when the judge says "Finish," the dog should move round to heel position as usual.

In "Retrieve on the flat," the handler throws a dumbbell (these come in different sizes, proportionate to the size of the dog); the judge then tells the handler when he wants him to order his dog to retrieve it. The dog is expected to return with the dumbbell and hold it in front of the handler but not to drop it until the handler is given the order to take it.

"Retrieve over the obstacle" is more complex. In this the handler throws the dumbbell over a hurdle while the dog stays. On the judge's command the dog leaps the jump, picks up the dumbbell, returns over the jump to the handler and sits in front of him, and again awaits the command to pass the dumbbell to the handler. These jumps for most breeds are set at $1^1/_2$ times the shoulder height of the dog, although the more cumbersome and heavy breeds have the jumps slightly lower.

"Broad jump" involves a jump over a spread of boards, not more than six feet across and not more than three times the shoulder height of the dog. The exact distance depends on the size of the dog.

Finally come "Long sit" for three minutes, and "Long down" for five minutes, both exercises being done with the handler going out of sight. In each of these there must be at least six dogs in the ring, for qualifying purposes, though not necessarily for placings only.

Utility class has five exercises, some of them quite difficult, and consequently, fascinating to watch. First comes "Scent discrimination," and for this 60 points out of a possible total of 200 for the whole class are awarded.

The handler has fifteen objects, five of leather, five of metal, and five of wood. The judge takes one from each type and gives them back to the handler. The remaining ones are placed on the ground by the judge. The handler handles the three selected objects

Italian Greyhound
A charming little dog, it has a sturdy strength which belies its outward appearing fragility. The pet and preferred companion of nobility as far back as the days of ancient Rome. There are two weight classes, one for dogs under 8 pounds and the other for dogs over 8 pounds. Registered by the American Kennel Club in the "Toy" group.

thoroughly so as to put his own scent on them, and then, without allowing the dog to see it, gives one back to the judge. The judge is careful not to interfere with the handler's scent, and places the object in the group on the ground. The dog then has to pick out that object by scent and take it to the handler. This is repeated with the other two objects.

"Seek back" involves the handler making a trail in the ring according to the judge's request, and on that trail dropping an object. When told to do so by the judge, he puts his hand on the dog's nose and commands him to find the dropped object. This can be by scent or sight.

For "Signal," the judge commands "Forward," and the handler must then take the dog through the heeling routine, without using the voice in instruction, only silent gestures that handler and dog have learned together.

The fourth exercise is "Hurdle and bar" in which the dog has the dumbbell placed in his mouth, and must on command go over the high jump and the bar jump and back to the handler, continuing to hold on to the dumbbell until the judge commands the handler to "Take it."

Finally, all the dogs (though not more than fifteen in all) are put in the ring, the handlers leave them, and the judge goes over the dogs for "Stand for examination" exercise. He then brings the handlers back to the dogs for the "Exercise finished" command.

Tracking involves the dog finding something which has been

"lost" on a trail of at least 440 yards in length and thirty minutes old. The handler must not guide the dog — in fact, it is better to let the dog do it on his own — and he should if he has been well trained — because attempting to help can frequently confuse. The trail has to have two turns in it, and the "pass" is only given if the "lost" object is found.

Before the dog can compete for Companion Dog Excellent (C.D.X.), it must pass the Companion Dog (C.D.) test, and to compete for Utility Dog (U.D.), it must have earned both C.D. and C.D.X. If a dog passes the Tracking test under two different judges and against at least three other dogs and already has at least the C.D. degree, it earns its T.D., Tracking Dog, title. But to be awarded Utility Dog Tracker (U.D.T.), the highest award, the dog must have all three titles: C.D., C.D.X., and U.D., and must have passed the Tracking test as well.

Obviously one of the great appeals of obedience trials is that the dog does not have to be an outstandingly beautiful representative of his breed. A well-trained family pet can compete on equal terms with the finest show bench companion. In fact, the family dog might do even better in the obedience ring than the big show winner. Sometimes the differences in approach between show ring and obedience work have been known to confuse a dog!

The obedience competitor can have a longer career than the show bench dog too, and many veterans continue to go through their paces

AKE WINTZELL

Japanese Spaniel (Japanse Chin Dog)
One of the loveliest of the toy breeds, natural and unspoiled. Originally from China, they were refined in Japan — hence the name. Bred for centuries as pets, they are ideally qualified to fulfill that function. Divided by weight into two size classes, dogs under 7 pounds and dogs over 7 pounds.

127

and beat all their younger competitors. Once a dog has won all his degrees, he may still continue to compete in Utility and Open B classes.

Most trainers advise leaving serious obedience training of the competitive kind until the dog is a year old, although there have been exceptions to this rule — the occasional youngster winning a Companion Dog award when a little over six months of age.

As for not teaching old dogs new tricks, there is a record of a dog that started its first lessons at the age of ten years and won all three degrees within one year.

Quite apart from the fun that can be had in training a dog to competition work, and the challenge there is in seeing how far you can take him, there is a perhaps more utilitarian aspect to it. Any dog that is trained well enough to compete in the ring — where he must be under control whether his handler is in sight or not — is going to be a civilized member of society. If more dogs were just that, there would be fewer nuisances on the public roads, fewer strays for the city authorities to impound, fewer complaints from farmers and stock owners, and maybe fewer anti-dog landlords and irate neighbors!

Trials in the Field

These are mostly for the sporting and hunting breeds, and they are intended to show off the dog's training and ability in the job for which his breed was developed.

Field trials are set up under natural hunting and sporting conditions, and constitute a complete testing of the dog's ability. There are bird dog trials, retriever trials, spaniel trials, Beagle Hound trials, Coonhound trials, and Foxhound trials. There are trials also for sheepdogs, and coursing for the sight-hunting breeds like the Greyhound, racing for sled dogs like the Huskies and Alaskan Malamutes. These trials are designed to be far more difficult than a normal day out in the field.

Field trials of various sorts are sponsored by several dog associations, including the American Kennel Club, the United Kennel Club, the American Field Stud Book, and the International Fox Hunters Studbook. It depends on the breeds, and the registrations.

Many a dog competes successfully in trials but rarely actually goes off with his master for informal hunting! Trials have become a

Karelian Bear Dog
A savage hunter from the border area between Finland and Russia, his courage and keen sense of smell make him ideal for hunting larger and more dangerous game such as bear, elk and wolf. Not registered by the American Kennel Club. Registered by the *Federation Cynologique Internationale* in Brussels, Belgium.

AKE WINTZELL

sport in themselves to competitors and spectators alike and have taken on something of the atmosphere of a social gathering. Serious enthusiasts on the other hand maintain that the spirit of competition between individual dogs helps to improve the qualities of the particular breed, and that is probably their greatest value.

Training for field trials is a specialized affair: in fact, it is exactly the same as that given to any dog to be used in the field. As much as possible it is done under natural conditions. At first the dog is taken, while still barely a puppy, out hunting with the older dogs, but serious training does not begin until the youngster has gotten the feel of the sport.

Learning a Trick or Two

A child will often tire of training a dog in obedience work — the discipline and control needed after the basic "Heel," "Sit," and "Down" work has been learned are sometimes too boring for the youngster to appreciate — and only the older boy is likely to be interested in field or trials training with sporting and working dogs.

Teaching tricks to the family pet is a different matter. Begging, shaking hands, fetching, and all the other clever things that dogs can learn to do are fun. Because they are fun and rely chiefly on the wish of the dog to please, children enjoy teaching them to their pets. There is more value in parlor tricks than fun, however. A strong early relationship between a child and his dog is usually the

129

foundation of a lifetime of sympathy with animals. This is one of the good facets of human nature. When children find that responsibility is a lot of fun, then it comes easier. That's where tne real value of parlor tricks lies.

To teach and to learn, child and dog must understand one another. With understanding comes affection, sympathy, and a sense of responsibility. So don't let anyone tell you that parlor tricks are a waste of time, and that it's undignified for a dog to do them. Most dogs, especially those that live as the family pet, love doing them anyway!

Teaching these tricks, incidentally, shouldn't begin until the pup is at least six months old, and preferably nine months or more.

Begging

It's a cute trick, and easy to teach. Encourage the puppy to rise on his hind legs. You can do this by snapping fingers over his head, or tempting him with a little piece of liver, or dog tidbit. As he rises, take his paws and gently push him on his rear, and hold him there while he balances. Gradually let go until he is sitting steadily,

Keeshond

Truly a dog of the common people, the Keeshond has been known and loved by the working class in Holland for centuries. He is particularly conspicuous as a companion to the barge people. Never used for hunting, he prefers to remain with his family rather than to roam. Height at the shoulder: male 18 inches—female 17 inches. Registered by the American Kennel Club in the "Non-Sporting Dog" group.

AKE WINTZELL

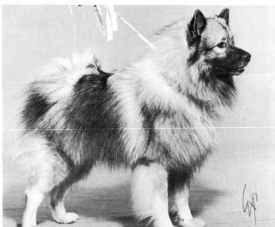

Kerry Blue Terrier

This lusty, medium sized dog from County Kerry at one time was used extensively as a fighting dog and as a vermin hunter. Today his smart appearance and bouncing good nature make him a favorite pet and companion as well as watchdog. Black when born, his color clears to blue as the adult coat comes in. Height at the shoulder: male 18 1/2 inches—female 17 1/2 inches. Registered by the American Kennel Club in the "Terrier" group.

and hold your finger just above his nose to keep his attention. All the time, repeat the command, "Beg." When he holds himself steady, even for a little while, reward him with the tidbit.

Repeat this practice the next day. Soon the pup will be doing it by himself, not only for tidbits, but to ask you for all sorts of other things.

Shaking Hands

Puppies will often extend a paw while they are playing. Shaking hands is teaching them to do the same thing when you command, "Shake *hands*." Get him sitting, then start by tapping at his right paw, and when he lifts it as he probably will, say "Shake hands," and take the paw. Keep repeating this. If he doesn't get the idea, gently push the opposite shouder, and he won't be able to resist lifting his other paw. Every time he lifts his paw, take it, shake it, say "Shake hands," and reward him.

Fetching

Well learned by a dog, this is a real "show-off" trick. An older puppy learns this easier than a young one, and dogs of the retrieving and sporting breeds learn it fastest of all.

Gun dog trainers teach fetching in this way. They offer an object to the dog, and when he takes it, command, "Fetch." Gradually they hold it farther and farther away from the dog, eventually putting it on the floor. You may find it easier to start this teaching by having the dog on a leash, with a choke collar; a little jerk on the collar will often get the dog to open his mouth so that you can put the object in it.

The dog must be kept alert and undistracted all the time, or he will lose interest. When he takes the object, say "Come," and when he comes to you, grasp the object with one hand and say "Give."

This last is the most difficult part, and one way of inducing the dog to give up what he has in his mouth is to tempt him with something else, a goodie of some sort, or a toy or chew that he likes. Of course you only reward the dog after he has given you the object, though you can praise him at each stage.

Teach each stage by itself if the dog it not responding quickly, and don't hurry any part of it.

When he has learned to fetch and give to you a ball or any object you throw for him, you have to teach him to fetch specific things for you from across the room. To do this, you must teach him its name.

You want him to fetch your slippers. Go back to the first stage of "Fetch" training. Offer him the slippers, or push them in his mouth when he opens it. Say "Fetch — slippers." He'll recognize the command "Fetch." Go through the stages again, using the double command all the time, so that the word "Slippers," (or "Paper" or "Gloves") becomes recognizable to him.

You can teach some dogs to fetch by using their sense of smell. Mostly they are dogs with hound blood in them, although German Shepherds, Working Collies and Retrievers will also do this well.

Komondor

A large, powerful cattle guard, bred for centuries in Hungary, the Komondor (plural, Komondorok) is a fine watch and guard dog. The heavy, matted coat serves to protect him from the cold and also in his battles with wolves. Height at the shoulder: from 23 1/2 to 31 1/2 inches, with the larger size preferred. "Working Dog" group.

AKE WINTZELL

Kuvasz

Originally from Tibet, the Kuvasz was brought to its present state of development and commanding appearance in Hungary. Like that other great Hungarian, the Komondor, he was used primarily for guarding cattle, although originally developed as a guard to the nobility. Height at the shoulder: 26 inches. "Working Dog" group.

EVELYN SHAFER

To do this, teach him the word for a particular toy or object, and teach him to fetch it, as has already been explained. Then put the object down in another room, let him in and tell him to fetch it. Don't hide it too well at first, maybe just putting it on the rug in the middle of the room. As he improves, you can hide it more carefully.

Dancing

This is a trick small dogs enjoy and do well. Start off as you would with begging, holding a tidbit over his head. He'll rise up on his hind legs. Don't hold it too high, or he'll jump for it, but keep it just above his nose. As he teeters on his hind legs, say "Dance."

133

Just as he is about to fall back on his four feet, reward him. As you repeat this, move your hand about a little so that he dances around on his hind feet, and keep saying "Dance" and keep giving him his reward just before he drops down on all four feet.

Don't practice this too long. Five minutes at a time is enough.

Jumping Through the Hoop

You'll know soon enough if your puppy dog has any natural ability for this—he'll leap over things like low hedges, bushes, and toys the children leave about. But most dogs can be taught. Start with a low hurdle, one the dog can step over easily; put the dog on a short leash and lead him over. The hurdle can even be a broom-handle on two wooden blocks. As soon as he goes over, say "Over." Reward him as soon as he is over. Keep repeating this, raising the hurdle a little as he progresses, and when you think he has got the idea try him without the leash. For this, go to the other side of the hurdle, and say "Come" and "Over." But make sure that he doesn't go around the hurdle.

Once he can do the hurdle, try him first with a half hoop and then with a full hoop. The hoop should be big enough for the dog to get through in great comfort.

You may find lots of other little tricks you'd like to teach your dog. A visit to an obedience trial might give you some ideas, or your dog himself may show you what he is particularly adept at, and you can encourage it. Most of these parlor tricks are merely an extension of the dog's natural habits.

There are three things to remember. First, don't let any training session run on long enough for the dog to get bored, and always end on a successful note. It is up to you to spot the last effort the dog is going to make. Second, rely heavily on the reward, this is the most effective bait for getting a dog to do something you want him to. Third, have patience, and don't try to teach too many tricks at once — one thing at a time is quite enough. Rely on regular short sessions every day, rather than one long session a week. Your dog will probably have forgotten it all by then anyway!

In the next chapter we'll talk about "beauty" shows, and the training that's needed for a dog to show off at its best.

Labrador Retriever SALLY ANNE THOMPSON

This, the most popular of the retrieving dogs, is about as fine an all around companion as one could wish. While the black variety is the best known, the golden or yellow is becoming increasingly popular. The Labrador is one of the breeds accepted for work with the Seeing Eye Foundation. Height at the shoulder: male 22 1/2 to 24 1/2 inches—female 21 1/2 to 23 1/2 inches. Weight: male 60 to 75 pounds—female 55 to 70 pounds. Registered by the American Kennel Club in the "Sporting Dog" group.

VII   Showing Your Dog

Sooner or later the dog owner gravitates to the dog show. If you own a registered purebred, this is where you may see some of his relatives, maybe even one that is a champion.

What are Dog Shows?

Dog shows are competitive events, which can now be numbered among sporting events. Dogs compete at shows for prizes, points towards gaining the title of "Champion" and some big awards.

The first dog shows in the United States were held less than a hundred years ago — just a few get-togethers quite unconnected with each other, in which some enthusiasts and fanciers matched their dogs against one another. Now dog shows, plus the field and obedience trials, held throughout the country every year can be numbered in the thousands.

Dog shows proper fall primarily into two kinds. There is the informal "match" show which is mostly attended by local people. This type of show often serves as a first outing and training ground for a young dog before he goes on to a bigger "point" show at which certain wins will gain points toward the total number required for the dog to earn the title of Champion, a coveted honor. As can be imagined, dog owners trying to win the title for their dog will travel all over the country to win the necessary number of points.

Who Organizes Dog Shows?

Mostly they are organized by local dog clubs, either those that cater to all breeds, or those that specialize in one breed.

A superintendent is appointed to manage the organization and administration of the show. Most of the dog shows are run under the rules and regulations of the American Kennel Club which is the largest of the several dog registration associations. Many of the specialized sporting and working breeds can be registered with other organizations, such as the United Kennel Club, or the American Field Stud Book, which encourage the utility rather than beauty of the various breeds they accept for registration. Only AKC registered dogs can compete in AKC regulated shows which are, nationally and internationally, the best known. When people talk about their dog being a champion, you'll usually find it is a champion through the AKC system.

What is the American Kennel Club?

It is basically an association of individual dog clubs. The American Kennel Club has grown out of the cooperation of dog enthusiasts and fanciers who in the early days got together to make some sort of sense and organization out of their hobby. It is a big concern now, with a permanent office and administrative staff, a permanent headquarters in New York City, and vast archives of records and files. It has great power over the dog fancy, but that power still lies basically in the hands of the associated clubs which are repres-

Lakeland Terrier

One of the oldest of the breeds of broken-coated terriers developed in England, the Lakeland has been a worker for generations. Originally valued for his ability to follow the fox underground and drive him out to the waiting hounds, the Lakeland, by his vivacity and bouyant nature, has endeared himself to those who know him as a housedog and companion. Height at the shoulder: male 14 1/2 inches—female approximately 13 1/2 inches. Registered by the American Kennel Club in the "Terrier" group.

Lapland Sheepdog

This is a fairly modern breed, created by crossing the old Lapland Spitz with the German Shepherd and Collie. He is a sturdy dog, used extensively as a companion and sheepdog. Height at the shoulder: 16 to 20 inches. Not registered by the American Kennel Club. Registered by the *Federation Cynologique Internationale.*

ented through their delegates. It is these delegates, through their meetings and committees, who make the ultimate decisions. Dog showing, and the AKC, have kind of grown up together.

Why Do People Go to Dog Shows?

The basic reason behind dog showing is to provide competition which will improve the quality of the breed. Each breed club has adopted a standard of perfection. This is a word picture of the ideal dog which breeders will strive to develop. Each dog entered in a show is measured against this theoretical perfection and the dog conforming most closely is the winner. It must be admitted, however, that many people enter their dogs in dog shows for the same reason that people enter into any competitive sport—because they are convinced they are better than anyone else and want to prove it—and that's a perfectly natural instinct! The fact that there is prestige and possibly some financial gain attached merely adds to the attraction.

Who Sets the Standard of Perfection?

The American Kennel Club publishes a description or standard of the perfect specimen for each of the 115 breeds of dog it officially registers. This standard not only describes the general appearance, colors, sizes, and specific details, such as movement and character, but also in many cases it lists the major faults that should be penalized and thus discouraged. Who sets the standard in the first place? In many cases, standards of perfection are like Topsy, they "growed." A big influence obviously is exerted by the enthusiasts who take a great interest in one particular breed—and eventually form a club devoted to that breed. They then exert themselves to get the breed officially accepted for registration by the AKC. The number of accepted breeds grows almost every year.

Another big influence are the kennel clubs of other countries. It is believed that there are from 400 to 500 distinct breeds of dog in the world. A distinctive breed, that is i.e., a purebred, is a dog which when bred to another dog that resembles it, will produce only puppies that look pretty much like their parents. In dog breeding parlance this is called "breeding true to type." As we can see, not all of these breeds are registered by the American Kennel Club, but many of them are accepted officially by a kennel club somewhere in the world. There are also many local or regional breeds of dogs which have never had the benefit of a formal organization to promote them. They are bred informally, but the lovers of that type take care not to cross them and thus the breed is fixed to a type. When a dog of a foreign variety is accepted for registration by the AKC, that organization will obviously take up basically the standard set in the country of the dog's origin. The AKC standards for most of the terrier breeds, which are nearly all British in origin, are based on the English Kennel Club standards.

What is a Dog Show All About?

This is a question you might well ask if it is your first time at a show. There seem to be so many dogs in and out of the rings, dogs in partitioned stalls with or without their owners and handlers around, and so much going on at one time. Stay until the end and you'll see a dog chosen as the Best in Show—but how did he attain that exalted position?

Imagine you are at a big AKC all breeds dog show where points can be won toward championship titles. Only a dog registered as a purebred example of any of the AKC registered breeds can enter into points competition. Some other breeds, not yet accepted for separate registration, can compete against one another in what are called miscellaneous classes, but there are no points awarded for this. A dog must be at least six months old before it can be shown, and must not be neutered or altered in any way, and should not have any of the faults which are quoted in the official Standard of that breed.

Dogs which are competing for championship points enter in one or more of the regular classes for their breed. Some entries have separate classes based on the sex or the variety—such as divisions based on color or size.

The Various Classes

The classes are as follows: *Puppy,* which is for dogs over six months and under one year. This can be divided into two, for the six to nine months old puppies, and the nine to twelve months old puppies.

Lhasa Apso

The "barking Lion Dog", as he is known in Tibet, was kept in his country of origin as a charming and attractive indoor burglar alarm. He has few peers as an intelligent, responsive pet, while his background makes him instinctively wary of strangers. Height at the shoulder: male about 10 or 11 inches—female somewhat smaller. Registered by the American Kennel Club in the "Non-Sporting Dog" group.

The next class is *Novice,* which is for dogs which have not won three first prizes in Novice, and none in any other classes, except Puppy classes, nor any championship points.

Then there is the class *Bred by Exhibitor,* which is for dogs which are not champions, owned wholly or partly by the breeder and shown by him or his family. The *American-Bred class* is for dogs born in the U.S.A., and resulting from a mating which took place in the U.S.A. Most competitive of the regular classes is *Open,* which is for any purebred dog.

These regular classes are scheduled separately for male dogs and females. It is possible to enter a dog which is already a champion in *Puppy* classes or in the *Open* classes, but this is not often done. Usually champions are entered in the *Specials Only* competition for the *Best of Breed,* which comes later.

Four ribbons are awarded in each class — blue for first, red for second, yellow for third and white for fourth.

The first prize winners of the regular classes go on to compete against each other in the *Winners* Classes. These are the important ones for the championship points.

The male dog that wins against all the other males becomes *Winners Dog,* and wins a purple ribbon and some points, according to the number of other dogs present. The best female in her *Winners class* power against the first prize winners of the bitch classes, becomes *Winners Bitch.* A Reserve to each of these is also chosen, and they earn a purple and white ribbon. Should the Winning Dog or Bitch be disqualified for any reason, the Reserve moves up to first place.

The *Winners Dog* and the *Winners Bitch* then compete for the *Best of Winners,* earning a blue and white ribbon, and sometimes extra championship points.

The *Best of Winners* then compete for the *Best of Breed* with any champions entered in *Specials Only,* and any outright winners of any special additional non-regular classes there might be in the breed. The *Best of Breed* wins a purple and gold ribbon. A *Best of Opposite Sex,* the best of the opposite sex to the *Best of Breed,* is also chosen, and this wins a red and white ribbon.

Each winner of the *Best of Breed* award then has to compete against the other breeds in its group for the Group Winner. You will have noticed that the AKC divides all the breeds that are registered into six groups. From all the *Best of Breeds* in each group will be chosen the Sporting Group Winner, the Hound Group Winner, the Working Group Winner, the Terrier Group Winner, the Toy Group Winner and the Non-Sporting Group Winner. A blue rosette is given to the winners of each group.

The six group winners then compete for the top award of all the *Best in Show.* For this, a red, or white and red rosette, or sometimes

Maltese

The Maltese has been known and valued as a pet for about three thousand years. For some reason, Maltese are frequently called terriers, but in reality they belong to the spaniel group. Bred and maintained as pets for so long, they are ideal for this purpose, being particularly valued by people of fashion and wealth. Weight: under 7 pounds, 4 to 6 pounds preferred. Registered by the A.K.C. in the "Toy" group.

Manchester Terrier

Originally known as the "Black and Tan Terrier," this breed was known for a time in America as the "Rat Terrier." This latter name referred to its skill and aptitude in despatching these vermin. Short-coated, cleanlimbed, game and intelligent, the Manchester Terrier makes an ideal housedog. There is also a toy variety.

a rosette in the colors of the Club sponsoring the show is given.

None of these wins, even *Best In Show*, automatically brings the coveted title of champion. Let's go back to the *Winners Dog* or *Winners Bitch* class. These are the ones in which championship points are awarded. The maximum number of points to be won in any one show is five. To become a champion, a dog or bitch must win a total of fifteen points under at least three different judges. In addition, a minimum of three points in each of two shows must be won under different judges.

The number of points that are available to be won at a show depends on the number of dogs which are entered. Supposing the *Winners Dog* wins in any entry that qualifies for four points, and the *Winners Bitch* gets her first place in any entry that qualifies for three points. You will have noticed that when the *Winners Dog* and the *Winners Bitch* compete for *Best of Winners*, it is possible for extra championship points to be won; this would be so if in our case the three point *Winners Bitch*, beat the four point *Winners Dog*, when she would be credited with a four point win. The *Winners Dog* wouldn't lose his four points, of course!

So you can see that to become a champion a dog has to win over fierce competition, perhaps in several shows. No dog needs to be a champion to win *Best of Breed*, but to do this he or she must compete against dogs that are already champions.

Who Does the Judging?

Obviously, to be able to decide from several dogs which is the one that is most like the ideal, and is in sound physical condition, the judge must have a good knowledge of the breed. Every judge has to be licensed by the American Kennel Club before he or she can judge at an AKC show. Before that association issues a license, naturally it checks up on the person. Perhaps he or she has bred a particular breed. If so, what is their reputation and character? Only when the AKC is satisfied about every point it will issue a license for judging.

Of course, when it comes to judging the *Best of Groups*, and *Best in Show*, the judge must have a knowledge of many breeds, and must be licensed by the AKC to judge those breeds. So it is no quick and easy job to become a judge at a dog show.

Who Shows the Dog?

Sometimes a judge has learned a lot about one or more breeds by show "handling," which means actually showing a dog.

This is one of the professional jobs in connection with dog showing which has really boomed in recent years. Owners, for many reasons, cannot always take their own dogs to shows. Perhaps they cannot spare the time to take a really good dog around the circuit to win the points necessary to his becoming a champion. In some breeds competition is so fierce, and the entries of good dogs so large, that the owner feels his dog would have his best chance if handled by a professional who knows how to show off a dog to its best advantage. As well as taking it into the ring, professional handlers usually prepare the dog beforehand, bathing and grooming and trimming him where necessary, and generally making him look his best.

Learning to Show

Making a dog look his best and teaching him to show himself off to advantage is an important part of dog showing. The professional handler, or the experienced owner/handler doesn't just put a show leash around the dog's neck, rush him into the ring and hope for the best.

Dog shows are something quite foreign to a dog's nature. He has to learn to behave quietly in what must seem, to a puppy at least, a rather frightening environment. There will be many, many dogs there, many strange people. For a long time he will be leashed on his partitioned bench. When he goes into the ring he will be expected to walk, stand posed on command, and he will be expected to allow a complete stranger to touch him, look at his teeth and feel him all over. All this time he will be expected to stand still and alert, looking his best.

If it is a breed in which the ears are expected to be alert and pricked and the tail curled confidently over the back, obviously if they are dropped through sheer fright, the judge's first impression is not going to be a good one.

First impressions do count. An outstanding dog — that looks outstanding — will catch the judge's eye, and although it would be ridiculous to imagine that a judge would be so naive as to be fooled by outward showmanship only, nevertheless many dog experts maintain that a dog that shows fearlessly and confidently is a dog of sound temperament. Good temperament counts.

An untrained dog is also a nuisance to other exhibitors, if it bothers, snarls at or generally makes itself unpleasant to others.

So, if you want to show a promising pup, start preparing him a long, long time before he ever reaches the entrance to his first dog show. Show training starts right from the time you get your puppy. All normal behavior training is part of it, as walking

Manchester Terrier (toy variety) SALLY ANNE THOMPSON

Except for its size, the toy variety is identical to the standard Manchester Terrier. Divided on the basis of weight, there are two toy classes: 7 pounds and under, and over 7 pounds to 12 pounds. The only other difference is in the ears; the toy ear must be naturally erect, while the standard may have either a button or a drop ear. In America, the standard is cropped to make the ear stand erect, but this is not permitted in England or Holland. Registered by the American Kennel Club in the "Terrier" group.

sensibly and without fuss on a leash, for instance.

There is one point to be wary of, however. If you are going to show your puppy later, don't teach him to "Sit" every time you stop. You don't want him to sit in the show ring; you want him to stand. You can probably introduce the "Sit" and other obedience work at a later stage when he is old enough to be able to distinguish between one activity and another.

Which brings up another caution — watch ou for anticipation. Often a dog will anticipate a command and react to it even before it's given. This is wrong! Vary the order of the lessons in order to avoid this. Also, if your dog starts to respond to a command prematurely, quickly give a command other than the one he expects. This will help keep him alert.

When you start taking your puppy out on a leash in public, take him with you as often as possible. Take him in stores, in crowds, walk him up and down the busy streets. If he shows any signs of being timid, extend the time gradually, and talk to him reassuringly. This will get him used to, and eventually oblivious to, strange surroundings and busy noisy places. When people notice him and stop you, encourage him to let them stroke him and talk to him. This will get him used to strange people in the most natural manner possible.

Show training proper can start once the puppy is over his elementary leash walking and learning period.

Find out how dogs of your pup's breed are shown. For instance, most toy dogs are walked in the ring at a normal pace. A Pekingese is walked rather slowly. Dobermans, German Shepherds and other active dogs are moved at a far quicker pace, the handler usually having to lope alongside the dog. Massive breeds, like St. Bernards, and slow breeds like Bulldogs, are moved rather majestically up and down the rings.

Toys, and other small dogs, are usually put on a table for the judge to examine. Bigger breeds are usually looked over while standing on the floor. What you have to do is find out which method is used for your breed and then practice it.

Practice both indoors and out. Using a short lead, get the dog walking close to your side. Keep him walking up and down at the correct pace for his breed, then quicken up a little, then slacken the pace again. Keep him going up and down in a straight line, jerking the lead lightly if he attempts to wander off course.

Remember to simulate ring conditions as far as possible, keeping the dog at your left side. Imagine a judge, and when you turn to back track, keep the dog on the inside of the turn, so that the dog is always between you and the judge. Vary the up and down path by going around in a circle, always with the dog inside.

Practice this every day, rewarding him frequently, until the dog does it well. Then you want to teach him how to pose and stand steady. Take a short walk and then stop. Turn the dog in profile to your imaginary judge, then step in front or to the side of the dog with the leash slack. Attract his attention with a tidbit, and if he is not in quite the right stance, with all four legs standing squarely, correct this. Do so by putting one hand under his chest, the other under his rear between his legs and lifting (or easing, in the case of a big dog) fractionally from the ground and placing the dog square. You may have to place each leg separately, with the weight distributed evenly over all four legs.

Teach him to remain standing steadily like this for several minutes. Talk to him quietly, and gently stroke his neck. Some dogs are shown on a slack leash, others on a short one, but if the leash is held up short and tight, don't rely on this alone to keep the dog in position. Better train the dog to stand steadily in the correct position than rely on "stringing him up" to keep him showing.

Some dogs, such as some gun dogs and most terriers, are shown with the handler holding either head and tail, or both, in the correct position. One or two trips to a dog show will tell you which style to use. Hold the dog's head out to show the full reach of neck, keep one hand under the chin, and with the other hand place the tail correctly and hold it there lightly. All this should give the impression that the head and tail are merely resting on your hands and you are not grasping them to keep them in position by force!

This will need patience on your part and plenty of practice, with suitable rewards for the dog when he does well. As with all training, don't make each session so long that the dog gets bored and tired.

Once the dog has learned to hold a pose for a while, enlist the aid of some friends. Have one or two of the dog owners among them bring over their dogs, and put on a mock show among yourselves. This will get your dog used to holding a pose with other dogs in close proximity. It is important that they learn to ignore other dogs completely when in the show ring.

Then have someone, preferably a complete stranger to the dog, act as "judge" and go over him thoroughly, handling him all over, looking at his teeth, eyes and ears. Have different people do this at different times, to accustom the dog to being handled by strangers.

Once you think he has learned his show manners at home, you can try him at a small local show. If he looks good, shows good, and matches up to the Standard for his breed, even if he doesn't win, you and he will feel more confident about taking on a bigger show.

Remember, in all training and in the actual event, never get excited or cross with your dog. Speak calmly always, and reward him often with a pat or a tidbit.

All Dressed Up For Show

Professional handlers prepare the dogs they are handling for the show ring with the special grooming that the breed requires. With most breeds this merely means that the dog is shown in his cleanest, smartest condition, everything perfect, coat bathed and clipped or stripped where necessary, toenails trimmed, ears and eyes clean and healthy.

Some breeds, such as the Poodle, are permitted to be shown only in certain clips. All details of grooming — and show grooming is merely an extension of everyday grooming — are given in the next chapter.

A point that should be made here is that no dog can be in peak condition on the day of the show unless he has been kept regularly groomed. It's no good thinking you'll make him look like a champion if you get the brush and comb out of storage only the night before!

Dog Shows in Russia

In Russia most purebred dogs are entered into local associations. These associations include fishing and hunting in their programs, and the number of members is unusually large. The local association in Leningrad, for instance, has 60,000 members.

These associations arrange for the dog shows and while they are not as extensive as shows in the Western world, they do include "beauty contests" much like ours. Only members can participate. The prize for winning is a metal *jetton* (medallion) which is affixed to a medal cloth around the neck of the dog. When one dog has won several prizes and can produce a required number of these jettons, he is awarded a larger one. Some victorious dogs are so loaded with *jettons* that they can hardly move around the ring.

Obedience trials are included in every show, and interest in them is great. Their tests are more difficult and extensive than are ours. Protection training is included in the tests and the "intruder" is sometimes hidden among the audience. The dog attacks the "intruder" and alarming situations sometimes arise, to the delight of the audience.

Special working tests take place. As late as 1964 a Russian racing hound, in order to become a working test champion, had to have killed a wolf, or at least to have shown such courage in hunting the wolf that it entitled him to the title. The prizes are also *jettons*.

According to the head cynologist in Leningrad (in Europe, the overall governing body of dog shows is the Federation Cynologique

Internationale (F.C.I.), in Belgium, which approves the shows and judges. The society's representative in various countries is known as a cynologist), an "international" show is held in Moscow every fourth year, in which all nations in the Eastern bloc and other communist countries participate. Only champions are permitted to enter.

A traveler reports that pet dogs are not too common in Russia; there are far more hunting dogs. In larger towns, it is unusual to find dogs running loose. The Russians appear to treat their dogs well and to take good care of them.

There are a number of local breeds which we in the West do not know at all. Special protection dogs and watchdogs have been bred, including several breeds which resemble the German Shepherd.

Maremma Sheepdog

A pastoral Italian breed whose origin probably goes back to the Roman herding dogs. Large, powerful and noble in appearance, he is frequently used as a guard, both in the home and in the yard. Height at the shoulder: male 25 to 29 inches—female 23 to 26 inches. Not registered by the American Kennel Club.

AKE WINTZELL

AKE WINTZELL

Mastiff

Fabled from time immemorial for his power and courage, the English Mastiff has probably been the subject of more legends than any other breed of dog. He is deserving of all of them, for as a guard his loyalty and courage have no peer. He is a sober dog with a deep personal dignity.

Miniature Pinscher

For some inexplicable reason, many people have the erroneous impression that this is a bred-down version of the Doberman. A far older breed than the Doberman, the Miniature Pinscher was developed in Germany and the Scandanavian countries. A fine, alert little watchdog, he is highly intelligent and learns readily.

VIII   Grooming Your Dog

A well-groomed dog is a well cared for dog. Grooming isn't just a matter of good looks, it is a matter of good health too. If a dog's cleanliness is neglected, he becomes very attractive to parasites and pests and any animal harboring an infestation of lice or fleas will not remain in good health for long.

So for health's sake, as well as appearance, spend a little time grooming your dog. Be he mutt or purebred, he deserves the comfort it will give him, and you'll enjoy him more if he smells clean and healthy, not grimy and odorous.

Most people's excuse for indifferent grooming is that they can't find the time. The simple answer to that is that everybody could

Newfoundland

Truly a noble dog, both in appearance and character, the Newfoundland (developed in the province of that name) is probably the finest water dog of all. He is particularly reliable with children. Height at the shoulder: male 28 inches—female 26 inches.

find ten minutes a day to tend to the dog's needs, and that is all the average dog requires. If time really is your enemy, then it is better to avoid the long-coated breeds which need more attention.

Another common excuse is that the cost of having a dog professionally groomed and clipped is high. Regular professional care of some breeds can be costly, but if care is going to be so much of a drain on the budget better not to indulge your fancy for one of these breeds.

One is reminded of a famous remark attributed to the great financier, J. Pierpont Morgan. Asked by a friend who was thinking of buying a yacht like Morgan's what the upkeep was, Morgan is said to have answered, "If you have to ask about the upkeep, you can't afford to buy it." Unlike Morgan's friend, however, you *could* learn to do the job yourself.

The task of grooming, whether it is merely bathing, brushing or complicated clipping, will be made easier if you train your dog right from puppyhood to cooperate. From the day you buy him, get him used to a gentle brushing, and then, as his coat grows, gradually extend the grooming.

Of course, he will object at first, perhaps quite vocally. Don't be brutal about it, but do be firm. With kind hand and calm voice make it clear that you intend to have your way — he *will* be brushed. If you regard early grooming as merely a matter of getting the puppy used to the idea rather than achieving anything fancy, and keep it as pleasant as possible, he will soon begin to enjoy it and look forward to his daily brushing.

You'll find the job a lot easier with the smaller breeds if you use a steady, waist high table to work on. It can be a folding table, provided it isn't rickety. Cover it with some kind of matting to give the dog a firm footing. You don't want him slipping and slithering around on a smooth plastic top. If he's insecure he'll squirm.

Work in a good light, and assemble all the things you will need before you start. Never leave a puppy or a dog loose and unattended on a table.

You can buy a halter and stand which are a great help if it is a long grooming job, such as a clip. You hitch the dog, front and rear to this, leaving both hands free to work.

Long-coated or short-coated, all dogs should have that daily brushing to remove dust and dirt. It also helps to stimulate the growth of new hair, the casting of dead hair, and it stimulates the natural oils of the skin. The type of brush to use depends on the kind of coat your dog has.

Short-Coated Breeds

Easiest of all to groom are the short-coated breeds. They need only attention with a hound glove or mitt to remove the dead undercoat and give them a sleek shiny look. The hound glove is a mitten with one side set with short bristles made of boar hair, wire or fiber. The kind to use depends on the harshness of your dog's coat.

The following dogs can be groomed with a hound glove:

In the Sporting Dogs group, the *Pointer*, *German Shorthaired Pointer*, the *Vizsla* and the *Weimaraner* — use a fiber glove. Among the Hounds the *Basenji*, *Beagle*, *Basset Hound*, *Black and Tan Coonhound*, *American* and *English Foxhound*, *Smooth-haired Dachshund* — use a wire or fiber glove.

TOOLS

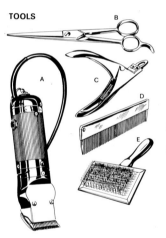 

GROOMING TOOLS:

A—Small animal clipper.

B—7 inch scissors.

C—Nail clipper.

D—Steel comb with two
    widths of teeth.

E—Carder or slicker brush.

F—Hound glove or mitt.

G—Bristle brush with wire
    center.

H—Rake.

I— Bristle brush.

J— Steel comb.

K—Dresser.

L— Stripping knife.

Among Working Dogs, the *Boxer, Doberman Pinscher, Great Dane, Rottweiler, Bullmastiff* and *Mastiff* — do a vigorous grooming with a wire or fiber glove.

On the few short-haired terriers — the *Bullterrier*, the *Staffordshire Terrier*, the *Manchester Terrier* and the *Smooth Fox Terrier* — Rub briskly to stimulate circulation, but use a fiber glove.

For the toys — *Toy Manchester Terrier*, Smooth-coated *Chihuahua, Italian Greyhound, Miniature Pinscher* and *Pug* — use a fiber bristled glove because their coats are rather fine.

On non-Sporting dogs as the *Boston Terrier, Bulldog, Dalmation,* and *French Bulldog* — use the fiber bristled glove.

On the *Schipperke*, brush first with a wire bristled glove, and then shine up by finishing with the fiber bristled glove.

That's all for the short-coated breeds, except to scissor off any whiskers around muzzle, ears and eyes, and to tidy up any long stray hairs.

Heavy-Coated Breeds

A bristle brush with a wire center is a useful brush for breeds with a thick coat composed of a dense undercoat and outer guard hairs. This brush gets right down to the base of the hair close to the skin, and that is what is needed. Brushing should be done with a twist of the wrist so that the bristles get right down into the undercoat.

Among the sporting dogs, the retrievers — *Chesapeake Bay, Labrador, Curly,* and *Flat Coated* — can be brushed vigorously with this kind of brush.

Other breeds which benefit from it are the working group — the *Alaskan Malamute, Belgian Sheepdog, German Shepherd Dog, Great Pyrenees, Newfoundland, St. Bernard, Samoyed, Siberian Husky,* the two *Welsh Corgis* — *Cardigan* and *Pembroke, Komondor, Kuvasz* and the *Puli.*

A stiff plain bristle brush is used on sporting dogs such as the *Golden Retriever, Springer Spaniels, Cocker Spaniels,* and *Setters* — although all these need some stripping or trimming at regular intervals as well, as do the *Afghan Hound,* the *Borzoi,* and the long-coated *Dachshund.* More about this later.

The *Collie* and *Shetland Sheepdog,* and the *Old English Sheepdog,* among the working dogs, can all be brushed with a bristle brush, and their featherings, whiskers, paw and ear furnishings should be trimmed neatly with a scissors.

The *Papillon*, the *Affenpinscher*, the *English Toy Spaniel*, the *Japanese Toy Spaniel* and the *Silky Terriers* are among the Toys that need ten minutes' daily brushing.

Long-Coated Dogs

More time will be required for the very long-coated dogs, and for these you will need a brush with really long bristles that gets right down to the base of the hairs.

Among the Toys that need above average grooming are the *Pomeranian*, whose coat should be brushed in the reverse direction of the hair growth to make it stand out. So should the coat of the *Pekingese*, be brushed to give it a wide full look, with the tail brushed to fall elegantly on either side of the body. In the Non-Sporting group the standout coats of the *Chow Chow* and the *Keeshond* should also be brushed in reverse direction.

There are one or two breeds with excessively long hair that often trails the floor. These are the *Skye* Terrier, in the terrier group, the *Maltese* and the *Yorkshire Terrier* among the toys, and the *Lhasa Apso* in the Non-Sporting group, and the *Shih-Tzu* which is usually classified among the miscellaneous breeds. All these dogs should be brushed with a long bristled brush, making sure you get through the undercoat; then a part is made in the center of the head and down the back right to the base of the tail. The coat will then fall elegantly from the parting, and the edge of it can be scissored evenly along the bottom.

With the *Maltese*, *Yorkies* and *Shih-Tzu*, the topknot or bangs are tied with a ribbon or barrette; the *Lhasa Apso's* eye-fall is allowed to drop completely over the eyes, and the *Skye Terrier's* fringe is combed down from a center parting to blend with the whiskers.

Dogs Needing Stripping and Clipping

The most complex form of grooming is that which involves stripping, plucking or clipping. In the main, it is the longer haired gun dogs and the majority of the terrier breeds which need this treatment, but so does the most popular dog of all, the *Poodle*.

There are dog beauty parlors which do this work for the dog owner, and the cost, considering the time involved is, for the most part reasonable, provided the owner doesn't want fancy clips, exotic rinses and other extravagances.

It is possible to learn to do a simple job yourself, particularly if your main concern is the comfort and neat appearance of a companion dog. The show dog needs far more extensive work, and unless the owner is prepared to take a short course in the proper technique for his chosen breed, it is best to leave the preparation of the show coat to the professional. Some breeds must be groomed in a definite pattern according to the kennel club show standards.

Electric Clippers

For grooming breeds which require more than a brushing or tidying up with scissors, some special tools will be needed. First and foremost, is the electric clippers. These should be the kind specially made for dogs, as they need to be strong. You'll need at least four different sizes of blades, so that you can clip hair to different lengths. There is a popular animal clipper on the market which has a changeable head to take these different blades. The sizes needed are numbers 15, 10, 7 and 5.

The higher the number is, the closer the clip. The number 15 blade, for instance, is used usually on the face, feet and tail to give a close shave, while the number 5 blade cuts the hair down to about half an inch.

The clipper is held like a pencil, and the blade used flat against the dog with a smooth motion. The motor and blades often get overheated, and should be cooled off before continuing. The blades should always be sharp and well oiled.

Before clippers are used for the first time, it is best to get the puppy used to the noise by turning them on and holding the clippers close to his ear. Get him used to the vibration by holding the clippers gently to the side of his head.

Clippers are used for grooming any long-haired dogs, and sometimes instead of stripping knives on terriers. On some dogs, a combination of the two is used.

Stripping is a far more tedious business than clipping, but for show purposes on certain breeds it is absolutely necessary. It is done either with a stripping comb, sometimes called a "dresser," which is a tool with a razor blade in serrated teeth, or a stripping knife, which is a steel blade with a nick in it, attached to a handle.

The idea of stripping is to get dead hair out so as to allow the healthy growth of the new coat. The blade of the stripping comb or knife is rested on the forefinger and with a twisting movement a few hairs are dealt with at a time. Obviously it takes a long time to do a complete dog, which is why clippers are often used instead. Clipping, however, does not remove dead hair, it merely shortens the coat and neatens the appearance.

Some professional handlers and old-time breeders groom the dogs they handle in the show ring by hand, using the thumb and forefinger. Done well, this gives fine results but is even slower than using stripping tools. The coat is usually chalked for hand stripping as chalk makes the hairs easier to grip.

Some other useful tools, which can be used to good effect on long-haired dogs other than those needing to be clipped or stripped, are: thinning shears, which have one smooth blade and the other serrated, and are used for thinning out the coat; a wire carder, which is a brush with tiny wirelike bristles set in a rubber base, used to loosen heavy mats and thick dead undercoat; and combs, if possible with several different teeth widths. There is also a tool called a rake, which has a single or double row of long metal teeth. There shouldn't be any need for this one; it is used when the mats in the coat are so bad that the carder won't shift them — and no dog should be allowed to get into such a state of neglect. The rake is a drastic tool and can be very painful if it is not used carefully.

The modern tendency is to go for the more natural look in most breeds — certainly in the sporting and working breeds — leaving the fancy clips and trims for the fancy pooches owned by sophisticated dog lovers.

The aim is to strip the coat just enough to keep down the dead hair and to neaten the appearance.

Among the sporting dogs, the *English* and *American Cocker Spaniels* and *Setters* get the fullest treatment. The head shape is fined down by a limited clipping, and the body hair, legs and tail are stripped and scissored to give a neater appearance. The other Spaniels, such as the *Welsh, Springer* and *Brittany*, merely have any unruly hair trimmed neatly, and the heavy-coated *Golden Retriever* and the *German Wire-Haired Pointer* are stripped slightly with dresser and thinning shears to give an orderly appearance.

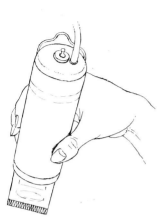

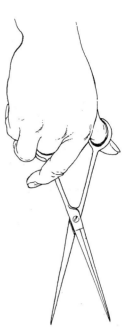

How to hold the clipper.   How to hold the scissors.

A similar neatening job is done on the long-coated hounds, such as the *Afghan, Borzoi, Irish Wolfhound, Scottish Deerhound* and long-coated *Dachshund*. The idea is to accentuate the characteristics of the breed; in the case of the *Afghan* and *Borzoi*, to enhance the essential lean grace by stripping and trimming accordingly.

Only a small amount of actual stripping is done on the *Collie*

How to use the stripping knife.

157

and *Shetland Sheepdog,* the *Old English Sheepdog,* the bulk of the neatening being done with scissors, and reliance for removing dead undercoat being placed on the brush. The *Giant* and *Standard Schnauzers,* however, with their harsh coats, need extensive stripping, though sometimes a clipper is used throughout.

Most of the terriers need extensive stripping too. Not only is the dead hair removed, but the new growth is trimmed to conform to the rigid standards for each breed.

Airdales, Welsh Terriers and *Lakeland Terriers* are all treated similarly. The *Wire Fox Terrier* is extensively treated to emphasize his trim type, so is the *Irish Terrier.* The *Scottish Terrier* also requires a lot of work to accentuate his chunky look, and the same "down to the ground" appearance is applied to the *Sealyham.*

The *Cairn, West Highland White, Norwich Terrier, Border Terrier,* and *Australian Terrier* are stripped only enough to keep them looking neat and orderly, leaving them with a natural look.

The *Bedlington* requires some careful work with the scissors, rather than clippers or stripping tools, to create the lamb like look, and the *Dandie Dinmont* similarly is scissored, although a stripper is used on him a little. The *Kerry Blue Terrier's* curly coat is also scissored carefully. *Miniature Schnauzers* are treated like the *Giant* and *Standard Schnauzers* with fairly extensive stripping.

Only two Toys have the harsher coats which require any stripping — the *Affenpinscher* and the *Brussels Griffon,* and they are stripped slightly to give a neat appearance.

In the non-sporting group is the dog with the most complicated grooming of the lot. He is also the most popular dog of all. It is, of course, the *Poodle.*

Poodles come in three sizes, the little *Toy* which is up to ten inches in height, the *Miniature* which is between 10 and 15 inches tall, and the *Standard* which is any thing over 15. All are treated in exactly the same way.

There are a dozen or more possible clips for the *Poodle.* Some are resemblances of other breeds, such as the *Bedlington Terrier,* the *Kerry Blue Terrier.* Others are just for fun, like the *Clown Clip* and the *Cowboy.*

Five clips are the most often seen, however, and we illustrate them here. Only three of them — the Puppy, which is for dogs under a year of age, the Continental, and the English Saddle — are permitted in the show ring.

Poodle Puppy Clip

The muzzle is shaved with a #15 blade from below the eyes, around the cheeks, and down the throat to the pith. The paws are shaved with a #15 blade up to the dewclaw area. They should be shaved clean, including inside the pads.

The coat should be brushed with a long bristle brush in an outward direction so that it stands away from the body. About one third of the tail at the base should be trimmed with a #15 blade, with the rest of the hair combed out and scissored into a ball. The hair over the eyes should be pulled away from the muzzle and tied with a ribbon, elastic, or barrette, into a topknot.

Scissor the body to make the coat look like clipped hedge; but very few of the long guard hairs should be scissored off. Pay particular attention to the ears as they should be left very long; a practical idea when feeding the puppy or letting it play is to put a cap around its head to keep this long hair from breaking off. A nylon stocking with the toe cut off makes a good cap.

Poodle English Saddle Clip

The English Saddle is the second of the three clips which is permitted in AKC shows.

Clip the muzzle clean, cutting horizontally below the eyes to the base of the ears, then down the throat to the pith of the neck. Use a #15 blade unless your Poodle has very sensitive skin, in which case use a #10. Hold his mouth firmly so that the tongue cannot protrude and get cut.

Clip the paws with a #15 blade. Do not shave higher than the dewclaw area.

From the dewclaw area to the first knuckle joint on the front legs leave the hair full. It is to be trimmed in a pompon. Shave above this area to the beginning of the elbow.

Scissor these bracelet pompons on the front legs to about 2 to 3 inches in length. Create a ball-like effect by combing the hair downward and cutting straight along the bottom edge, then combing upward and scissoring lightly a rounded edge on top.

With the #15 blade clip a band about $1^1/_2$ inches in width around each rear leg just above the hock joint. Shape the bracelet pompon below this band just as you did on the front legs. You will create

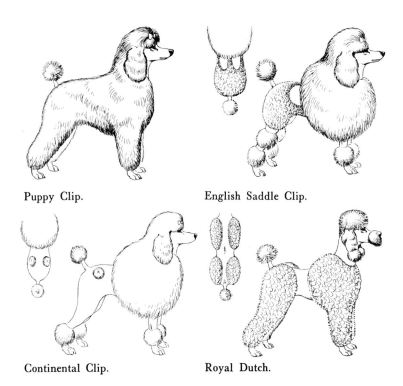

Puppy Clip.   English Saddle Clip.

Continental Clip.   Royal Dutch.

another pompon above the band later. Leave the hair around the hock joint a little heavier than the hair on the front pompons.

Clip the base of the tail with a #15 blade on top and a #10 underneath. If the tail is unusually long, expose less of the tail to make a larger pompon. If the tail is very short, shave almost to its end but leave the pompon hair longer than usual.

All of the hair forward from the last rib is left on for a lionlike appearance. The rest, from the last rib back, is scissored down evenly, and a full amount of hair is left from the stern to the first stifle joint on the back legs. This fullness on the hindquarters is called the "pack." Between the mane and the pack make a long, crescent-shaped indentation on each side. You can use soft chalk to drawn the outline. Shave this area close with a #10 or #15 blade.

Make an indentation about 1¹/₂ to 2 inches below the pack on the stifle joint. Shave this area with a #15 blade. When you trim the pompon which is left, cut the bottom and top edges straight across. Fluff out the hair on the pompon and scissor it into a ball.

Trim the edge of the mane at the saddle with your scissors. Comb the hair downward and cut along the edge. Then comb upward and

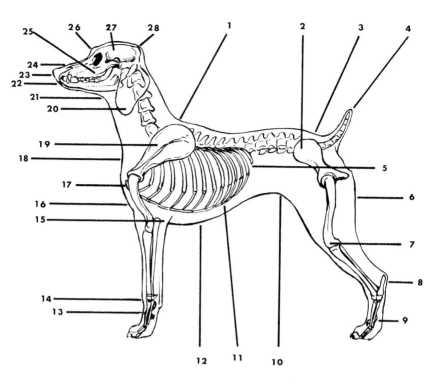

DOG TERMINOLOGY

1. Withers.
2. Hipbones.
3. Rump.
4. Tail.
5. Last rib.
6. Stern.
7. Stifle.
8. Hock.
9. Dewclaw.
10. Loin.
11. Ribs.
12. Brisket.
13. Dewclaw.
14. Pastern.
15. Elbow.
16. Chest.
17. Breast bone.
18. Pith.
19. Shoulder.
20. Ear leather.
21. Throat.
22. Lip.
23. Nose.
24. Muzzle.
25. Cheeks.
26. Stop.
27. Skull.
28. Occiput.

cut along the edge, making a definitive line. Fluff out the rest of the hair on the mane and scissor to the desired length.

Remove shaggy hairs from the inside of the legs with a #7 blade or with your scissors. Clean the stomach as well as the private parts with a # 10 blade.

Grip the hair above the eyes and attach a barrette (the clip-on type) or a rubber band for a topknot effect. Your dog is now ready to step into the show ring.

Poodle Continental Clip

This is the third cut acceptable in the show ring and is a variation of the more formal English Saddle clip. The same procedure is

AKE WINTZELL

Norwegian Elkhound
An extremely fine breed, this ancient Swedish farm dog is not really a hound, but an all-around working and hunting dog. This picture, taken in Sweden, shows its original build. American breeders have changed it to a shorter legged, heavier bodied dog, more pleasing in appearance.

Norwich Terrier
Unlike the American Cottontail, the European rabbit lives in warrens or holes in the ground, and small terriers like the Norwich are used to drive them out. Unlike most broken-coated terriers, the Norwich does not require clipping, sheds very little, and makes an excellent housedog. Height at the shoulder: 10 inches.

followed as with the English Saddle clip except for the hindquarters.

The rear the last rib (the back edge of the mane) is shaved all the way down to the hock joints with #15 blade.

At the hock joint on each rear leg you are to have one large pompon. Leave a great deal of hair on these pompons as they are the focal points of the Continental clip. The pompons are fluffed out, trimmed straight across on the top and on the bottom edges, and then trimmed in a ball or a square design. (Whether round or square is a matter of personal choice and will not affect your Poodle's candidacy in the AKC ring. The pompons on all four feet must be the same however — do not leave some square and some round.)

You may, if you wish, put rosettes on either side of the rump. The rosettes should be approximately over each hip bone, which you can find with your hand. Make the rosettes from 2½ to 3 inches in diameter. They should be separated on top by the width of the clipper blade. Comb the rosettes from the center outward and scissor them evenly at the edges, giving the design sharp definition. Fluff the tops of the rosettes and round them with the scissors for a ball-like appearance.

Poodle Utility Clip

This clip is also known as the Sporting clip, Working clip, Utility clip, Field clip, and Business Man's clip. It is very easy to maintain, since you need trim it only four or five times a year.

Shave the muzzle and the neck with a #15 blade.

Leave the ears full.

The pompon should be full and round with a point at the rear of the head blending into the hair on the back of the neck, as in the Clown clip.

Shave the paws with a #15 blade to the dew claws.

With a #7 blade (#10 if you wish it closer) shave the body to the top of the shoulders at the front and to the loins at the rear. Shave over the top of the rump. The shoulders in front should each be like the point of an arrow when the dog is viewed from the side, with the heavier hair expanding away from the shoulder toward the pith of the neck and toward the belly.

Use your scissors to blend the hair on the shoulders and rump into the fullness of the legs. Trim the hair on the legs to about 3 inches.

Poodle Royal Dutch Clip

The Royal Dutch, or Dutch Boy, is the most popular Poodle clip in America.

The muzzle is shaved with a #15 blade but full whiskers are left. These should begin at the back corners of the mouth. Square them off by combing them forward then scissoring straight along the bottom edges and straight up and down at the front of the mouth.

The ears usually have ball-like tassels. Full ears are also very attractive with this clip.

Leave full pompons on the head and tail.

The neck and throat are shaved with a #15 blade.

With the #15 blade shave a strip the width of the clipper all the way along the ridge of the back to the base of the tail. Use smooth, steady strokes to make a very clean line. Don't jerk the clippers.

Between the last rib and the point where the loin joins the hindleg shave a band around the stomach with a #15 blade. You want to make the shoulders and rear legs look very full, and the Poodle look short, so don't make this band too wide.

Shave the paws to the dew claws with the #15 blade.

Fully comb out the hair on the legs and then scissor this hair evenly for a hedge-like look.

Rub, Dub, Dub — in the Tub!

Most dog owners either bathe their dogs too little or too much. Bathing is necessary, but for the average, clean-living housedog, twice a year is quite enough. Of course, if the dog rolls in filth, or gets excessively dirty for some reason or another, he'll need a tubbing.

Too frequent bathing, however, dries out the natural oils in the skin, can cause patches of dry skin, and take the life out of the coat. Daily brushing will keep the coat clear of the everyday dust and dirt.

Some long or heavy-coated dogs, especially the low to the ground ones, get dirty underneath, and if the feet and legs are heavily coated with hair, this can get very grubby too. These dogs can be dumped into a shallow tub of water between bath times and given a thorough rinsing on the bottom half.

Brush and comb the dog thoroughly before bathing. Use a fair sized tub and a shower spray — one of the portable attachments will do. Before wetting the dog, plug his ears with cotton, and smear a little vaseline round the eyes to keep the water out.

Use a good dog shampoo — your pet store will offer a wide selection. It is a good idea to buy one which contains an insecticide and antiseptic, as a preventative against fleas and lice and other external parasites. There are also special shampoos for Poodles and for white dogs.

Wet the dog thoroughly, right down to the skin, with warm water. Work in the shampoo, but don't touch the face yet; leave that until last. Don't rub a densely-coated or long-coated dog, either when applying the shampoo or later when drying, as this may cause mats to form. Squeeze the shampoo through the coat instead.

Rinse the dog well, and then shampoo again. Give a really thorough rinsing until every trace of shampoo is rinsed quite clear. Any shampoo left in the coat will dull and dry it. The hair should "squeak clean" when you rub it between your fingers.

Finally, do the dog's face very carefully, taking care not to let any foam get into the eyes or ears. On the face use a mild shampoo such as those prepared specially for babies, as these do not sting the eyes.

Have some heavy terry towels ready, warmed if possible, and dry the dog on these. A short-coated dog can be rubbed briskly, but with a long or densely-coated dog just mop and squeeze out the excess water.

Dry with a hairdryer if possible and brush the dog as you dry. The dog should be kept out of drafts while being bathed and dried, and should not go outside while still damp unless the weather is hot and dry. Check that the insides of the ears are dry, and take care to dry carefully between the pads of the feet.

Dogs needing clipping or trimming should be bathed and clean before any work is done on them.

If a dog is rather dirty but cannot for some reason or another be properly bathed, dry clean him. There are aerosol foam shampoos on the market, and also powder cleansers.

Ears, Eyes and Nails

These should all be checked regularly. When you are doing your grooming is as good a time as any. Spot troubles early and clear them up before they get too painful or uncomfortable for the dog.

Drop-eared dogs are particularly prone to ear infections, so check the ears for any redness, or any dirt or secreted matter that may be there. Many dogs have a lot of hairs actually inside the ear cavity, and these should be plucked out. Use blunt ended type of tweezer and pull the hairs out singly with a quick, twisting motion. Remember that the ears are sensitive, so be gentle, and if the dog objects too strongly, do only a few at a session. Wipe the ears out delicately with cotton damped in rubbing alcohol, but don't probe into the ear.

If you feel you cannot tackle the tweezing job yourself, ask your veterinarian to do it for you. Also consult him right away if the dog seems to have painful or foul smelling ears.

Make it a routine part of your grooming to wipe the corners of the dog's eyes with cotton moistened in warm water. Check during the summer months that no grass seeds or husks are clinging round the eyes. If the dog's eyes are running excessively, or there is any mucus, consult your veterinarian.

Toenails will usually stay worn down if the dog gets a lot of walking and running on hard surfaces. A dog that spends most of his time in the house or on grass, however, will probably need fairly regular clipping.

Use an animal nail clipper, not one meant for people because these are not strong enough except for the tiniest dogs. Clip the nails if they are hooked, but beware of cutting into the quick, which is the spongy growing area of the nail. On light colored nails this can be seen quite easily, because it is darker than the actual nail.

Dark nails must be done more carefully. The best way is just to clip a tiny piece at a time, and you will soon spot the difference in "feel" should you touch the quick. By studying the undersurface of each nail after each cut, you can see the texture change, becoming flaky or spongy as you near the quick. If you should cut into the quick, use a styptic pencil on it right away to stop the bleeding.

Pay particular attention to the dewclaws if they have not been removed. These are the extra claws, like a thumb, which are higher than the foot. As they do not come into contact with the ground, they are not worn down, and if neglected they can grow into a hook and inbed themselves into the leg, with obviously painful results. Badly neglected dewclaws should be seen by your veterinarian.

Old English Sheepdog
Developed from the ancient working sheepdogs of England, the "Bobtail" finds little employment on the farm or ranch today. His buoyant manner, brilliant personality and unique appearance have created a great demand for him as a housedog and companion. His coat is never clipped, but it must be cared for regularly.

SALLY ANNE THOMPSON

IX Feeding Your Dog

Most pet dogs in our affluent society are overfed. Many commercially raised kennel dogs are underfed. Both kinds would be a lot healthier if they were nearer the happy medium.

Food is the basis of the dog's health. Good feeding increases chances of good health. Poor feeding condemns the dog to an existence under par, never up to peak condition, never reaching his full potential for living.

There are three basic principles of dog diet which, if followed, will guide you along the right lines.

First — *a balanced diet.* This means a diet that contains all the necessary elements and in the proper proportions — protein, carbohydrate, fat, water and a full complement of vitamins and minerals.

In primitive times, the dog, which is basically a carnivore — a meat eater — had to hunt for its food. Sometimes it got it, sometimes it didn't. Those that got enough survived.

Because of this, many people say that a dog needs only meat, forgetting that in the wild, meat was in poor supply and the early dog existed on whatever it could find. In any case, the dog ate the whole of its prey, including the small soft bones, the organs, as well as the vegetable contents of the stomach.

167

Following this "natural" parallel, we might say that primitive man was also a carnivorous eater, and ate when and what he could. There are few people today who would honestly say that this was the natural way for mankind to eat.

Man and dog have grown civilized together, and their patterns of eating have been adapted and modified. In primitive times things were pretty hit and miss; lifespan was short. Greater knowledge of nutrition nowadays enables us to insure complete balanced nourishment to develop and maintain strong bodies, good health, and longer lives.

Nowadays the protein a dog needs is fed in the form of meat of all kinds — raw, canned, frozen, and dried — as well as in fish and eggs, and in cheese.

The carbohydrate is in the cereal foods, brown bread, dog meals, kibbles and rusks, and so are many of the necessary vitamins and minerals.

The necessary fats — and most dogs need about 15% of their caloric intake to be in the form of fat — are usually found in the meat content or can be added in the form of fatty tablescraps, meat fats, lard or oils.

Vitamins and minerals are present in most foods or they can be added in the form of commercially prepared supplements.

Drinking water, of course, must always be available.

Things are made easy for the modern dog owner. The market is full of a wide variety of commercial dog foods that help to prevent confusion for the nutritional novice.

You can feed nutritionally complete dog diets — these are all the basic foods put together, including added vitamins and minerals, and you feed them by merely following the package's instructions.

You can compromise and feed fresh or frozen meat, or all meat

EVELYN SHAFER

Otter Hound
The ancestor of many of our rough-coated terriers, a sturdy, courageous and tough vermin hunting dog. Height at the shoulder: 24 to 26 inches. Weight: 66 to 70 pounds. Registered by the A.K.C. in the "Hound" group.

canned food, along with commercially prepared cereal foods (frozen foods should be defrosted and fed at room temperature.)

But if you are a strong believer in home cooked foods, you can do it all yourself by feeding fresh meat, plus toasting whole wheat bread in the oven, and feeding that — in which case you should add a vitamin and mineral supplement, too.

Plan it however you like, provided you read the labels of the cans and packets you buy, and add to the dog's diet any basic food element that is not listed among the contents.

Dogs, of course, don't always respond as science decides they should, no more than people do. There are lots of people who prefer hamburger to chicken, or food served dry rather than with sauces.

Dogs have their fancies too. Some prefer cereal soaked and mixed with their meat ration. Others prefer to eat it dry and separately.

Some dogs like mashed vegetables, others don't. Give them as an extra if they like. I've known dogs that liked fruit — a Pug I had adored strawberries and would pick them right off the plants.

You can indulge these fancies to a limited extent, provided they don't affect the general principle of the balanced diet. Let your pup have his meat and meal mixed or separate, whichever he prefers, provided he gets enough of both.

The second principle in dog diets is *regularity*. Dogs have a built in time clock, and there is no doubt they do better if they are fed at much the same times every day and without tidbits and treats in between — except for special purposes such as training rewards.

The ideal situation is when your dog greets the arrival of his food dish with waving tail and appreciative barks, devours the food with obvious enjoyment, licking the dish clean, and settles down happily for an after dinner nap. If he doesn't know what time he's going to get it, but his stomach says it's overdue, he is going to fuss and bother. His digestive system is going to be so overanxious by the time the food arrives he will probably knock it out of your hand before you set in on the floor.

At the other extreme is the pampered over-indulged pooch who asks for and gets tidbits, chocolates, candy, cookies and cakes all day. "Feeding time," in effect, covers all the waking hours. When the real meal comes, fat Fido can barely raise enough enthusiasm to sniff at it, let alone eat it. The results: irregularity of feeding, leading to unbalancing of diet!

Papillon

Often called the "Butterfly Dog" because of his large, fringed, erect ears, this charming little fellow from Spain and Italy deserves to be better known. Remarkably hardy for a toy dog, he is at home almost everywhere and has no inherited weaknesses. Height at the shoulder: 11 inches or under. Registered by the American Kennel Club in the "Toy" group.

The actual time you feed your dog depends on your household habits. Adult dogs really need only one meal daily, and most people find it convenient to fit this in to the same time that the rest of the household has its main meal.

In really hot weather, it is probably better to give the main meal

Pekingese

For centuries this was the royal dog of China where it was known as the "Lion Dog," a tribute to both its appearance and courage. A charming companion, the Pekingese takes up very little space and requires little grooming, except for brushing. Registered by the American Kennel Club in the "Toy" group. Weight, up to 14 ponds.

in the cooler evening. Another point in favor of a late afternoon or evening feeding is thaat the long night of rest that follows probably aids the digestion.

It may be preferable to give a small portion of the day's food as a snack at another time of day — perhaps the cereal can be given in the mornings in the form of hard biscuits or kibbles. If so, this should be a regular thing, so that the dog can look forward to it.

Puppies need feeding more frequently than the adult dog. Very old dogs also find it easier to have their food split into two, perhaps three, smaller meals.

But however frequently you feed your dog, the same rule applies — make mealtimes regular.

Principle three is *cleanliness*. Dirty dishes provide a breeding ground for bacteria that can cause digestive upsets. Stale food is a source of trouble. Bits and pieces left to lie around in the dog dish attract flies, ants and, worse still, vermin and pests.

The most expensive food on the market is of no value to your dog if you don't serve it cleanly. You might just as well throw your money in the garbage can.

Don't save any leftovers. If bits are regularly left in the dish, you are feeding too much. Throw away the bits today, and feed less tomorrow.

Pointer

Styles constantly change in gun dogs, but the Pointer, developed many years ago in England and much the same today as it has been for several hundred years, still maintains his pre-eminence. The instinct to point is inherited and needs only refinement and training for the dog to become an expert. Height at the shoulder: 19 to 24 inches. Registered by the American Kennel Club in the "Sporting Dog" group.

A feeding bowl should be cleared within ten minutes. Any remainder should not be left lying around, nor served the next time.

Your dog's food should be stored with the same care as your own. The contents of opened cans, and cooked or fresh meat or fish which are not going to be fed right away, should be kept in the refrigerator. Packages and boxes of cereals, kibbles, toast and biscuits should be stored in a dry place, and be inacessible to dust, dirt, mice, ants and other pests. Vitamins, oils, and other supplements should be stored in cool, dark places, not on a sill or shelf in full sunlight. Tops and lids should always be replaced.

Dog bowls for both food and water should be washed out after every use every day. Stale old water, floating with dust and dirt in a slimy grubby bowl, is a common cause of minor upset.

Two Kinds of Feeding

Young growing dogs and adult dogs need different patterns of feeding.

Let's deal with the mature adults first. You've already seen the importance of a balanced diet. The next obvious question is, "How much food does a dog need?"

Like people, dogs vary in their needs. Not only does quantity depend on size, but on basic metabolism too. Pound for pound in weight, an active dog needs more food than a slow, lethargic type.

A rough guide is to feed about $1/2$ to $3/4$ of an ounce of moist food per pound of body weight every day. Dry dog food (meal, kibbles) goes further. One half pound will keep a 22 pound Beagle happy and well. Small and medium sized dogs need more per pound than do the larger breeds. Active working dogs need more than do pet dogs living a sedentary life.

For instance, a 25 pound adult Beagle, living as a family dog and getting moderate exercise, would need about one and one half pounds of moist food daily. A 75 pound Old English Sheepdog living under similar conditions would need not quite three times as much. If you feed canned dog food exclusively, remember that most brands supply 450 calories which is half enough for a healthy Beagle or Cocker.

If either were working regularly, however, and getting a great deal of exercise, their food intake would need to be increased considerably.

A 5 pound Chihuahua is a tiny dog, but because small active adult dogs need more food per pound of body weight than larger ones, he'd need at least 6 ounces of moist food a day.

These quantities refer to mixed meat and meal. *Dry meals,* complete in themselves, are becoming more and more popular, especially for people who keep more than one dog or who have a big active breed.

As these foods are usually fed moistened, the amounts required are slightly different from the above estimates. As a rough guide, one pound of dry meal for every 35 pounds of dog can be considered a reasonable maintenance diet for an adult animal.

Do remember, incidentally, when feeding dry meals that plenty of fresh water should *always* be available. *This is very important.*

All these suggested quantities can only be a rough guide. Each individual dog varies in his needs, and the only way you can be sure your dog is being correctly fed is to watch his response to food, and to weigh him regularly to see that his weight is being maintained over a long period.

If you regularly have food left on the dish, you are probably feeding too much.

If your dog is always ravenously hungry and doesn't seem to put on weight, you could be underfeeding him.

If, however, you are already giving him far in excess of the above suggested amounts, and he's still hungry all day and never gains an ounce in weight, you'd better consult the veterinarian.

Feeding the Growing Dog

Puppies and young growing dogs need far more food per ounce of body weight than do mature dogs — two and a half times as much — and a considerably higher proportion of protein, so important for good strong growth.

Puppies also need feeding more frequently than adult dogs because their digestive systems obviously cannot cope with the necessary bulk at one time. Like babies, they do better on small amounts of food several times a day than large amounts once or twice a day.

Sudden changes of food may upset the young digestive system, too, so when you first bring home a new puppy, ask for, and continue to follow, the diet that he has already been receiving. Make any changes gradually, introducing only one new food at a time and giving the youngster three or four days to get used to it before making another change.

Nevertheless, don't delay too long in putting the pup onto the kind of food you are going to give him more or less permanently. Better get his ideas about food set in the direction you want them to go, and not too much according to his whims and fancies! By six months of age, he should be having the kind of food — be it canned, fresh, dry meal, or whatever — you've chosen as a regular diet.

Feed puppies four times a day — the most convenient times usually being at the three family mealtimes and just before going to bed. At three to four months of age, reduce the schedule to three times a day, and at seven to nine months to twice a day. At a year of age, the youngster can go to the adult routine of one meal a day, although some people prefer to continue on two meals daily. There is nothing wrong with this. The dog usually has most of his day's ration in a main meal, and the remainder as a breakfast, or a bedtime treat.

Two points about feeding the growing dog:

First, puppies have a lot of growing to do in a short time. They start out at birth weighing a few pounds and, with the really massive breeds, by eight months may have increased their weight to a hundred pounds. A great deal of good quality protein — the basic body building element — and the calcium, phosphorus, and vitamin D that go into making good bone, are needed for that kind of growing. If you can't afford to feed on this scale, then buy a pup of the smaller breeds.

Secondly, vitamins and minerals are especially needed by the youngster — not only are they active building materials themselves, but they are frequently needed to regulate the use of the other nutritional elements. The adult dog on a well-balanced diet probably gets enough in his normal feeding, but it is usual to give a vitamin and mineral supplement to the young growing puppy, until he is twelve months old. Your veterinarian will advise you on the kind and amounts to give.

The feeding charts that follow will give you a guide to the amounts needed by puppies as they grown into maturity. These amounts are only a guide. You must adjust them for your individual dog's requirements.

Amounts of cereal should be measured *after* soaking to a crumble consistency. Use hot water or broth when mixing with meat.

Unless you feed a complete commercial diet, a vitamin and

mineral supplement should be given daily up to twelve months of age.

Commercially pre-cooked baby cereals are useful and readily digestible by young puppies.

Until three to four months of age, the milk in the diet may be commercial baby milk food, mixed with a little hot water.

Hard or kibbled biscuits can be given from the age of about four months, at first, a few as a "treat," but later, especially with an adult dog, in addition to or as a substitute for soaked cereal. Give them in the morning or at night separate from meat.

Classify your dog by the adult weight of its breed. Chihuahuas and Toy Poodles, for instance, come under Very Small Breeds; German Shepherd Dogs are Large Breeds. The average weight for puppies at varying ages is given, and will provide a useful guide to check against your own puppy's progress.

In borderline cases, if you know your pup's parents were large specimens of their breed, step up into the next group. All the quantities given are based on the eventual weight of the adult dog. These are suggestions for those who love to fuss. To those who don't, commercially prepared dog foods will do just as well, if not better. These are discussed further on.

Poodle

Several countries in Europe contributed to the development of this, probably the most popular breed of all. Available in all solid colors, as well as three sizes: Toy (under 10 inches), Miniature (10 to 15 inches), and Standard (over 15 inches)—there is a Poodle for everyone. His intelligence is legendary and there is a certain human quality in his thinking that is unique. The American Kennel Club registers the Toy Poodle in the "Toy" group, and te Miniature Poodle and Standard Poodle in the "Non-Sporting Dog" group.

AKE WINTZELL

VERY SMALL BREEDS — (5 to 15 pounds)

American Fox Terrier, Small Boston Terrier, Cairn Terrier, Chihuahua, Miniature Dachshund, English Toy Spaniel, Griffon, Italian Greyhound, Small Lhasa Apso, Maltese, Miniature Pinscher, Papillon, Pekingese, Pomeranian, Toy Poodle, Silky Terrier, Small Schipperke, Toy Manchester Terrier, Miniature Schnauzer, Yorkshire Terrier.

Age 2 Months — (1 to 3 pounds)

Breakfast:	2 fluid ounces of milk mixture with 1 tablespoonful of pre-cooked baby cereal.
Noon:	Heaped tablespoonful of raw ground meat.
Afternoon:	Same as breakfast.
Dinner time:	Same as noon.
Bedtime:	2 fluid ounces of milk.

Age 3 to 4 months — (2 to 6 pounds)

Breakfast:	$1/4$ cup of milk mixture with 2 tablespoonsful baby cereal.
Noon:	2 heaped tablespoonsful of raw meat.
Dinner time:	2 heaped tablespoonsful raw meat with 1 tablespoonful of soaked puppy cereal.

Age 5 to 6 months — (4—12 pounds)

Breakfast:	$1/4$ to $3/4$ cup of cow's milk (plus egg yoke if liked) with puppy cereal (to make 2 to 6 tablespoonsful soaked cereal).
Noon:	2 to 4 heaped tablespoonsful meat (raw, canned, frozen) with equal amounts soaked puppy cereal.
Dinner:	Same as noon.

Age 7 to 8 months — (5—15 pounds)

Breakfast:	$1/4$ to $1/2$ cup of cow's milk, with puppy cereal (to make 2 tablespoons cereal).
Dinner:	2 to 5 heaped tablespoonsful meat with equal amounts soaked cereal.

Age 9 to 10 months — (Maturity)

Daily:	$1/4$ to $3/4$ cup of meat. Equal amount of soaked cereal mixed with it. As an addition or alternative to soaked cereal, hard dog biscuits, rusked or kibbled cereal can be given as morning or bedtime snack.

SMALL BREEDS: (15 to 30 pounds)

Beagle, Bedlington Terrier, Boston Terrier, Cocker Spaniel, Dachsund, Dandie Dinmont Terrier, Fox Terrier, French Bulldog, Irish Terrier, Lhasa Apso, Keeshond, Manchester Terrier, Miniature

Poodle, Pekingese, Sealyham Terrier, Scottish Terrier, Schipperke, Standard Schnauzer, Shetland Sheepdog, Welsh Corgi, Welsh Terrier, West Highland White Terrier, Whippet.

Age 2 months (3 to 6 pounds)

Breakfast: 2 to 4 fluid ounces of milk mixture with 3 tablespoonsful baby cereal.

Noon: 2 heaped tablespoonsful raw ground meat.

Afternoon: Same as breakfast.

Dinner: Same as noon.

Bedtime: 2 to 4 fluid ounces milk.

Age 3 to 4 months (6 to 12 pounds)

Breakfast: $^1/_4$ to $^1/_2$ cup of milk mixture with 4 tablespoonsful baby cereal.

Noon: 2 to 4 heaped tablespoonsful meat (raw, canned, or frozen).

Dinner: 2 to 4 heaped tablespoonsful meat with 2 tablespoonsful soaked puppy cereal.

Age 5 to 6 months (12 to 24 pounds)

Morning: $^3/_4$ to $1^1/_2$ cups cow's milk (with added egg yolk if liked) with enough cereal to make $^1/_2$ cup when soaked.

Noon: 4 to 8 heaped tablespoonsful meat with equal amounts soaked cereal.

Dinner: Same as noon.

Age 7 to 8 months (15 to 30 pounds)

Breakfast: $^3/_4$ to $1^1/_2$ cups milk with enough cereal to make 4 to 8 tablespoonsful when soaked.

Dinner: $^3/_4$ to 2 cups meat with equal amount soaked cereal.

Age 9 to 10 months — (15 to 30 pounds)

Breakfast: $^1/_2$ to 1 cup milk with cereal to make 2 to 4 tablespoonsful when soaked.

Dinner: $^3/_4$ to $1^1/_2$ cups meat with equal amounts soaked cereal.

Age 11 months — (to maturity)

Daily: $^3/_4$ to $1^1/_2$ cups meat with equal amounts soaked cereal. As an addition or alternative to soaked cereal hard dog biscuits, rusked or kibbled cereal can be given as morning or bedtime snack.

MEDIUM BREEDS — (30 to 50 pounds)

Bassett Hound, Bull Terrier, Chow Chow, Dalmatian, Elkhound, English Bulldog, Foxhound, Kerry Blue Terrier, Saluki, Samoyed, Small Setter and Pointer, Springer Spaniel.

Age 2 months — 6 to 8 pounds

Breakfast:	¹/₂ cup of milk mixture with 3 to 4 tablespoons-ful baby cereal.
Noon:	2 heaped tablespoonsful raw ground meat.
Afternoon:	Same as breakfast.
Dinner:	Same as noon.
Bedtime:	¹/₂ cup milk.

Age 3 to 4 months — (15 to 25 pounds)

Breakfast:	¹/₂ cup to 1 cup milk mixture with enough puppy cereal to make 4 to 8 tablespoonsful when soaked.
Noon:	4 to 8 heaped tablespoonsful meat (raw, canned, or defrosted frozen kind).
Dinner:	4 to 8 heaped tablespoonsful meat with equal amount soaked cereal.

Age 5 to 6 months — (25 to 35 pounds)

Breakfast:	³/₄ cup to 1¹/₂ cups cow's milk (with egg yolk added if liked) with cereal to make ³/₄ to 1¹/₂ cups when soaked.
Noon:	1 to 1¹/₂ cups meat with equal amount soaked cereal.
Dinner:	Same as noon.

Age 8 months — (weight 30 pounds)

Breakfast:	1¹/₂ cups milk with cereal to make 1 cup when soaked.
Dinner:	2 cups meat with 1 cup soaked cereal.

Age 8 months — (weight 45 pounds)

Breakfast:	2 cups milk with cereal to make 2 cups when soaked.
Noon:	1¹/₂ cups meat with 1 cup soaked cereal.
Dinner:	2 cups meat with 1 cup soaked cereal.

Age 9 to 10 months — (weight 30 to 50 pounds)

Breakfast:	1 to 1¹/₂ cups milk with cereal to make ³/₄ cup when soaked.
Dinner:	1¹/₂ to 2¹/₂ cups meal with 2 cups soaked cereal.

Age 11 to 12 months — (30 to 50 pounds — maturity)

Daily:	1¹/₂ to 1³/₄ cups meal with equal amounts of soaked cereal. Hard dog biscuits, rusked or kibbled cereal morning or bedtime.

LARGE BREEDS — (50 to 80 pounds)

Airedale, Terrier, Afghan Hound, Bloodhound, Borzoi, Boxer,

Collie, Doberman Pinscher, German Shepherd, Greyhound, Husky, Large Pointer, Large Setter, Malamute, Old English Sheep Dog, Retriever (all types), Giant Schnauzer.

Age 2 months — (8 to 10 pounds)

Breakfast:	$1/2$ cup milk mixture with 4 to 6 tablespoonsful baby cereal.
Noon:	3 to 4 tablespoonsful ground raw meat.
Afternoon:	Same as breakfast.
Dinner:	Same as noon.
Bedtime:	$1/2$ cup milk.

Age 3 to 4 months — (20 to 30 pounds)

Breakfast:	1 to $1^1/2$ cups milk (with added egg yolk if liked) with cereal to make 1 to $1^1/4$ cups when soaked.
Noon:	1 to $1^1/4$ cups meat.
Dinner:	1 to $1^1/4$ cups meat with 1 cup soaked puppy cereal.

Age 5 to 6 months — (30 to 50 pounds)

Breakfest:	$1^1/2$ cups to 2 cups milk with cereal to make $1^1/2$— 2 cups when soaked.
Noon:	1 to $1^1/2$ cups meat and equal quantity soaked cereal.
Dinner:	2 to 3 cups meat with equal quantity soaked cereal.

Age 8 months — (45 to 65 pounds)

Breakfast:	2 cups to $2^1/2$ cups milk with cereal to equal when soaked.
Noon:	$1^1/2$ cups to 2 cups with equal quantity soaked cereal.
Dinner:	2 to 3 cups meat with equal quantity soaked cereal.

Age 9 to 10 months — (50 to 75 pounds)

Breakfast:	$1^1/2$ to 2 cups milk with cereal to equal $1^1/2$ cups when soaked.
Dinner:	$2^1/2$ to 3 cups meat with equal quantity of soaked cereal.

Age 11 to 14 months — (50 to 80 pounds — mature)

Daily:	$1^3/4$ to $2^1/2$ cups meat with equal quantity of soaked cereal.
	Hard dog biscuits, rusked, or kibbled cereal in morning and/or bedtime.
Note:	Vitamin and mineral supplements are vital until maturity with the Large Breeds.

VERY LARGE BREEDS — (80 to 100 pounds plus)

Great Dane, Great Pyrenees, Irish Wolfhound, Large Burzoi, Mastiff, Newfoundland, St. Bernard.

Age 2 months — (10 to 12 pounds)

Breakfast:	$^3/_4$ cup milk mixture with baby cereal to equal.
Noon:	5 to 6 heaped tablespoonsful raw ground meat.
Afternoon:	Same as breakfast.
Dinner:	Same as noon.
Bedtime:	$^3/_4$ cup milk.

Note: Increase amounts rapidly according to growth.

Age 3 to 4 months — (30 to 45 pounds)

Breakfast:	$1^1/_2$ cups to 2 cups milk mixture with cereal to equal when soaked.
Noon:	$1^1/_2$ cups to 2 cups meat.
Dinner:	$1^1/_2$ to 2 cups meat with equal amounts soaked cereal.

Age 5 to 6 months — (60 to 80 pounds)

Breakfast:	2 to $2\frac{1}{2}$ cups cow's (with added egg yolk).
Noon:	2 to 3 cups meat with 2 cups soaked cereal.
Dinner:	3 to 4 cups meat with equal quantity soaked cereal.

Age 8 to 9 months — (70 to 90 pounds)

Breakfast:	$2^1/_2$ cups to 3 cups milk.
Noon:	3 to 4 cups meat with 2 to 3 cups soaked cereal.
Dinner:	4 to 5 cups meat with equal quantity soaked cereal.

Age 9 to 10 months — (80 to 100 pounds)

Same as 8 to 9 months feeding.

Age 11 to 12 months — (100 to 110 pounds)

Breakfast:	3 to 4 cups milk with cereal to equal when soaked.
Dinner:	$2^1/_2$ to 3 cups meat with equal amounts soaked cereal.

Hard dog biscuits, rusked, or kibbled cereal as bedtime snack.

Age 14 to 16 months — (100 pounds plus — mature)

Daily:	3 to 4 cups meat with equal amounts soaked cereal.

Hard dog biscuits, rusked, or kibbled cereal as snack.

Note: Vitamin and mineral supplements are vital until maturity with the Very Large Breeds.

As was pointed out, the foregoing menus are for folks who love to fuss. Admittedly many do. But there are other ways of feeding dogs, too.

One way is to trust the manufacturer who tells you his food is complete. Feed it as he directs. The best are the meal type foods to which you add only water. To these you should add fat up to 15% of the amount of the food. Any edible fat will do. This category includes cooking oils. But any butcher will gladly sell you animal fat ground in hamburger form and chilled, for only a few cents a pound. One pound of this fat contains over twice as many calories as a pound of the best dry food.

Your dog doesn't need variety. This simple feeding regime is all he needs for his entire life.

Fact — or Fiction

It is *fiction* that milk, sugar, candy, raw meat, cause worms.

It is *fact* that dogs need protein, not necessarily beef. Raw meat is preferred; but dried, frozen (served defrosted and at room temperature), or canned mesats are equally sufficient, if not better, in vitamin content.

It is *fact* that commercial dog cereals are more nutritious than home toasted bread.

It is *fiction* that raw meat makes dogs vicious.

It is *fiction* that bones make dogs vicious unless children worry them trying to take bones away.

It is *fact* that chicken and chop bones, and all bones that splinter, are bad for dogs.

It is *fact* that beef marrow bones and soft rib bones are the only safe bones to give a dog.

It is *fiction* that grass is a tonic.

It is *fiction* that garlic is a tonic.

It is *fact* that seaweed products are a tonic.

It is *fiction* that dogs do not like fat. They need a certain amount in their diet, and some should be added when feeding only commercial dog foods.

It is *fact* that you can overdose a dog with vitamins. Your veterinarian can advise on dosages and specific types.

It is *fact* that feeding a dog is a lot simpler than many folks would have you believe, thanks to modern research and your common sense!

Pug

A true gentleman — from China by way of England — amiable of disposition, sound of structure, and with a great deal of courage and self-respect. An ideal housedog. Weight: 14 to 18 pounds. Registered by the American Kennel Club in the "Toy" group.

AKE WINTZELL

X   The Why and How of Breeding

The Why

You have a female dog; you think she's the greatest character, the lovingest dog. You think it would do her good to have some puppies, and do the kids good, too, to watch the little things grow up. Besides, you've heard that people sell pedigreed pups for a good sum, so maybe they'd pay for their cost, perhaps some profit, if you sold some of them. You know you'll love them all, and you won't want to part with them, so perhaps you'll keep just one, a little female and later, perhaps, she can have puppies too.

If those are the reasons why you'd like to breed some puppies *don't*. They are all wrong.

A female that is basically the family pet and was bought as such, with no particular regard to how good or poor an example of her breed she is, should not be bred. It serves no useful purpose and, contrary to popular opinion, it has no particular benefit from the health point of view; in fact, it may lead to future trouble. At worst, with an inexperienced owner, an inexperienced female dog, probably unchecked by the veterinarian as to her physical and mental suitability for breeding, could die in "child-birth" or at least develop a mental or physical disability causing unhappiness to the family.

Breeding puppies, and eventually selling them, does not inevitably lead to a nice little profit either, or even to covering the costs! Pregnant dogs and their puppies need to eat — and eat — and eat. Conscientious owners who love their animals will feed them what they need (and any other kind of owner isn't fit to own an animal, certainly not to breed from it). Dog food, eggs, milk, and meat cost money. The conscientious owner finds that he is spending far more on rearing his puppies than he expected. If he is inexperienced in knowing how and where to sell them, or happens to have picked the wrong time of year, or the wrong breed (that is, one which at the moment is not the current fashion), he may find that after fourteen or more weeks he still has a horde of hungry animals. Then he must either give them away to willing friends (if he has any left), or hang on to them in the hopes that somebody will come along and pay a good price for them.

I am reminded of a comic strip I saw some years ago which expressed the whole story in three panels. In the first, a private suburban home displayed a sign on the front gate, "Pedigreed German Shepherd Puppies." In the next panel the same house now displayed a sign, "Dogs for sale Cheap." In the final panel the sign had been changed to, "Beware of the Watchdogs."

So, if your female is your adored pet and companion, and nothing more, and it merely crossed your mind that it might be fun for her to have some puppies, forget it, please! Let her live her life as the favorite pooch of the family, without the problems of motherhood.

If she some funny habits — like thinking she is going to have pups, stealing your socks and pretending (it happens sometimes) — don't let anyone tell you that having a litter will cure her — it could make it worse. Talk to your veterinarian; he may suggest spaying or hormone treatment.

In fact, anyone buying a female pup as a house pet, would be wise to consider spaying. It prevents a lot of future problems if it is done properly and at the right time — usually before the first "season." Usually, six months of age is recommended, as some females come in season as early as seven or eight months.

However, let's consider the situation from a different angle. Some people, it is true, make a lot of money out of dogs. But they may not make it entirely from breeding them. The larger portion may come from the side lines of dog breeding and dog showing, or from buying and selling stock, or boarding other people's dogs.

Most people who breed dogs seriously do it because they really enjoy it. They may or may not make money out of their puppies. People who breed poor specimens, or run "puppy" factories, or otherwise exploit man's best friend, shouldn't be allowed, we all agree... But remember, these people only get rich through the gullibility of those who buy their products.

However, perhaps to you making money is a secondary consideration (though, naturally, you'd like to make a dollar or two — your pride wouldn't let it be otherwise). You've a really good female, a fine specimen of her breed. Maybe you've even taken her to a show or two and she has won some prizes. You are really interested in breeding her to see if you can produce some good youngsters. You've the interests of the dog and the breed at heart.

So read, and listen and learn. Consider every angle, steep yourself in dog knowledge, particularly of your chosen breed, study your female, study others of the same breed, talk to other breeders, keep your ears open and your thoughts to yourself. And then, if you still are as keen, go ahead and join the host of people who throughout the centuries have been fascinated by the domestic dog.

The How

The first step in successful breeding is to know something of the physiology and the reproductive cycle of the canine species.

The bitch comes "in season," on the average, twice a year, though it varies from breed to breed and even with the individual animal. Twice a year is twice as often as is nature's usual plan, but it doesn't mean she should be bred that often.

It is usual to wait until the second season before breeding. By that time the bitch is more or less mature, with all her growing and developing behind her so that she is better able to stand the strain of having puppies.

Normally, it is believed that a bitch should have her first breeding by the time she is three years of age. Nature has curiously adaptive ways, and a female left a maiden that long before breeding, some folks say, suffers ill effects. Some say the shock to the nervous system is too great — that she suffers temperamental upsets which are good neither for her nor the puppies; that sometimes her fertility has lessened and she doesn't become pregnant — this is particularly so with a bitch much older than three; and that sometimes physical problems arise in either mating or whelping. But if these claims are so, I have never seen them.

It is probably better, although not essential, to breed a bitch before three — particularly with some of the late maturing and exceptionally long-lived breeds — but is serves as a useful guide.

It is only during her season that the bitch is really interested in the opposite sex. At all other times she will reject his advances. The season, or heat period, is in three stages.

First, is the period when she is coming on, lasting roughly a week. This often goes unnoticed by the owner, especially if the bitch is showing only slight signs, or if she is particularly docile in temperament. The first stage is when the vulva, as the entrance to the reproductive organ is called, begins to swell. A behavior sign which the alert owner may notice first, is a more frequent stopping in the street to pass water, leaving a series of little puddles, or, when visiting or receiving friends who own a dog, falling from grace in her housetraining. Even the most impeccably mannered female has been known to leave a little puddle in the middle of the carpet after a male dog has paid a visit. At this stage her appetite increases.

The second stage of the heat period comes after a week or so, when a bloody discharge from the vulva is noticed, and the swelling gets more obvious. The discharge gets gradually lighter in color as the days go on. This is the time when, if you live in a rural area where dogs are not confined, the neighborhood dogs will definitely be calling around to check up on your female's progress, and if you haven't caught on to what is happening by now, these eager callers should warn you.

The earlier you notice the onset of the season, and prevent the bitch from leaving her calling card for all the dogs of the neighborhood (in the form of the before mentioned series of puddles) the less

AKE WINTZELL

Puli

A medium-sized dog from Hungary, the Puli (plural, Pulik has a history as a sheepherder going back more than a thousand years. His heavy coat, composed of a thick under and harsh outer coat, was normally allowed to become matted and corded although today, this heavy protection is no longer required for his duties.

you will be bothered with visitors. She should certainly be confined to the house and yard (preferably in a wired-in run inside the yard, well away from the gates), by the time the second stage is reached. If you have to take her out, make sure she is on a leash *all the time,* and carry her to the car, or at least five hundred yards from the house, before you let her feet touch the ground.

In the city, or in those suburban areas which require all dogs to be leashed, these elaborate precautions are not really necessary. There are cloth and rubber contraptions available which can be worn by the bitch to prevent staining the rug. Ask your pet department about them.

There are also pills and sprays available which mask the odor that attracts the males.

If you are going to mate her during the current season it is best

Rhodesian Ridgeback

A large, powerful breed, created by a blend of the Bloodhound and native African breeds. While Bloodhounds are gentle creatures, many of whom hardly know that teeth are made to bite with, in disposition the Ridgeback has much of the sharpness of the African dogs. He is more suitable for work as a guard dog, and in Africa he is used to hunt such big game as Lions. Height at the shoulder: male minimum 25 inches—female minimum 24 inches. Registered by the American Kennel Club in the "Hound" group.

R. W. TAUSKEY

Rottweiler

SALLY ANNE THOMPSON

This dog's ancestry goes back directly to those large, powerful, Mastiff-type dogs used by the Romans to guard the herds of cattle which accompanied their armies. Well-known in Europe as a police dog, guard dog, and a prominent contender in obedience competition, it is slowly becoming better known in the United States and deservedly so. Height at the shoulder: male 25 3/4 to 27 inches—female 21 3/4 to 25 3/4 inches. Registered by the American Kennel Club in the "Working Dog" group.

not to use any of the special anti-mate preparations that are now on the market.

As the color of the dischage grows lighter, the bitch gets more ready for breeding. The best time is usually anywhere from ten to fifteen days after the first show of color. Many breeders mate their bitches on the tenth or eleventh day, sometimes again two days afterward, but this second mating is not absolutely necessary.

There's a glucose fertility test utilizing "Tes-Tape" which is available at drug stores. A piece is inserted into the vagina, and if it turns bright green quickly, the bitch should be mated 24 hours later.

A bitch being mated for the first time may not show clearly by her behavior that she is ready for mating, but an experienced female usually indicates the best time quite clearly. Most bitches, even first timers, will flirt with a dog during the first ten days of the colored discharge, but whereas an experienced girl will co-operate during her ready period, a "maiden" may suddenly turn frightened, nervous, and a little snappy at the male's approaches as he ceases to flirt and wants to get down to business.

A maiden should always have her owner with her during her first mating (provided the owner is not a fusser) as this can make things easier and more reassuring. It isn't really kind to ship her off to strange people and different surroundings. It may scare her, and a bad experience could affect her behavior and at another time make her difficult to mate.

The last stage of the season is when the bitch is "going off" — when the discharge gradually stops and the vulva swelling goes down — this is usually the last few days, up to a week, of the heat period, which in all lasts approximately twenty days or three weeks. However, it can last 28 days, so don't relax your vigilance too soon!

Again, the timing of these stages, and indeed of the whole season, varies slightly from breed to breed and from animal to animal. Some females have very short heats and are ready by the sixth or seventh day of the colored discharge. Others drag it out until as late as the seventeenth or eighteenth day, but neither of these are typical.

Before being bred, the bitch should be treated for worms. This is not safe to do later when the pregnancy is advanced. She should also have been prepared for her breeding time by being kept in the pink of condition, not too fat or too thin, but really fit and healthy.

The Who

Of course, before the bitch can be bred, you have to find a dog to mate her to! This is not as simple as it sounds.

Just any dog of the same breed will not do. No dog, however big a winner, is a perfect specimen; there will be some faults from the show bench point of view. The ideal is to find a dog who is strong in those points in which the female is weak. For instance, if she has too long a nose for perfect beauty, she should be mated to a dog with a nose of perfect length, provided, of course, he is good and typical of his breed in other respects. There is no point in compensating for one fault and introducing another — perhaps more serious — one.

The way *not* to choose a dog is: a] using the dog down the road because he is nearest, or b] using the dog that is the current big winner, or has the most wins to his credit, just because he is the big winner. Neither may be right for your female.

Where, then, to find the right dog for your bitch?

You could do a round of shows, and study all the individual dogs. This could take a long time.

A quicker way, and a surer one, is to know something of the

Russian Laika

This is the common farm dog of northern Russia. An all purpose dog, he is used for bird hunting, tracking, as a beast of burden and as a herder. This breed made headlines when the Russians sent one around the world in a capsule. Height at the shoulder: 16 to 18 inches. Not registered by the A.K.C.

AKE WINTZELL

animals in the various bloodlines, especially those that appear in your bitch's pedigree. You may not have this knowledge, but there is one person who may well have it, and that is the breeder of your bitch. The first step, then, is to consult him or her for advice.

Dog breeding by pedigree is pretty complex, involving for any hope of success an understanding of genetics and an extensive knowledge of the faults and outstanding virtues of the animals in the pedigree of any given dog.

It is probable that your breeder will suggest what is called "crossing back" to the bloodline of one of the dogs in your bitch's pedigree if it is a line that is good in the points on which your

SALLY ANNE THOMPSON

St. Bernard

His name comes from the hospice of St. Bernard which was established to aid travelers who might encounter difficulties in the snow and ice of the Alps. The St. Bernard dog was trained to locate and assist lost wayfarers from which work he achieved a world-wide reputation. This is the heaviest breed of all, but docile and intelligent, he finds a place in many homes. Also known as the "Good Samaritan" dog and the "Avalanche" dog.

female is weak, for example, a line noted for its good nose!

This is not inbreeding and will not result in abnormalities, neurotic dogs and terrible temperaments!

Inbreeding is the breeding together of close relatives, father and daughter, mother and son, full brother and full sister, for several generations. It is a potent force. It fixes virtues, but it also fixes faults. So it must be done only with the finest, soundest animals available. In the hands of experts using animals whose background they know for many generations back, inbreeding can be effective. In the hands of the novice, with animals whose backgrounds they know nothing of, it can be disastrous. Better, then, simply to "cross back" into a line that is related and is good for the points you want to improve.

The extreme from inbreeding is outcrossing or outbreeding, using an animal completely unrelated. Not a good idea unless its advantages are going to compensate for the problems it introduces.

To put it scientifically, when you breed completely away from your bitch's bloodline, you will be introducing a completely new genetic pattern, which may cause a real mix-up of faults and virtues in your pups, or introduce something completely new that you didn't have before. It may take several generations to sort it all out again.

The only real reason for outcrossing is when the line is getting too many faults fixed, or producing too many untypical of the breed. Then the best and most fault free dogs of the line are aften "outcrossed" to a really strong inbred line to correct the faults that have been creeping in. Again, this is a method for the expert who knows his breed well enough to experiment.

There are some faults that one should never overlook. Never, ever breed from an animal with a bad temperament — nervous or completely neurotic, or really vicious.

There are other faults, physical in origin, that in extreme cases can cause crippling abnormalities — hip dysplasia, progressive retinal atrophy, slipping patellas, and many more. Some breeds of dogs are more affected by these than others. Any animal suffering from them should not be bred either, because it is *suspected* that a predisposition to some of these abnormalities may be hereditary, passed on genetically from parents to offspring. That is one of the reasons why it is always wise to buy breeding stock from a really reputable source, not just casually or on impulse. And it is another reason for having a veterinarian give any animals you intend to

Saluki

Mohammedans consider dogs to be unclean. The sole exception is the Saluki. This noble and ancient breed of gaze, or sight, hound is the only dog permitted entrance into the tent of the Arab. Height at the shoulder: male 23 to 28 inches—female may be considerably smaller.

breed a really thorough examination.

Genes and All That

There's an old country truism that you can't make a silk purse out of a sow's ear. This applies to dogs too — you can't breed a champion from poor quality or untypical animals. And all breeders of livestock will vouch for the fact that the silk purse animal will often produce less than silk — sometimes surprisingly so!

The sudden appearance of the unexpected in a litter of puppies a light eyed puppy born to parents both having dark eyes; an overshot mouth when the parents are both level mouthed — these shocks are not so surprising to the breeder who understands something of the law of genetics.

All that has gone before, all the breeding practices of inbreeding and outcrossing, are the methods of using genetics, the science of heredity.

Even if you know nothing of this science, but choose a mate for your female with care, so as to counter her faults — in other words, practicing selective breeding — you are applying genetics.

191

Samoyed
Sturdy is the best word to describe this smiling dog from the far north — sturdy in body, sturdy in habits, sturdy in disposition. Happy go lucky, at home in all climates, to know him is to love him. Height at the shoulder: male 21 to 23 1/2 inches—female 19 to 21 inches. Registered by the American Kennel Club in the "Working Dog" group.

The laws of heredity operate whether we are conscious of them or not. If the breeder knows something about these laws, he can make them work for him to improve his breeding stock, helping towards bettering color, coat, conformation, temperament, length of muzzle, eye color, length of leg — every characteristic, in fact, that makes up the individuality of any given breed of dog.

Genetics is the scientific study of the laws and principles of heredity. It is a relatively young science. Of course, man has always been intrigued to notice that blond parents usually have blond children; or that the offspring of two dogs with strong herding instincts are good sheepdogs too. In improving his domestic animals, man has made use of the fact that these things happen, and in his ingenuity has put forward all sorts of reasons how and why this should be. Mainly, these reasons were only inspired guesses.

Schnauzer (Giant)
The largest of the three varieties of Schnauzer, the Giant is an impressive looking dog. Evolved in Germany from the smaller Standard Schnauzer, probably through crosses with such dogs as the Bouvier des Flandres, the Giant was developed for working cattle and as a guard. In Germany he has made a distinguished record as a police dog.

The real "break-through," the beginnings of the answer to those questions, how? and why?, came only a little over a hundred years ago when an Austrian Monk, Gregor Mendel, published the results of some studies he had made, although it was not until the end of the 19th century that the significance and importance of Mendel's discoveries was realized.

By using controlled breeding and recording the results, Mendel discovered that physical characteristics were inherited mathematically and precisely, according to particular pattern. This pattern of inheritance applies to all living things, plants as well as animals and human beings.

Each different characteristic is carried by a certain chemical factor; these chemical factors exist in pairs, and one half of each pair is inherited from each parent. So the possession by an individual of a certain characteristic is dependent on the presence of a pair of these related chemical factors. The chemical factors were later called genes — thus, the name of the study of genes and their inheritance is genetics.

The genes from each parent come together in the fertilized egg, and with their interaction the characteristics and qualities of the new living thing are decided. The genes can regroup and recombine into a multitude of patterns.

Mendel experimented by breeding garden peas. He crossed tall peas with dwarf ones, red flowered with white flowered, round and wrinkled seeds, green and yellow seeds. He discovered that in the first generation after the crossing of, for instance, red flowered peas with white flowered, he got only red flowers. Then he crossed all this generation together, and got some red and some white; the proportions were calculated on the average at 75 % red and 25 % white. So that despite the fact that in his first generation all the flowers were red, when bred together they could produce white flowers. The white appeared to have skipped a generation.

Mendel further experimented with this second generation of pea flowers. He discovered that some of the red flowers (25 %) produced only red flowers. Others of the red flowers produced red and white flowers; and that white flowers produced only white. The ratio was 1 pure breeding (homozygous) for red; 2 hybrid (heterozygous i.e., breeding either color); 1 pure breeding (homozygous) for white.

Even though Mendel's first generation from his purebred red and white peas, all had red flowers, the white had not disappeared; the

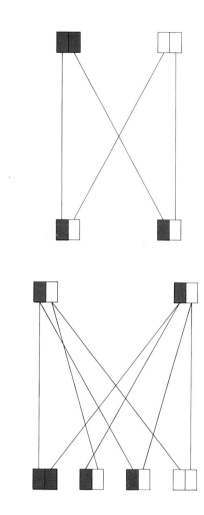

Figure 1.

Figure 2.

color genes, in fact, were distributed as shown in Figure 1. From this it can be seen that as the flowers showed red, the red color *dominated* the white.

So some genes are *dominant*, and some, like the white in Mendel's peas, are *recessive*.

With the next generation, when these hybrid or mixed were crossed, the pattern of dominant and recessive genes became even more interesting (see Figure 2).

The important point from the breeder's point of view is that of the proportion of those showing red, only one in three is pure breeding for red, the recessive white being masked in the others. The white can only be purebred for white.

Thus the heterozygotes or hybrids must always produce further hybrids in their turn.

When these rules of inheritance and the pattern of dominant-recessive genes are applied to dogs, the same pattern emerges, and this is how — slowly if left to nature, but more rapidly if the principles are selectively applied by the breeder — certain characteristics, physical and temperamental, can be emphasized.

Of course, the genetic makeup of the dog is far more complex than Mendel's pea experiments — for instance, in the more complex structure of the advanced animals — the dog among them — many genes are linked together in particular patterns and are inherited only in those patterns. Some genes are sex linked, carried only by male or female the disease hemophilia, in which only males are affected, but which is carried by females, is the classic example of a sex linked recessive. Environments, basic changes called mutations, and many other factors complicate matters further.

But this summary of the elementary basics of the principles of inheritance must show that a knowledge of genetics can be a powerful weapon for the dog breeder who is determined to improve the quality of his dogs. It can help to detect and get rid of hereditary faults, to introduce good points and fix them. Properly used, genetics combined with the traditional breeding techniques — (selection, crossing and inbreeding, plus the natural "eye" for a good dog) — can help the breeder more quickly towards what should be every dog breeder's aim — to produce stock which breeds more and more "true" to good and correct type. A study of genetics, even only the elementary facts, is never time wasted, and at more advanced levels it is fascinating.

Schnauzer (Miniature)
A smart and sturdy little dog whose popularity, particularly in the United States, is growing by leaps and bounds. Originally developed in Germany as a utility dog, he has lost none of his spirit, but with it all he has a sweetness of disposition and devotion to his family which has few equals. Height at the shoulder: 12 to 14 inches.

XI   Care of the New Family

Preparing for the Happy Event

The bitch carries her puppies for about nine weeks — usually between 60 and 65 days. During this period of gestation, as it is called, she needs care, a good diet, and no fussing.

There will not, usually, be any obvious signs of pregnancy for the first five or six weeks. The first indication, as a rule, is a little corpulence or breadth in the flanks. This may be spotted in the leaner breeds, or if the litter is to be large, about the fourth week, but normally not until the fifth or sixth week, even later, perhaps, if there aren't going to be many puppies.

The observant owner may notice some differences in behavior — a normally lively dog may become a little quieter, more *matronly* in her manner. There may be an increase in appetite, but not always. In fact, sometimes she may become finicky about her food! All one can say is that an alteration in behavior could be a sign of pregnancy.

Sometimes a skilled veterinarian, by gently feeling, can tell if she is "in pup" at from three to five weeks. He can be more sure during the last couple of weeks when the uterus drops lower in the abdomen. But he can never tell you for sure how many puppies there will be. Neither the owner, nor anyone except an expert, should attempt to make any examination which would be painful or uncomfortable to the mother.

There are two other signs of possible pregnancy. One is an enlargement of the teats in the later stages, and the other, most exciting and certain, during the last week or ten days before they are due the pups can sometimes be seen moving about if you are able to catch the expectant mother lying stretched out relaxed on her side. However, whether sure or not, a bitch that has been mated should be treated as if she were expectant, and given all the necessary care.

After the actual mating, she should be kept apart, away from other dogs until her heat is completely over. Then she can resume her normal life — with certain exceptions.

She should not be fussed over or treated as if she were sick. She isn't. What is happening to her is perfectly natural. However, she will need extra care. Watch her diet. At first she will not need a greater quantity of food, but her diet should be well-balanced and adequate in all the things she needs for her own strength and to

Scottish Deerhound
The royal dog of Scotland was described by Sir Walter Scott as "the most perfect creature of heaven." The Scottish Deerhound enjoys, and in fact only thrives, when he has human companionship. Height at the shoulder: male 30 to 32 inches or more—female 28 inches and up. Registered by the American Kennel Club in the "Hound" group.

Scottish Terrier
Until about a hundred years ago, any of the short-legged, wire-coated terriers which went to ground after the fox was called a Scottish Terrier. In 1880, a Standard was drawn up to describe the breed very much as we know it today. This stocky and dignified little Scot it at ease everywhere, whether the field or the home.

pass on to the developing puppies. She will require sufficient amounts of bone and body building foods, together with vitamins and minerals, to keep up her own health, and to virtually bring into existence new creatures — the puppies have no other way of receiving nourishment except through their mother.

She should have meat, egg yolk, fish and liver in plenty, as well as a good whole wheat cereal, and milk, and the additional supplements of vitamins A and D, some extra bone forming material such as calcium, and a yeast preparation. Alternatively, a complete proprietary vitamin and mineral supplement can be given. It all sounds rather complex, and if you are not sure of what to feed, ask your veterinarian. He may recommend a complete commercial food which is less expensive.

The emphasis in the early weeks should be on quality, not quantity. In the middle weeks, the expectant mother's appetite will probably increase a little, but by the last couple of weeks she will be requiring more of the concentrated foods like meat, yolk of eggs (not the white, as this tends to destroy one of the B-complex vitamins) and milk. Probably by this time it is better to feed her two meals a day, because as she gets heavier she may find it difficult to cope with a large meal at one time, as the distention it will cause can be very uncomfortable.

The aim should be to give her the maximum nourishment in concentrated form. She should not be allowed to get too fat as this could cause difficulties while she is actually giving birth.

She should always have access to plenty of fresh drinking water, of course.

Exercise is very important for the expectant mother. She should be allowed plenty of freedom, and not permitted to become lazy and idle. In the later weeks, as she grows heavier, more gentle exercise will be in order, perhaps just short walks on a leash. Regularity is the key; this is what keeps the muscles toned and the circulation healthy, all of which will be of great help later.

When the Time Comes

As the expected time of arrival draws near, the owner will naturally be on the lookout for the first signs of the imminent birth. A few days beforehand a certain amount of restlessness may be noticed.

A few hours before, the expectant mother may refuse all food. This last may, in fact, be the first sign, particularly in a dog having her first litter. So, if suddenly, for no apparent reason and seemingly otherwise in perfect health, she refuses her food about the time the puppies are due, you can be almost certain she is ready.

Further confirmation is a slight drop in temperature. The temperature is taken with a rectal thermometer. Control the dog with the left forearm, holding up her tail in the left hand. Grease the thermometer with petroleum jelly, and insert gently, holding the dog steady. Normal dog temperature is $101.5°$ — a degree or so below this indicates that she is due.

AKE WINTZELL

Sealyham Terrier
Squarely built and low slung, this Englishman looks almost like a toy representation of a dog. And yet, this powerful fellow was bred to tackle the badger in his lair, an act requiring strength and courage. A quiet home companion who retains all his ancestral grit.

199

A week before this, the mother should have had a whelping box provided, and have been introduced to it. This can be a wooden box, with a floor raised an inch or two off the ground. It should be kept in a quiet place, in a warm room or at least have a mild infra-red lamp over it. A guard rail around the sides, fixed a few inches off the floor of the box, will protect the puppies from the mother's lying on, and crushing them.

The box itself should be big enough for her to lie comfortably and allow enough space for the puppies; and it can continue as a sleeping box until the little ones are old enough to leave their nest. With this in mind, a movable sliding front should be included.

The box can be lined with heavy paper or newspapers — these keep out drafts, and are easily removed and destroyed when soiled. Bulky blankets or rugs should not be used because the pups when tiny can be smothered in them as the mother scratches about to "make her bed."

Some breeders use a basket, or even a cardboard box, but the disadvantage with these is that some maternal minded females may chew and scratch them into bits. It depends how strong the "bed-making" instincts are!

Some breeders prefer a whelping bed that is saucer shaped. For the bitch kept in a kennel, fill the box two thirds full of some soft bedding material (not shavings), such as soft hay, straw, or dehydrated sugar cane, and form it into a saucer shape. This is the natural kind of bed. When the bitch whelps, the puppies lie in the bottom and stay together. When the mother lies down she steps around them and lies outside of the pile of pups with her teats in reach. Many find this preferable to a flat floor where puppies are often sprawled everywhere, some even behind the bitch when she lies down.

Warn the veterinarian of the expected date in advance. Not that you'll need his assistance necessarily, but it is easier for him, especially when called out in the middle of the night, if he knows something of what is happening, and knows the dog personally. If you keep in touch he'll be familiar with any problems that might arise. He may want to have a look at the bitch anyway a day or so before her puppies are due, just to check that all is well.

Of course, if you know of any particular breeding problems that have arisen in your dog's line, let your veterinarian know. Very tiny breeds or breeds with abnormally broad heads occasionally give

Shetland Sheepdog

In the stormy Shetland Islands, many domestic animals are bred to a small physical size, but retain an over-sized heart and intelligence. He is not, as he is sometimes called, a Miniature Collie, but a separate and distinct breed though with some of the same ancestry as his larger cousin. Height at the shoulder: 13 to 16 inches. Registered by the American Kennel Club in the "Working Dog" group.

trouble. Unless you are an experienced breeder you should never attempt to cope with the birth of these breeds without forewarning the veterinarian.

If the expected date comes and goes with no sign of birth, there is no need to worry for a day or two more, provided the dog is acting in a normal manner. However, if three or four days go by and her temperature is down a little, if she is restless and in obvious discomfort with no sign of any puppies arriving, then it is necessary to get veterinary advice. There just *may* be a problem. This is particularly important if it is the first litter the owner has ever attended.

Any delay longer than five days after the due date calls for expert advice.

Should You Be There?

Even the dog that has never had puppies before seems to know instinctively what to do when the time comes. But this doesn't mean that she should be left entirely alone. Better cancel that dinner date or trip to the country if it is obvious that the addition to the family is soon to arrive. Also anticipate a disturbed night if she starts telling you what is about to happen by fidgeting and whining late in the evening.

Not that you should bustle around and interfere. Misplaced agitation and fussing can only make her more uneasy. And if you really can't face it without worrying, better call in an expert!

However, a dog who is affectionate, and regards you as her greatest friend, will often welcome your presence — indeed, may even demand it. To be near her when she is having the puppies doesn't mean taking the box into your bedroom or living room. The writer well remembers once allowing a favorite dog to have the whelping box in a quiet corner of the bedroom. As each puppy was about to arrive the mother left her warm box, jumped up on to the bed and produced her wriggling offspring on the covers!

So better to put the expectant mother in a quiet room on her own. When it is obvious that birth is imminent, line up a comfortable chair for yourself, and once the puppies start to arrive, stay with her, quietly just keeping a watch. With the big breeds, who often have large litters, this may be too long a time, but at least visit her every half hour or so to see that all is well.

Only by devoting this attention — particularly with a dog having puppies for the first time — can the owner know that all is going well and that no problems are arising.

The mother-to-be will push and contract her muscles, strongly and regularly, until the pup is born, and then chew off the umbilical cord and lick and push the puppy roughly around the box to stimulate it. She should need no assistance, and seems to know what to do. Let her eat each placenta as it comes away. When the pup is lively enough and cleaned up it will nuzzle its way to a teat, and

Shih Tzu
One of four breeds from Tibet, this shaggy, vivacious, intelligent and attractive little fellow is highly valued as a pet and watchdog. Weight: 9 to 16 pounds. Not registered by the American Kennel Club. Registered by the Shih Tzu Club of America and the Kennel Club of England.

the mother will settle down quietly until the next pup announces its arrival. This is usually about half an hour afterwards.

If the dog is in obvious discomfort and is straining powerfully for an hour or more and nothing happens, then something may be wrong, and the veterinarian should be called. She should not be allowed to exhaust herself uselessly, or she and her unborn puppies may be lost unless she gets expert aid.

With large breeds and large litters, several puppies may be born, and then the mother will take a rest before delivering the remainder of the litter. This is quite normal. The mother's behavior will soon tell the owner whether all is going well.

While the puppies are being born the mother will not want to eat or drink very much, but she will probably welcome a little warm milk and glucose now and them, particularly if there are several puppies.

The owner can only guess from the bitch's behavior if the last pup has been born. She will probably settle down quietly with her new family and indicate quite clearly that she doesn't want you to bother her.

Should she be restless, and the pups all crying and whimpering, better get expert help, because she may be having trouble feeding them.

In any case, ask the veterinarian to stop in after you are sure the last of the pups has arrived, and have him check her over to be sure that everything has gone well.

The New Family

Now that the newcomers have been launched, the hard work begins — for mother and owner.

For the first two weeks of their lives, the puppies will do nothing but sleep and eat. The mother will be disinclined to leave her babies. She will settle in her box and spend her time, day and night, licking and nuzzling them, keeping them clean, well fed and contented.

She will probably not welcome visitors and it is better for her not to be pestered by strangers. Children should be told not to bother her, but just peep, under adult supervision.

Of course, she will have to be taken out to relieve herself, and it is well to sponge her down with a mild disinfectant solution before

SALLY ANNE THOMPSON

Siberian Husky
Outstanding in appearance, the Husky has, like most arctic sled dogs, a gentle and friendly nature. His dense coat is almost unique in that it is entirely free of body odor. In spite of this heavy coat, he can be kept in all climates. Height at the shoulder: male 21 to 23 1/2 inches—female 20 to 22 inches. Registered by the American Kennel Club in the "Working Dog" group.

Silky Terrier
This wee fellow from Australia is a cross between the Australian Terrier and the Yorkshire. Bred solely as a pet and companion, he retains his terrier spirit and fire while adding a sweetness of disposition which endears him to all. Height at the shoulder: 9 to 10 inches. Weight: 8 to 10 ponds. Registered by the American Kennel Club in the "Toy" group.

AKE WINTZELL

Skye Terrier
One of the oldest of the terriers of the British Isles, you can find traces of the Skye in the ancestry of most of the other native British breeds. His character is exemplified by the motto of the Skye Club of Scotland — "Wha daur meddle wi me".

putting her back with the puppies. This helps cut down the risk of infection. A bitch nursing puppies should never be taken out on the streets where other, perhaps unvaccinated, dogs can infect her.

All should be contentment in the nursery, and any puppy that persistently cries should be checked to see the reason why.

In colder weather, an infra-red lamp over the nest will keep things cozy; this is perhaps unnecessary with larger breeds, but the very small breeds, particularly the tiny toys, appreciate it. When the mother leaves them to go outside, it is amazing how the pups, their eyes as yet unopened, wriggle along on their bellies to the circle of warmth under the lamp, like so many baby chicks.

During the first week their dewclaws will have to be attended to — these are a no longer used claw high on the foot, a kind of thumb. If left on, they can cause trouble later on, either in the short-coated dog by catching in things and tearing, or in the long-coated dog growing unnoticed until they curve right around and imbed themselves into the dog's leg. It is better to trim them off, and the veterinarian will do this when the puppies are about a week old.

Tail docking, if called for by the breed Standard, is usually done at this time too.

Puppy nails should be checked regularly from now on. Trim them down occasionally with dog nail scissors because they grow quickly, and until the puppies are old enough to go outside on pavements, there is nothing in the nest to wear down the claws. Left to grow they get needle sharp, and scratch the mother as the pups clamber over her. Puppies can also scratch each other in play. The writer has seen more than one tiny puppy with a badly damaged eye caused by such a scratch. Trim the nails carefully, taking great care not to cut into the quick. Hold the puppy on the lamp, control its wriggly body with the left forearm, and hold the foot out with the left hand to cut.

The only other important event in the first weeks of the young lives is the opening of their eyes. This usually happens at ten days. It occurs gradually over two or three days, and it is best to keep the pups out of bright light, artificial or sunlight, for that time.

You come into the picture again when the puppies are from three to four weeks old. They'll crawling about the nest now, and it won't be long before they can get out of the box, so you should give them a wide space. It is quite a good idea to use a child's play pen, as a sort of raised run, with the nest box in one corner. The

Soft-Coated Wheaten Terrier

This breed has been known in Ireland for hundreds of years. Like his cousins, the Kerry Blue and the Irish Terrier, the Wheaten is active and alert, strong and eager. Height at the shoulder: 17 inches. Not registered by the American Kennel Club.

Springer Spaniel

The best known of the spaniels used for field work, the Springer will flush and retrieve on land or water. Medium-sized, active and alert, he makes a fine companion for a day outdoors. Like most English dogs, he has the good disposition so desirable in a house pet. Height at the shoulder: about 20 inches. Registered by the American Kennel Club in the "Sporting Dog" group.

Staffordshire Terrier

Developed in England from a cross between the Smooth-Coated Terrier and the old style Bulldog, he was used for many years as a pit fighter. Astoundingly powerful and agile for his size. Unless encouraged to do so, he avoids fights and is extremely trustworthy with the family.

play pen can have fine netting attached about 18 inches high all round, and its floor should be covered with newspaper. The bitch will still be cleaning up after her babies, but they will get accustomed to coming out of their bed to relieve themselves, and as you will be needing newspaper for their later housebreaking, it is a good idea to start getting them used to the feel of it under their feet.

At about three to four weeks of age you can also start thinking of another kind of training — teaching them to lap milk. As yet, this won't be counted as part of their feeding; it is simply a lesson in the way they'll be eating later on.

Give them warm milk, reinforced with egg yolk, or dried egg powder, and a little glucose or Karo syrup. You'll mix in one egg yolk and a cupful of light cream.

Put some of the mixture in a shallow saucer and, taking each pup in turn, push its head gently into the liquid. Some pups will take to it eagerly right away. Others will sputter and splat, but they will quickly learn how. You can, in a day or two, have them on this formula four times a day; it will start them on the road to weaning, and reduce the strain on the mother.

After about a week — gradually increasing the amounts up to about double — add a little pre-cooked baby cereal, and the milk and cereal meals will have become part of the regular puppy feeding.

At this stage, the mother should be spending a good bit of time away from her puppies, although some bitches are reluctant to do so. She will probably leave them in the morning, go in with them after the midday feeding and be out all afternoon until night.

At five to six weeks of age, you can start adding meat to the puppies' diet. The best kind is good fresh beef, scraped with a serrated edged knife so that it is like a puree, with no fiber or gristle. Commercially prepared strained baby beef is also good. About a teaspoonful daily for each pup is sufficient to start with. Tiny breeds, maybe even less. Or you can use a specially prepared puppy food.

Most puppies will eat this meat with great enthusiasm. Don't be surprised when the puppies are about three weeks old if you find the mother vomiting up her food, semi-digested, for the puppies. This is a perfectly normal thing; it is the way the female would wean the puppies if she had no human friend to help her. It is a sure sign that a milk diet is no longer sufficient. The thing to do at this stage is to feed the mother separately from the puppies, and not to let her in with them for a while after her meal.

As you begin to wean the puppies, and they rely less and less on their mother for nourishment, it is important to see that each gets his fair share of food. The only way to do this is to give it to them in individual dishes (if there are only a few puppies); or at most two to a dish when the litter is big. Stay with them to see that the greedier pups don't gobble up all their rations and then push the slower, less aggressive ones out.

Egg yolk may be given fairly frequently. It should be mixed with the milk and baby cereal, at the rate of one yolk to four puppies. If the eggs are cooked it is perfectly all right to include the egg white, which can be chopped up. Cooking destroys avidin, the substance which makes egg white partially indigestible.

After the puppies have been having scraped meat and egg yolk for a week or so, you can vary their diet with fish, which should always be cooked. By six weeks of age, the meat need not be scraped, but it can be finely minced. Along with the cereal feeds, a fine puppy meal can be substituted for the mushy baby cereals as the puppies grow older.

Puppies six weeks old should be having five meals a day, two of milk and cereal, two of meat or fish, and a little milk the last thing at night. A complete puppy food will suffice even if fed at every meal.

The idea is to feed them little and often, gradually increasing the amounts as they grow older and more active. The amounts, of course, will vary according to breed. A small toy breed will need far less food than a large one.

You will find the feeding charts in this book a useful guide to the amounts of food the different breeds need.

All young puppies should be given water to drink as well as milk. As I said, remember to regard milk as a food rather than a drink.

Puppies six weeks old can spend some time outdoors, provided the weather is mild, and particularly if there is sun. They should have some shade, if the weather is very hot and sunny. A little wooden puppy house, raised somewhat off the ground, but not so much that they cannot get in and out easily, is perfect. Ideally, it should be set in a wired run, partly concreted and partly grassed, and with a tree to provide some shade. The run not be very big for the smaller breeds.

In clement climes, pups even as young as six weeks could spend all day in this kind of run. If it isn't possible to have the puppies out, perhaps because the weather is very cold, wet or windy, they should have space to play where there is plenty of natural light and air.

Even at this age, the habits of cleanliness can be started. Relieving the bladder and bowel control is involuntary in the young puppy and will happen quite naturally after every meal. Exploit this habit by either putting them out, or onto a heap of sawdust or a sheet of newspaper after they have eaten.

The mother will not be having a lot to do with the puppies now. She will probably only spend the night with them, and she should have a bed which they cannot reach. By seven or eight weeks she will have little milk left for them. It is best to keep her away all the time now, and get her used to giving up maternity as an occupation.

By eight weeks the puppies can go to their new homes, although you may want to keep them for another couple of weeks. But don't keep them more than twelve weeks or you'll never want to part with them!

Since puppies should be fed several times a day until they are ten weeks old, do give the new owners full instructions and careful diet details of their present and future needs foodwise. The amount of food should be increased regularly. As we saw, a growing puppy needs more food for its weight than an adult dog. Again, the feeding charts will help you with this and with the kinds of food needed.

Remember that vitamin and mineral supplements are necessary for youngsters, to help with the development of bones and teeth. A little special vitamin concentrate in whatever form the puppies will take willingly — as "treats" or mixed in with their food — should be given regularly.

The right kind of feeding, clean surroundings, plenty of light and air, space to romp and play — for all puppies need the stimulus of playing together — and the opportunity to rest in between, these — with a lot of love — are the things that set puppies up, give them a sound and healthy beginning to their lives, and make you the proud breeder of plump, sleek, friendly pups that people will be delighted to take home with them.

Sussex Spaniel
A slow, steady, thorough field worker, this medium-sized, rich liver colored spaniel is an excellent gun dog. Refined and developed by a Mr. Fuller of Sussex. England, he was used for rough shooting in England. He is readily trainable and makes an excellent retriever. Height at the shoulder: 15 to 16 inches. Weight: 35 to 45 pounds.

EVELYN SHAFER

XII Your Dog's Health

Your Friend, the Veterinarian

Any self-respecting dog owner has made the acquaintance of a "family vet." Dogs get ill just as people do. Healthy puppies need inoculations against dog diseases. Unexpected accidents happen.

The relationship between veterinarian and dog owner is a delicate one. It is built up over the years, and should be one in which the veterinarian knows and takes an interest in his patient (the dog). The dog likes and does not fear the vet, and you, the dog owner—the client — need to have confidence in your veterinarian and know the right times to call on him.

The relationship begins when you first buy your pup. Have the veterinarian look him over, checking that you did all the right things when you chose the pup, looking for bright eyes, a lively, healthy manner, a clean nose, a clear pestfree coat and scabfree skin, no signs of Diarrhea or stomach upsets. If you bought the pup in spite of one of these things because he was just the dog you wanted, now is the time for the vet to put things right.

Usually the first task for the veterinarian is to give the newly bought pup his inoculations against the dreaded dog diseases (if he has not already been inoculated). These shots are to immunize him against the most common dog diseases: Distemper, Hepatitis, and the Leptospirosis group, and perhaps, if the local laws, or the frequency of its occurrence demand it, against Rabies.

When you consider the investment in years of companionship and pleasure you have in your new pup, the cost of these things is little enough. In exchange for a few dollars you will be getting insurance against future heartbreak — and against heavy veterinary bills too, perhaps, should the dog contract one of these scourges.

Dogs do build up a certain amount of immunity against the local varieties of all these diseases (with the exception of Rabies), but still too many dogs suffer — yes, really suffer, from them, for during a virulent outbreak in the neighborhood it is the uninoculated animal that most easily succumbs and is frequently the one to die. With "shots" for every dog, these far too common ills could become almost things of the past.

Puppies are particularly susceptible, and it is among the young that the highest death rate occurs. They receive a certain amount of natural protection from their mothers, both before birth and during nursing. This protection lasts for about six weeks. But as they grow older they must build up their own immunity to disease, and normally this takes time. The inoculations give them that immunity immediately.

When you buy a new puppy you are taking it to a completely new environment, and exposing it to a variety of germs and viruses never encountered before, so the chances of any immunity at all are small, and the consequent risks even higher.

Best then to take your pup to the veterinarian as soon as you buy him, and get the youngster the protection he needs. The visit will also serve to introduce the doctor to his patient.

A friend is what the veterinarian should be and, for the dog's sake, it is a friendship not to be abused. You will expect your veterinarian to cure your dog of his ills, to spare his suffering when he is in pain, to ease his discomfort, and to be there, quickly, when an emergency arises.

In his turn, your veterinarian will expect you to keep a level head,

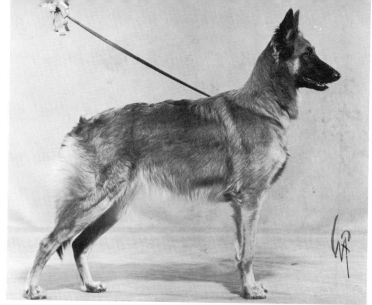

Tervuren

This fine Belgian sheepherding dog was registered together with the Groenendael, but since 1959 it has been registered in the United States as a separate breed. A fine working dog with a steady disposition, the Tervuren does especially well in obedience and police work. Height at the shoulder: male 24 to 26 inches—female 22 to 24 inches. Registered by the American Kennel Club in the "Working Dog" group.

to be able to spot the symptoms that could be dangerous, and not to fuss unnecessarily.

It will help the veterinarian if you know something of the obvious symptoms that might mean serious illness. If you can take the dog's temperature and know the normal (which is 101.5° — a bit above human temperature), you will be able to tell him the pattern of the fluctuation in the dog's temperature over the past day or so.

It helps, too, if you can quickly spot any divergence from normal in the behavior or appearance of your dog, and can describe it in detail. Your veterinarian would rather be called in for a slight illness early, and cure it quickly and easily, than be called in late for a serious illness because you didn't want to bother him. Then he might have a hard job to save an ailing, suffering animal.

Never ignore any divergence from the normal, such as frequent vomiting, Diarrhea or other gastric disturbance, refusal to eat, coughing, mucousy nose and/or eyes, which persist for more than twelve hours, or recur with alarming frequency over a few hours.

A combination of all these things, any violent symptoms, or racking vomiting should be dealt with immediately. A fever indicated by a raised temperature should also be the signal to get in touch with your veterinarian quickly.

For instance, if a dog that normally eats well refuses a meal at his regular time, it may be something very minor — he's had too many tidbits, or found a store of kibbles. If he refuses again later in the day, and looks listless and miserable, all may not be well. If, in addition, he has a raised temperature, or other symptoms, something is certainly wrong.

Your common sense and the background knowledge in this book should then tell you whether to assume that it is a case of poisoning and take emergency action because there isn't even time to rush round to the veterinarian, whether you should put out an urgent call for professional help, or whether you can wait for the veterinarian's next visiting hours.

It is wise, incidentally, to ask your veterinarian if he likes an obviously sick dog to visit him; some vets prefer to make a house call on infectious patients. This is particularly so with sick puppies.

Many dog illnesses have similar symptoms, which is one reason that the veterinarian, with his training, is the best person to diagnose and prescribe.

Coughing may be due to Asthma, a respiratory infection, a sore throat, Tonsilitis, Pneumonia, or Heartworm; if it is a dry cough it could be Distemper; a gagging cough could be a symptom of Kennel Cough, or fluff or grass in the throat.

A mucousy nose can be associated with Distemper, Pneumonia, Housedog Disease, a nasal infection or tumor. Running eyes occur in cases of worm infestation and in Distemper. So does Diarrhea.

Loss of appetite may indicate many ailments, from eating sticks and stones, Distemper, worm infestation, or one of the Leptospirosis diseases, or merely an upset stomach. Violent head shaking can be because of ear canker or mites, lice around the head and ears, an injury from a fight, or an abscess in the ear.

And so on. . . the list is endless.

Diarrhea

Diarrhea is one of the problems most frequently met with in a dog. It

213

Tibetan Spaniel
Long preserved from foreigners by the Tibetan monks, a few of these spritely and alert companion dogs are now being bred in England and America. Somewhat similar to the Lhasa Apso, but as we can see by this picture, not as exaggerated in form or coat. Not registered by the American Kennel Club. Registered by the Indian Kennel Club.

AKE WINTZELL

means the frequent passing of loose and watery feces, and is due to the intestines becoming irritated. This can be caused by viral infection, poisons, worms, coccidiosis, unsuitable foods, or even a sudden change of diet or environment. It is a symptom rather than a disease in itself. Puppies normally have frequent bowel movements, often as many as six or seven a day. These are not always fully formed, particularly when the puppy has been very active, but they should not be watery.

When young puppies are affected, obviously it is best to call in the veterinarian. Apart from anything else it is very debilitating, and

AKE WINTZELL

Tibetan Terrier
The only thing "terrier" about this dog is its name. He is really a sheepherding dog, of a small size suitable for very rugged country. Agile and responsive to training. Height at the shoulder: male 14 to 16 inches—female somewhat smaller. Not registered by the American Kennel Club. Registered by the Indian Kennel Club.

214

puppies need to make constant and regular progress if they are to grow strong and resistant to disease.

An older dog, suffering from an isolated attack of Diarrhea, provided it is not too acute an attack, will probably respond to sensible treatment.

Mild Diarrhea can be treated with a kaolin preparation such as Kaopectate or milk of bismuth. Give a tablespoon every three to four hours for each 10 pounds of body weight. This both soothes the inflammation and absorbs any poisons. Also give frequent small drinks of glucose (glucose is dextrose in solution) and a pinch of salt dissolved in boiled water, to counteract the debilitating effects and dehydration that can occur. Lacking glucose, use Karo or pancake syrup diluted with warm water. Plenty of rest and warmth is

TOM CARAVAGLIA

Toy Fox Terrier

In point of numbers, this is probably the most popular small dog in America. Not much, if any, larger than a Chihuahua, his clean-limbed look, superior intelligence combined with neat and dainty ways insure his ready acceptance. A uniquely American breed, he has not yet received registration privileges from the American Kennel Club. Weight: not under 3 1/2 pounds nor over 7 pounds when fully matured. Registered by the United Kennel Club, Kalamazoo, Michigan.

called for. After 24 hours with little or no food, a bland, easily digested diet, such as meat and boiled rice (equal amounts of each), can be tried. However, a veterinarian should be called in if the trouble does not clear up within a few days with these simple treatments.

Constipation

The other extreme is Constipation, the difficult or infrequent passing of food residue. Dogs, digestively speaking, are basically simple creatures, and the stimulus is usually quite regular and natural. The bowel action is a result of the contraction of the intestinal muscles. These work best if they are in good tone from a regular amount of exercise and a well-balanced diet.

Constipation may occur during illness, when little food is eaten, or through regular underfeeding, through a diet which contains too little residue and "roughage," through lack of exercise — in other words, an unhealthy way of life. It may also occur if there has been a blockage of the bowel — quite common in youngsters, who seem to love to swallow the oddest things, such as stones, lumps of wood and plastic. Puppies can also suffer from this ailment if their diet does not contain enough whole meal, biscuit meal, fats and plenty of water.

It is surprising the number of people who forget that even quite small puppies need frequent access to clean drinking water as well as milk, although milk should be regarded as a food, not a drink.

Treatment of straightforward Constipation is simple. Check the most obvious causes; if there are signs of an obstruction — a bloated stomach, some pain and perhaps vomiting as well as constipation — call in the veterinarian. In other cases, revise the diet, give mineral oil (one teaspoon for 10 pounds of dog), and make sure there is plenty of opportunity for play and exercise.

Never expect a dog, young or old, to be shut in for long periods without the opportunity of getting out to relieve himself, particularly after meals. A well housebroken dog will often suffer agonies rather than disgrace itself indoors, and it doesn't take long for bad habits to be established — and usually, this is all that Constipation is.

No dog should be given strong purgatives on a regular basis — this can only worsen the trouble eventually. Long established cases of constipation become a job for the veterinarian.

Rabies

The most serious illnesses are those caused by a virus. This is because, as yet, we have no really effective medicines to attack the virus directly. We can and do immunize against many diseases of viral origin. However, once the disease has actually been contracted the basic treatment is supportive therapy. That is, it is designed to strengthen the dog until his own body's defenses can throw off the infection. The so-called "wonder drugs" (antibiotics) are not effective against most viruses. They do affect a few of the larger organisms like rickettsias. However, they are valuable in preventing secondary bacterial infections which frequently attack a dog when his body's defenses are weakened by a virus.

A virus is invisible under an ordinary microscope. It invades the cells of its host (unlike the other enemy group, bacteria) and grows and develops there. This makes its destruction by medication very difficult. A disease caused by a virus is infectious.

The oldest known viral disease is probably Rabies. The virus that causes Rabies affects the nervous system, grows along it and ultimately causes inflammation of the brain. It is the brain inflammation which is responsible for the symptoms and abnormal actions so often associated with the disease such as loss of appetite, morose and wild behavior, aimless running and biting, and trying to eat unusual items such as wood and carpeting.

The one symptom peculiar to Rabies is the paralysis of the throat which prevents the dog from satisfying his craving for water — it was this symptom, which in the past was mistakenly thought to be a fear of water, that gave the disease the old name of "hydrophobia."

Rabies can pass from animal to animal — foxes, bats, in fact all species of animals can suffer from it as well as dogs — and, of course, it can be transmitted to humans. The virus is usually present in the saliva, and when the animal bites another, the infection is introduced into the blood stream of the bitten animal or human. Obviously it is sensible to have every dog bite treated by a doctor, but in an area where Rabies is prevalent or when the dog has been behaving strangely, *it is essential.*

There is no need for the disease to be regarded with the fear and dread that it once was, because there are precautions — apart from the obvious ones of isolating any dog that is behaving in an odd manner — that can successfully be taken against it. Annual vaccination of dogs can give the dog an immunity, protect its human friends, and also be of service to the community by helping to keep the incidence of the disease down. Certainly in an area where Rabies is prevalent, any responsible dog owner should consider it a must.

Care and precautions can keep an area Rabies free — New York City is reputed to have been clear of Rabies since 1954. In Great Britain, where there is a quarantine on dogs entering the country, whether vaccinated or not, there hasn't been a case of Rabies for forty years.

SALLY ANNE THOMPSON

Viszla (Hungarian)
This Central European Pointer is noted for his precise, careful ranging and excellent scenting ability. Developed primarily as a bird dog, he has been used on rabbits and also as a water fowl retriever. He is also kept as a pet by those who appreciate his aristocratic bearing and manner. Height at the shoulder: about 23 1/2 inches. Registered by the American Kennel Club in the "Sporting Dog" group.

SALLY ANNE THOMPSON

Weimaraner
Originally bred to hunt such large and dangerous game as wildcats, wolves, mountain lions and bears, today the Weimaraner is best known for his work as a bird dog. He has a flashy style and sureness of manner that have earned him the sobriquet of the "Grey Ghost."

AKE WINTZELL

Welsh Corgi (Cardigan)

While the Pembroke has been known in England for about 900 years, the history of the Cardigan extends into prehistory, to about 1200 B.C. For almost 3,000 years he has served the farmer as a guard and companion, as well as a cattle driver. An excellent house companion and watchdog.

But, to be on the safe wide, we give below an emergency first-aid treatment recommended for *all* animal bites by the U.S. Public Health Service.

Rabies Treatment[*]

First-aid procedures are recommended in all Rabies exposures, but particularly when a delay is anticipated before competent medical treatment can be obtained. Fortunately many purported exposures to Rabies are dubious or consist of bruises, abrasions, lacerations, and other minor wounds. Wounds should be encouraged to bleed freely whenever practical. The effectiveness of simple first-aid procedures in guinea pigs suggests that similar procedures may be effective in man also. Marked sparing effect has resulted from the treatment of deep cutaneous wounds three hours after infection with approximately 1,000,000 LD_{50} of fixed Rabies virus by scrubbing and flushing the wound with cotton pledgets impregnated with warm tap water, 20 percent soap solution, 1 percent aqueous benzalkonium chloride, or Ivory Soap and water, both with and without the addition of topically applied rabies antiserum. Despite severe challenge as manif-

* Dean, Donald J. Local Wound Treatment of Animal Bites.
  In: Proceedings, National Rabies Symposium, 1966.

Welsh Corgi (Pembroke)

Well-known in England as the favorite dog of the royal family, the Corgi has an ancient and honorable tradition as a worker. "Corgi" comes from the Welsh word *cor*, which means dwarf, and *ci*, also spelled *gi*, which means dog. His small size notwithstanding, he is excellent at driving cattle.

Welsh Springer Spaniel

This is an extremely attractive red and white dog. An excellent worker in all sorts of terrain and in all sorts of weather. A convenient size, midway between the Cocker Spaniel and the English Springer Spaniel, he is thoughtful of children and a fine home companion. Height at the shoulder: 16 to 18 inches. Weight: 35 to 45 pounds.

Welsh Terrier

Somewhat less bumptious than most terriers, this Welshman lacks none of their traditional courage and energy. His good manners and ready trainability as well as his smart appearance, earn him high marks as a family dog.

ested by 90 percent mortality in the control animals, not more than two animals in each treated group died of Rabies; these differences between controls and treated groups are highly significant statistically. Trappers, laboratory workers, and others in high risk occupations should, in addition to being vaccinated prior to exposure, have ready access to first-aid supplies including 1 percent aqueous Zephiran and/or 20 percent soft soap solution. Wherever practical, hyperimmune serum or its gamma globulin preparation should be available for possible topical application.

Medical Treatment

Treatment by the physician should include thorough cleansing and debridement followed by thorough swabbing and irrigation of the wound with copious amounts of a 1 percent aqueous solution of benzalkonium chloride (Zephiran) or 20 percent soft soap solution. Such treatment has been shown to be effective by many workers. However, Zephiran should be used judiciously on or near delicate tissues. Other substances should not be used without adequate prior testing. Quaternary ammonia compounds, for example, are not equally effective in preventing Rabies. Adequate cleansing with benzalkonium chloride or soap is believed to be at least as effective and probably more so than fuming nitric acid in wounds that permit its application. Immediate suturing of the wound is not generally advised since it may contribute to the development of rabies. Antibiotics presently available do not affect rabies virus but may be helpful in preventing bacterial infection.

Distemper

Once upon a time "Distemper," another virulent disease, was the scourge of the dog owner. Breeders and kennel owners feared the onset of an epidemic, when they saw their valuable breeding stock suffer and die, and the survivors were often left with aftereffects. Distemper comes in varying forms. The classical type, called Carre's Disease, is no longer so frequently met. This is probably a case where preventative vaccination has had its effects. By conferring widespread immunity against the disease, the conditions in which the virus can flourish are reduced and so the virus is weakened.

Therefore, the absence of the disease in its worst form is due to the protective measures. Any lessening of the number of animals

West Highland White Terrier
At one time, he was considered
an all white version of the Cairn.
At other times, he has been
mistakenly called a "White Scottie." He is neither; this charming, spirited and attractive
little dog is a separate and distinct breed, welcome in any
home. Sprightly and vivacious
without being obtrusive.

AKE WINTZELL

protected by vaccines could reduce the general immunity and cause
the disease to recur in its most virulent form, or be replaced by a
variation of the virus.

Of course, several types of distemper are still common. The
symptoms are very much like many other infectious diseases in the
early stages, i.e., raised temperature, Diarrhea, vomiting, sore throat,
Tonsilitis, loss of appetite, running nose and eyes, coughing—all or
any of these symptoms might be present. If it is true Distemper
(Carre's Disease), in the later stages there may be hardening of the
pads of the feet, a dislike of light, Conjunctivitis and a temperature
that ranges up and down over a period of days. Death, or permanent
brain damage, can be the end result.

The most obvious defense against Distemper is vaccination, both
of puppies and of grown dogs. The veterinarian will usually suggest
the initial inoculation at ten weeks of age, with booster shots at
intervals in later years. The booster shots are particularly important
for dogs which travel around to different places with their owners —
to shows and trials or on vacations and visits.

Canine Hepatitis

Immunization can be provided against several other diseases too. One of them is another virus disease, sometimes giving symptoms similar to distemper. That is Canine Hepatitis, or inflammation of the liver.

One form is very acute, death coming very rapidly. Many a dog owner has unjustly accused his neighbor of poisoning his dog when the animal may well have died of Hepatitis. If the animal survives the first week, he will, with good nursing, recover. Obviously the grown dog has more hope than the susceptible puppy, and the inoculated dog more chance than the uninoculated. In some cases Hepatitis is very mild, and may go unnoticed. Jaundice usually occurs in the milder forms. One aftereffect of Hepatitis may be a blueing of one or both corneas. This is temporary, the translucency disappearing by itself in a few days.

The vaccine for Hepatitis can be combined with the one for Distemper in a single shot.

Leptospiral Diseases

At the same time, protection can be given against two of the more serious bacterial diseases. One, Leptospiral Jaundice, also occurs in other animals and in humans too, where it is known as Weils Disease. It is an acute infection of the liver with jaundicing and hemorrhaging of the body tissues. This disease is spread by rats, so rodents should be eliminated and dogs should also be kept away from garbage dumps and other areas which attract rats.

More common among city and town dogs than their country cousins is the other Leptospiral disease, *canicola fever*. This attacks the kidneys, and many elderly dogs with kidney ailments might well trace their troubles back to a mild attack of Canicola.

Canicola is transmitted by the urine of an infected dog, and lampposts, fire hydrants, and similar street objects attractive to the normal dog are probably a common source of infection.

As it is also transmissible to humans, it is obvious that habits of cleanliness around the home are essential. All the more reason for preventing the disease from ever occurring by having the appropriate inoculations. Today it is common for the veterinarian to give four inoculations in one — that is, to combine Distemper, Hepatitis, and the two forms of Leptospirosis.

Common Ailments

Just like people, dogs can get ill, sometimes with ailments that are fairly minor, at least to the older dog.

Many a dog, as if about to throw up, has had an attack of gagging coughing, the sniffles and a slightly raised temperature. He seems off-color for a few days and then appears perfectly recovered. This particular type of infection in caused by a very lively virus. In the more severe cases, the veterinarian will probably prescribe antibiotics, not to cure the virus but to prevent bacterial infections which start in virus weakened tissue.

Dogs can get sore throats and develop Tonsilitis. Sometimes this is a symptom of a more serious illness, sometimes it is an isolated occurrence. The latter is more usual in man made breeds where the heads are less "natural," such as Bulldogs, Bostons and Pugs. Antibiotics are the usual treatment.

Streptococcic infections are not uncommon. These usually affect the throat. The dog runs a high temperature, as high as 105° F., and because of an extremely sore and swollen throat he frequently cannot swallow food and is therefore disinclined to eat. These infections can pass from dog to dog rapidly. The veterinarian can quickly get them under control with sulfa drugs or penicillin.

Pneumonia is more serious, particularly as it usually follows another illness, attacking when the dog's resistance is at its lowest. However, it is not the danger that it used to be, if it is caught in time, thanks to the wonder drugs.

Pneumonia is an illness that needs good nursing; the dog should be kept warm. An old-fashioned treatment was the Pneumonia jacket; the dog was sewn into a warm blanket. This is still a good idea, enabling the dog to be kept in a cooler room more beneficial than an overheated, dried out atmosphere. Caught in time and treated well, the illness should be over in five or six days.

All these ailments are more easily borne by older, mature dogs. Greater care is obviously needed when the ailing animal is a puppy; even the slightest departure from the normal in the young should not be overlooked. Just as a child depends on his parents for help and comfort when he is sick, so does the dog, young or old, depend on his owner. He doesn't know why he feels so miserable and ill, he just knows he does. So if you nurse and care for a sick dog as you would a sick child, you won't go far wrong.

How to Give Medicines

In any illness, there are bound to be medicines prescribed for the dog. Some owners have difficulty in giving them, and dread, just as much as the dog does, the "twice daily" administration.

But remember that no liquid medicines should be given with food, unless they are palatable in themselves. Try to disguise a foul smelling medication in the dog's meat or milk and he will probably refuse to eat at all — and be highly suspicious of every meal for days after. Medicines which are not objectionable in themselves may be mixed with pancake syrup, but ask your veterinarian about this first.

It need not be a fight to get the stuff into the dog, provided you have the know-how. First you must be gently firm. If it will give you more confidence, get someone to assist until you get the knack of quickly and surely giving the dose.

Liquids are perhaps the most difficult to give for the inexperienced. The first two or three doses usually end up all over you, all over the dog, and all over the rug!

Here's the right way to do it: the dog's lips are usually fairly loose at the sides. You can make use of this. Hold the dog's mouth closed and his head up (or get someone else to do this for you). Then pull the lips out at the loose corner to form a pocket. Into this pour small amounts of the liquid from a bottle, allowing him to swallow each dose. Holding the head up, but not straight up, and stroking the throat will make it impossible for him not to swallow.

Giving pills or capsules is not so obviously easy, though with practice, it is no trouble either.

Place the palm of your hand flat on the top of the dog's head, press with thumb one side, fingers the other, where the jaws meet. The dog will open its mouth. Tip the mouth upward. Have the pill ready between index and middle finger of the other hand, and then push it as far back in the dog's throat as you can. Close the dog's jaws and hold them, keeping the head up. He will then swallow — and you can see the movement in the throat. It helps to gently stroke the throat to encourage the swallowing reaction.

Using the index and middle fingers to push in the pill is easier than using thumb and finger, because you can get the pill further down with less chance of the dog being able to spit it up.

Internal Parasites

Knowing how to administer pills and liquids is a help if you have to treat a case of worms.

Most dogs seem to get a crop of worms of some sort sometime during their lives. Generally an infestation starts with the dog or puppy swallowing the eggs of the worm. Some types of worm eggs are passed in a infected dog's feces. Other kinds need an intermediate host — the tapeworm, for instance, can only infect the dog via the flea or rabbit, which act as intermediate host for the eggs. So cleanliness and sanitary habits are obviously the first precaution against worms.

No dog with worms can thrive, even though older dogs seem to build up a resistance to them, so that their infection may not be a serious one; nevertheless they lack the full bloom of tiptop condition.

Puppies, with so much growing and building up to do, should never have their strength depleted by heavy infestations of worms. As a matter of course, whether there are obvious signs of worms or not, puppies should be checked for worms by the veterinarian at an early age.

Generally, the symptoms are a variable appetite, a bloated stomach — particularly after meals — intermittent Diarrhea, and slimy mucus in the feces. Dragging his rear end along the ground is not necessarily a sign of worms — it is more likely to indicate that the small glands in the dog's anus are impacted.

The most common type of worm is the *Roundworm;* certainly most dog owners are likely to meet this one first because it is very common in puppies. A bitch should be treated for this worm early in pregnancy, because she can infect the unborn puppies.

Even if the mother has been treated, however, the puppies could still have a mild infestation which should be corrected as a matter of routine. The veterinarian will probably prescribe a medication that contains a drug called piperazine. Unlike the old kinds of worming medicines, this does not require any special fasting or purging. It is safe enough to be given as early as three weeks of age. This early dosing is usually followed by another in about 11 or 12 days. The first treatment gets rid of adult worms; the second, which usually results in fewer actual worms, is to deal with those that were in the puppy's blood during the first worming.

In recent years, some ailments among young children have been traced to infectious conditions picked up from a certain type of roundworm in dogs and cats. Family dogs, especially puppies, make great playmates for young children, so it is even more important to be sure that your housedog is free of any worm infestation — and to keep him that way. One of the values of the drug piperazine is that it is effective against a wide range of roundworm types, including the type thought to lead to ailments in children.

The veterinarian is able to check whether the dog is harboring worms, and can prescribe the right treatment and dosage.

Less frequently found in puppies, but quite often in adult dogs, particularly farm and country dogs, is the *Tapeworm*. This is a long, flat, segmented worm. As the worm matures and grows, some segments break off and are passed out with the feces. These segments carry eggs.

However, the dog cannot be infected directly from Tapeworm segments. An intermediate host is needed, usually either the rabbit or the flea. It is by eating either infected rabbit meat, or swallowing fleas nibbled from his coat that the dog can become host to Tapeworms.

A certain sign of Tapeworm infestation is the segments that have been passed, seen either in the feces or sticking like dried grains of rice around the hair at the rear.

Easiest precaution is to keep the dog clear of fleas. Once you see that your dog is harboring a Tapeworm, best to get veterinarian advice on how to get rid of the parasite. The Tapeworm is possibly the most difficult to eradicate because of the head, which is hooked into the dog's intestine and must be eliminated — sometimes a tricky job.

Whipworms are more common in warmer parts of the country. They incubate in the soil, and mainly affect older puppies and dogs.

Hookworm can cause anemia which in a young animal can be very debilitating. They are tiny parasites which can burrow through the skin of the dog, and eventually attach themselves with small hooks to the intestine. Like Roundworm, they can be passed to the unborn puppy.

External Parasites

Dogs can also harbor parasites externally — fleas, lice, ticks, mites. There is no excuse for any of them, because mainly they arise from dirty, unsanitary conditions; and because there are modern treatments to eradicate them quickly and safely.

Never forget, though, that curing the dog is only half the battle; every effort should be made to prevent reinfestation.

Fleas are the commonest, irritating the dog and causing him to scratch and infect the skin. As we have seen, the flea is an intermediate host of the Tapeworm. The first places the flea makes for when he gets on to the dog are around the neck, ears, and the base of the tail. During the dog's regular grooming, keep an eye open for the telltale dirt the flea leaves behind — if you haven't already noticed any persistent scratching. All dogs scratch to some extent. However, flea infested dogs scratch and bite themselves constantly. Flea bites are more easily seen (they look like mosquito bites) on the stomach.

Obviously, frequent grooming, regular bathing in special insecticidal shampoo, or dusting witlh a good flea powder are the precautions as well as the cure. Don't forget to wash the dog's bedding and dust his quarters with flea powder regularly too. For a heavy infestation use a good dip.

The latest and simplest method of flea control is by the use of a new pesticide called Vapona. This can be purchased incorporated in a resin strip about ten inches long. It can be hung close to the dog, either in the house or in the kennel. Its fumes — completely unobjectionable to human noses — will kill all the fleas on the dog and in his bed or immediate environment.

The most effective flea control consists of using the 90 Day ™ dog collar. When worn around the dog's neck, the collar eliminates fleas anywhere on your pet for three full mounths. It also helps in the control of ticks.

Lice thrive in dirty conditions on unwashed, unbrushed dogs. They come in two kinds, biting and sucking. Both seriously debilitate young puppies, and make any dog unthrifty. Sucking lice live on the blood of their hosts and attach their eggs to the hairs. Biting lice eat skin scales.

Antiseptic baths are the usual treatment, but these kill only the lice not the eggs (nits), so they must be repeated at regular intervals until no more lice live long enough to lay eggs. Obviously, all this must be done under veterinary supervision, particularly with young puppies who will also need extra dietary supplements if they are badly infested.

Ticks are quite large — about half an inch long when mature — and, therefore, usually are easily spotted on short-coated dogs. On the long-coated dog which is not brushed and groomed as often as it should be, they can exist unnoticed for quite a while. Ticks attach themselves to the skin and feed on the blood. They are becoming more and more common. Country and farm dogs tend to host the American Dog Tick, but there is a type that is not unknown on city dogs, the Brown Wood Tick.

Ticks should never be pulled off, or the head may be left embedded and cause an infection. They can be treated individually by a drop or two of turpentine, which will usually make them drop off whole and they can then be picked up with tweezers and burned. Heavy infestations need more drastic treatment, and your veterinarian will prescribe a dust, rinse, dip or shampoo which will be effective.

Mites (obviously!) are tiny creatures. *Harvest mites* are little red insects hardly visible to the naked eye, and can be picked up in brush or grass, or growing crops. They cause great irritation, and can affect human too. They usually settle down in areas in which two skin surfaces rub. A favorite spot is between the toes, and the dog will chew and nibble frantically to rid itself of them. Many preparations used as a preventative against fleas also control these mites.

Mange, both of the skin and ear, is caused by mites. The skin parasites come in two forms: sarcoptic and follicular (or demodectic or red). Suspicious patches should be looked at by the veterinarian, especially slowly balding areas on the cheeks and front legs.

Constant shaking of the head and scratching at the ears may mean the dog has picked up the mite that burrows into ears and causes great irritation. Its presence can be seen by a crumbly brown discharge in the ear itself, and an affected ear gives off an unpleasant smell. It can be treated simply with special ear drops. You should never probe deep into the ear or try to scrape out the discharge; most modern remedies, as well as destroying the mites, aim to soften the unpleasant deposits so that they are shaken out quite naturally by the dog and then wipe out the ear flap very gently with cotton.

Whippet AKE WINTZELL

This delicate beauty, a Greyhound in miniature, is remarkably strong and outstandingly fast. For his size, he is the fastest domesticated animal known, having been clocked at speeds as high as 35 miles an hour. And yet his size and cleanliness alone would entitle him to a place in the home for, except when called on to give his all in a burst of speed, he is quiet in manner and gentle in deportment. Height at the shoulder: male approximately 19 to 22 inches—female approximately 18 to 21 inches. Registered by the American Kennel Club in the "Hound" group.

XIII   First Aid and Emergencies

There are occasions when you may have to do a veterinary job; in times of accident, prompt emergency treatment can often save a life or limb — if you know what you are doing.

It may be that there isn't time to get veterinary help. Perhaps you live many miles from your veterinarian, and the time taken in getting a poisoned or injured dog to him would be too long to save the dog's life. Perhaps some urgently undertaken measure will help and ease the dog until the veterinarian can get there.

Here, then, are some answers to the question, "What do I do?" in the event of accident or sudden illness in order to save the dog's life, or ease pain and suffering until the veterinarian can come to the dog's aid.

It is just what it says — *first* aid. It is not intended to replace the professional expert aid that only a veterinarian can give. So in every case, after even the most minor of accidents or mishaps, get the veterinarian to check the dog as soon as possible.

An injured dog is usually in pain; if you move him you will make its pain worse. A dog in pain is a frightened dog, he will lose all reason and may well bite if you attempt to touch him. Even your dearest companion, who has never hurt you in his life, may well go for you in his agony.

So make sure he is rendered harmless before you do anything else. To move a small dog, you may be able to drop a blanket over him and roll him gently into it, making sure his head is covered. Keeping him straight, holding him under the head and the hindquarters, you should then be able to get him to the veterinarian.

To deal with a larger dog, or if you have got to take emergency action with a small one, you will probably have to muzzle him to protect yourself from bites. You'll need a long strong piece of cloth or soft belting, even a necktie will do for small dogs. Make a loop in the middle, slip it over the nose quickly with the knot under the chin, and pull tightly; then take the ends up behind the ears and tie firmly at the back of the neck. Tied this way, it also gives you something to hold the dog with and control the animal.

If the dog is very large and quite out of its mind with fear you may not be able to get near enough to muzzle him. In that case you will have to try to lasso him with a rope, straddle him over the back and pull up around the neck while someone else ties the mouth.

The secret is to make the dog harmless right away before he realizes what is happening and gets enraged. Firm, unhesitating movements without too much noise and fuss will usually achieve this. Always remember that the dog cannot get his mouth round to bite you if you are behind and in control of his collar at the back of the head. Once the mouth tie is on, you can usually calm a dog down, although you may also have to tie the legs.

An injured dog, in fact, is best laid on his side with legs outstretched. If you have to move him, ease him on to a blanket, and then use the blanket as a stretcher, one person carrying each end.

The dog, if it has been injured in a road accident, or in a bad fall, may well be suffering from shock. He will seem hardly conscious, and unless moved will probably not feel any pain. The heartbeat and breathing are slow, perhaps hardly perceptible.

Shock should be treated at once, before anything else is done. The dog should be covered with a blanket and kept warm. A little sweetened coffee will act as a stimulant, if you can give it and the dog can swallow. Give half a cup to a dog of Beagle size; a cupful to a German Shepherd. Make a cup shape with the side of the lip and pour some in. Alcohol, despite what is commonly believed, is useless and even dangerous in shock cases.

If the dog appears uninjured otherwise, it is probably best to move him gently, keeping him as flat as possible, and get him to a veterinarian. Speediness in getting help is absolutely necessary if he doesn't appear to be gradually coming out of the state of shock.

Accidental Poisoning

It is surprising the number of dogs every year who get an accidental dose of some toxic substance or other. Or is it, when one considers the number of common household items that contain poison? Perhaps the real surprise is that there aren't even more dead dogs from poison.

Children can never resist touching, then tasting, anything bright, different, or looking like candy. Nor can dogs, especially puppies, to whom everything is chewable and edible. Unfortunately, unlike children, dogs cannot tell you which package or bottle they got the substance from.

It is important to know, because there are all kinds of poisons, some quick acting, some slower in their effect. If you know which poison, you know how to act and which antidote to give. Some cases of poisoning require immediate action, otherwise it will be too late; others can wait even the few minutes it will take to get to the veterinarian.

There is probably only one general, sound rule: empty the dog's stomach. In other words, make him vomit.

For this you need an emetic. Every home usually has an ordinary household item on hand that will serve for the first emergency treatment — particularly if you don't know exactly which poison the dog has ingested.

A good emetic is hydrogen peroxide, the ordinary 3% strength bought from the drug store. Mix it with an equal amount of water. For a medium sized dog (Springer Spaniel, Basset, Chow Chow) you will want about two ounces of the peroxide and water mixture to make the dog vomit within a minute or two.

It is safe to repeat the dose after five minutes if it isn't successful the first time. Peroxide, incidentally, is the antidote for phosphorous, a poison often found in rat baits.

If there is no hydrogen peroxide on your shelf, common table salt will do — one heaping teaspoonful in a third of a glass of water. Salt is the antidote for thallium, commonly used in insect and rodent poisons. Thallium is a slow poison, showing symptoms days after it has been consumed, when veterinary help will be needed.

When you buy insect killers, paints, sprays, cleaners — all the ordinary household and garden items we use every day — there are two things to do. First, take a good look at the label and see what is in the stuff. Second, keep it stored well out of harm's way on a shelf or in a closet where the dog (or children) can't get at it.

Should an accident occur, you'll have more of an idea just what poison the dog has ingested if you know exactly what is in the items you've been using. It might be a good idea, too, to know something of your neighbor's habits. If he has put down Warfarin against rats or mice, or sprayed his weeds with a potent weedkiller, it is just possible your dog might swallow some of it.

Poisons take different effects. Some act very quickly. Some are corrosive, burning the mouth, throat, gullet and stomach. These need urgent action with the right antidote. Other poisons act more slowly; you may not realize the dog has taken a poison until hours, or even days later, when odd symptoms develop.

Always suspect poisoning if a dog that moments before was full of life and play suddenly acts or looks strangely. The symptoms listed below may help you to identify the toxin. In any case, take emergency action to empty the dog's stomach, and then get him to the veterinarian — fast.

Alkaline Poisoning

Drain cleaner is an alkali. It is, obviously, easily "getable" by a dog when used for its intended purpose. A little can cause a lot of trouble. The dog that has taken it will drip and dribble, sometimes vomit and appear to be in pain. Antidote: several teaspoonsful of vinegar, or lemon juice, to neutralize the caustic effects of the alkali.

Acids

These have a corrosive effect on the internal organs, and even a little can cause intense pain for many weeks while the healing takes place. The dog will show signs of pain and nausea. Antidote: neutralize the acidic effects with bicarbonate of soda, or crushed plaster.

Radiator Antifreeze

This is a frequent source of poisoning. Dogs lick it from the pavements or garage floor where it has dripped from cars. It is ethylene glycol, which changes to oxalic acid in the stomach. Antidote: bicarbonate of soda dissolved in water, followed by a quick trip to the veterinarian.

Food Poisoning

This is common. Loving owners don't often feed their animals bad food, but dogs, ungrateful creatures that they sometimes are, seem to feel they have to investigate every garbage can and dump they come across. The organisms that develop in these decaying messes can kill, or at least make a dog very ill indeed. Fantastic weakness is usually the result, with trembling and prostration. The dog is limp, often quite unable to vomit. Antidote: an emetic, that is dilute hydrogen peroxide, followed by a teaspoonful of Epsom salts in a little water to empty the intestines.

Cyanide

This is a quick killer in sufficient doses. Your dog may be lucky enough to get just the small amount that is usually put into mole poisons. Digging for moles is quite normal behavior for a dog, particularly terriers, and if something interesting has been pushed in the mole's burrow and the dog spots it, it is quite natural for him to chew it. The dog with cyanide poisoning will act sick, in pain, and have trouble breathing. His gums and tongue will turn blue, and you will smell almond on his breath. Antidote: an emetic quickly, and then speedily to the veterinarian.

Warfarin

This kills rats and mice by causing internal bleeding. Very unpleasant. It isn't completely harmless to domestic animals; several doses of it would be needed to kill, but a little bit of the stuff will certainly make a dog ill. Antidote: there is none. Unless you have the most undog-like dog, best get rid of the rodents some other way.

Thallium

Another poison used a lot in clearing rodents and insects. Eating large amounts will eventually cause the dog to drool and vomit, suffer from pain and diarrhea. As mentioned before, it is slow acting, and is therefore extremely dangerous since the owner may not even realize the dog has consumed it. Antidote: table salt, but unless this is given soon after the poison has been taken, only the veterinarian can help.

Phosphorus

Another potent toxin used in rodent poisons; taken by a dog it causes excruciating pain and Diarrhea. It gives off a garlicky smell. The phosphorus gets into the bloodstream and causes internal damage. The dog is completely prostrated, goes into a coma and dies unless immediate treatment is given. Antidote: luckily, our old friend, the hydrogen peroxide emetic, is also the antidote for phosphorous poisoning. Many a dog has been saved because of this. However, speedy, urgent action is absolutely essential, or the dog will die.

Lead Poisoning

This is not so often caused these days by dogs chewing paint, because lead isn't used as frequently as it once was in paint. However, to be on the safe side, if the dog has been at a tin of paint, or chewing at painted wood or furniture, watch for any symptoms, however slight, such as abdominal pain, trembling, or general weakness. Antidote: an emetic, followed by Epsom salts, a teaspoonful dissolved in water.

Arsenic Poisoning

This may result from some paint eating, because arsenic is a pigment often used in paint. Many plant sprays contain arsenic, so do some of the products sold for killing ants and other pests. Severe pain, trembling, rapid breathing, fidgeting, eventual weakness and prostration are the symptoms. Antidote: the label on the bottle or packet will give the antidote, but if you are not sure what was taken, but suspect arsenic, give an emetic, followed by Epsom salts, and then a teaspoonful in water of sodium thiosulphate, which is photographer's "hypo." Pest killers also include other poisonous substances — copper, chlordane, sodium fluoride. Give the dog an emetic if he's just taken the poison. Get him to the veterinarian anyway, particularly if time has elapsed since the dog ate the poison.

Miscellaneous Poisons

DDT has no published antidote.

Mercury poisoning will respond to a dose of egg white and milk — about six egg whites to a cup of milk.

There are some plants and their leaves and their seeds, that are poison to dogs. Numbered among these are laurel and rhododendron leaves, some types of aconite, lupin and laburnum seeds. Somehow these things seem to have a strong attraction for dogs. Ingesting them makes the dog sick. The antidote is to make him sicker by giving him the peroxide emetic, then Epsom salts. Sedatives and sleeping pills are frequently eaten by dogs. If you find your dog very drowsy, or he comes home barely awake, it could be barbiturate poisoning. Antidote: peroxide emetic followed by a cup of black coffee. If this doesn't brighten him up a little, take him to the veterinarian.

Watch out for the behavior of dogs coming out of a period of doping — some dogs take a long time to throw off the effects. Certain drugs certainly lead to odd behavior. The dog as he arouses is only semi-conscious for a while, and seems to be without all reason for several hours. Once you are sure he is over the drowsy effects of the barbiturates, and his stomach is emptied of the poison, the only way to avoid getting a nasty and unexpected bite is to confine him in a quiet, semi-dark room and wait for him to come to his senses. If the stomach has been well cleared and has settled, it sometimes helps to give a light and nourishing meal.

"Careless" Accidents

Many, many mishaps are caused by the carelessness of the dog owner. Innumerable dogs every year get electrocuted not because they run into high tension cables, or anything dramatic like that, but simply because their owners left a radio, record player, toaster, any electrical appliance, with a trailing, live cord. Dogs love to chew at electric cords and wires. Somehow the shape is right, and they can just keep on chewing; it never ends.

The live wire can cause bad burns, or worse. If the dog should wet the floor when shocked he becomes a perfect conductor of electricity. And so do you if you touch dog or wire.

The first thing to do is to shut off the current at the switch which controls the wire; if there is no switch, use a dry wooden stick to remove the wire from the dog's mouth.

If the shocked dog's heart is beating, apply artificial respiration and you may save him. To do this, gently press down on the rib cage, then quickly release the pressure. Keep repeating this, stopping as soon as he starts to breathe normally. Then get him to the veterinarian. There may be burns to tend, around the mouth and tongue perhaps, and these will need veterinary attention.

All that is needed to prevent this kind of electrocution is a little thought — perhaps some rearranging of the family's habits. Take a good look round the house for electrical hazards. No dog should be shut up by himself in a room with trailing wires and cords. All wall switches should be turned off, and if possible, removable plugs should be pulled. Never leave a dog alone with any electrical appliance turned on, including electric fans, heaters, irons. Because they carry a heavier current, they are far more dangerous than a table lamp. Christmas time, with all the extra lights on creches and trees is a particularly hazardous time.

Wounds — Honorable and Otherwise

Cuts and bites don't seem to bother the dog as much as they would a human, unless they are very deep, or extensive. The most common cut met with is the cut pad. It is instantly noticed because the dog starts limping. It is difficult to heal (if big) because with every step the dog takes the cut opens up again. Bandage it and every self-respecting dog will have the bandage nibbled off in no time!

Check first that there is no thorn or chip of glass in the cut. Then, if the cut is minor, leave it to the dog to clean it. The dog's saliva seems to have some healing properties — at least for his own wounds. Keep an eye on it to see that it doesn't constantly open up and bleed and get infected, but otherwise, it should heal in a day or two.

A badly cut pad, however, will probably need more attention. The bleeding should be stopped with a pressure bandage. To do this, put a pad of cotton over the cut, bandage it tightly in place, keep it there and neaten the job with adhesive tape. Once the bleeding has stopped, get the dog to the veterinarian who will probably suture, or stitch, the cut. The task for the owner will then be to keep the bandage on and the stitches in while the dog tries to nibble both away! A pressure bandage should not be left unattended. Properly applied it retards circulation and, therefore, must be loosened once the bleeding stops—certainly within a few hours.

With cuts that are deep or difficult to get at, the veterinarian will probably want to give an injection of antitoxin to prevent tetanus (lockjaw) from developing. Be sure to tell him if the dog has had this shot before, and it is also a good idea to keep a note of the date when the shot was given, for future reference.

If the cut is on the leg or higher up the foot, and is bleeding profusely, you will probably need to apply a tourniquet *above* the cut to stop the loss of blood. Tie a bandage loosely over the cut—a handkerchief can be used in an emergency, or any clean manageable piece of fabric. The ends should be tied into a double knot. Push a stick under the knot and twist it until the blood stops flowing. It is important not to keep the tourniquet on for too long or the circulation will be affected. Release the pressure every ten minutes or so. When you've got the blood flow under control you can get the veterinarian to stitch the cut if necessary.

All the above treatments apply equally well to dog bites. The only thing with bites is that often the tears and wounds are jagged and ugly, and the antagonist's teeth may sink deeply. These deep bites can be a source of trouble with Lockjaw, particularly if a scab forms over the top, keeping the air out and allowing pus to develop underneath.

It is best to get bitten dogs, however minor the bite, to the veterinarian as soon as possible after emergency first aid, and the prior necessity of stopping any excessive blood loss. Apart from an injection against possible tetanus, the veterinarian may also feel it advisable to give an antibiotic.

Heat Stroke

Another common mishap due to thoughtlessness on the part of the owner is heat stroke. All too often, in the heat of summer, one sees dogs left in cars — and when the thermometer is soaring this is the last place they should be, even in the shade. Of course, it is possible for a dog to suffer from the effects of the heat anyway in a hot

Wire-Haired Pointing Griffon Originated in Holland and developed in France, where it is known as "Korthals Griffon," this powerful and sagacious pointer has a unique, wiry coat. A slow but thorough worker, he faces any type of cover boldly and will retrieve on land as well as water. His sturdy nature also fits him for use as a guard dog.

R. W. TAUSKEY

climate, or on a journey, perhaps, through the desert. If you know you are going on such a trip it is well to know what to do should the need arise.

The human being reduces his body temperature by sweating all over. The dog cannot do this. He keeps his temperature at normal in hot weather by evaporating moisture through the throat and tongue. Because at the point of evaporation the water temperature is low, the dog has, in effect, a built in thermostat.

Trouble comes when the amount of heat is too much for the dog's normal mechanism. He pants ineffectively and eventually collapses completely.

To help him you need to soak him in cold water and put him in a current of air to make the water evaporate. Remove him from the sun, and away from pockets of dead air. Get him either into the bathtub, or under the backyard hose, or simply keep pouring water over him. Then fan him vigorously near the air conditioner, with a portable fan, or if outdoors, with a wide piece of board which you can wave about to create a strong current of air.

If the dog collapses while you are travelling, you can use the air flow from the cowl ventilator, remembering to wet him first. Anyone living or staying for any length of time in a hot summer climate should always keep some emergency containers of water in the car.

Broken Bones

Most frequent is a broken leg, and before moving the dog it is best to splint the break. Any straight stick will do as a splint. Get the leg as straight as possible, and if it is a compound fracture, make sure that no point of bone has broken through the skin. Tie a strip of material round the lower leg and the splint below the break. Set the splint against the dog's straightened leg and tie it above the break also.

With other kinds of more serious fracture — pelvis, ribs, shoulder — it is best to leave the dog alone until you get the veterinarian's advice.

Danger! Porcupine

This animal is an increasing menace to dogs. Somehow dogs seem to feel they must attack them, and mostly the adversaries meet in the late afternoon or evening, in woodlands. Make no mistake, a porcupine is a mean beast to mix with.

Pliers are essential equipment for dealing with the situation should a dog tangle with a porcupine. When attacked, the animal will slap at its attacker with its heavy tail, depositing its short black quills wherever it strikes the dog. These tail quills do far more damage than the long white body quills. There isn't time to get back to town and to the veterinarian, so you must pull as many of the black quills as quickly as you can. The quills move inward with every movement the dog makes, and those around the ribs and body can cause death if they penetrate the vital parts of the dog's body.

After such an experience the dog will be frantic; he could even go into a state of shock. Tie him to a tree. If he's a big dog you may have to straddle his back to keep him under control. A stick across his mouth will force it open so that you can get at any quills in the mouth, tongue and throat.

Also among the first quills to be pulled should be those around the eyes, and around the body, over and under the ribs. You may find that those in a shallow layer of flesh, such as around the mouth or feet, are easier got out by pushing them right through and out the other side.

Every quill that you can see must eventually be pulled, and for the next few days, keep running your hand over the dog's body to find any more that are still traveling.

Jammed Up Mouths

It isn't unusual for dogs to get bits of bones, needles and pins, pieces of stick, and other things stuck in their mouths. You'll find it easier to get at whatever it is if you push a stick across the mouth to keep it open. Straddling the dog is usually the best way of controlling him if he's big. Extract the foreign object with pliers.

Fish Hooks

It is quite common for a dog to snatch at a fish hook. And the hook is easily removed if you know how. Cut it in the middle with the cutting pliers that most fishermen carry, and pull half from each side. Never try to pull the hook out the way it went in, or the barb will cause the dog agony.

Snake Bites

As when a poisonous snake bites a human, there is little one can do, particularly if the bite is far up the leg or on the body. A tourniquet on a low bite to keep the poison from spreading upwards may help to stave off the effects while you hurry to a veterinarian. Lancing and sucking out the poison might help. The latest treatment is to make a small oval cut over each fang mark. Cut in at least 1/4 inch and remove the little plug. Suck out the blood to remove the poison.

Drowning

Yes, it does happen sometimes. A dog may fall in water and knock himself unconscious on a submerged object. If there is a pulse (find it high on the inside of the thigh of the hindquarter) there is a good chance of saving him. Give artificial respiration; lay the dog on his side and pull the tongue out and try to drain out excess water; then press down on the chest and draw up rhythmically twenty times a minute. This should expel any water and get air into the lungs instead.

Bloat

This is a condition not uncommon in cattle, and seemingly on the increase among dogs, particularly the larger breeds. It is frightening and frequently fatal. It is caused by gas developing in the abdomen, and usually happens about five or six hours after a meal. The swelling is tremendous in a true case of bloat, and the pressures on the internal organs are immense.

Caught early, it may be possible to squeeze and prod the abdomen so that the dog belches and expels some of the gas. But, truly, this is a case where getting the dog to the veterinarian urgently is the only thing to do. In a dire emergency, dogs have been saved by their owner's puncturing the stomach wall with a sharpened hollow knitting needle to allow the gas to escape, and following this up with a couple of teaspoons of strong black coffee. But this drastic action should be taken only if veterinary help is unavailable.

It is presumed that some types of food may be responsible for bloat. Some veterinarians recommend feeding only very fine cereals, never anything lumpy. Other specialists say that wheat products can cause trouble, particularly if the wheat germ is included.

But research is still needed into this frightening condition. All that can be said is that some strains and some breeds seem to suffer more than others, so some hereditary element may be involved.

Conclusion

To repeat, many of these accidents and mishaps occur because of owner carelessness and thoughtlessness. One must remember that a dog is as vulnerable as a child when it comes to the day-to-day hazards of life — eating things he shouldn't — like needles, dangerous drugs and so on. He is ignorant of the power of electricity, and quite incapable of realizing that if he runs suddenly into the street an automobile or truck may knock him down and kill or maim him. But the dog has an added disadvantage over the child, he doesn't have the power of speech or of understanding. Realize this and take normal sensible precautions every day and you may save your dog much suffering — and you and your family much heartbreak.

Yorkshire Terrier
This spirited toy is not old as breeds go. Developed about 100 years ago as the dog of the people, he was skyrocketed in recent years to popularity. In spite of his size he is extremely spunky, neither asking nor giving quarter.

AKE WINTZELL

XIV   Does the Dog Think?

Sooner or later, the owner of a much loved dog will say, "He's so intelligent. He knows exactly what I'm saying to him."

On the surface, this is true — the dog shows a quick and complete understanding of his human friend, and seems to be really using his mind to think.

The dictionary defines intelligence as "intellect; quickness of understanding." Intellect is defined as the "faculty of knowing and reasoning." Looking at it through the eyes of a fond owner, you might say the dog is indeed intelligent, because it does things that the owner thinks are clever.

The dog knows when the master's footsteps are approaching, and wakes from his doze wagging his tail in eager greeting. He sees the family putting on their coats, and knows they are going out, and asks to go, too. He knows which is the cookie bin, and might even be able to open it. He knows that when a certain person comes to visit there are doggie treats to come, and he may even know which pocket they are kept in. So he makes his knowledge obvious in the real welcome he gives the visitor.

When you go down a certain street, the dog knows that at the end of it there's a run in the park; let off the leash he'd probably find his own way there. He also knows that a certain door probably leads to the veterinarian's clinic — and he may not be so eager to go there.

Some dogs can do quite complicated tricks, like dropping a ball into the right one of a series of holes, to release some food.

A very maternally minded female dog the writer once owned housebroke her own puppies. All canine mothers teach their puppies from the start not to dirty their bed. This particular mother carried the process a stage further. As the puppies began to walk around, she would insist they go outside into the yard whenever she did. Every evening, when she was put out for the last time before settling down for the night, she would fidget and whimper, and run back to the puppies, trying to shepherd them to the doorway, too. Until she was allowed to take them with her, she wouldn't go out herself, and if pushed out without them she would scratch and whimper at the door.

A certain toy spaniel could turn on an electric heater, and the dogs that can open doors to get at what they want are legion.

A particular Farm Collie bitch, known to the writer, was the inseparable worker and companion of the farmer—except when his wife was near the birth of a child. Then, the Collie would never leave the woman's side, showing distinct signs of distress if taken away from her self-imposed vigilance, and at the first opportunity would slip off and make her way back to the house. As soon as the child was safely born, she would lose interest and return to her master and her duties.

Viewed by human standards, all these things seem to indicate intelligent, thoughtful behavior. Dogs are different from people, however, with a different kind of mind, and we must be careful not to compare their behavior with the human's, but to try to understand it from the dog's point of view.

Comparisons are difficult anyway, because the senses in the dog — sight, hearing, smell, touch — are, in general, more developed than they are in people, enabling the dog to get firsthand information denied to us.

The *senses* are the means by which the dog receives signals and information from the world around. In many respects, the dog's senses are *far* superior to man's. Most dogs have a far better sense of smell than the human being does. Any who has watched Obedience Trials will have seen how each dog can pick out from several objects one touched by his master and one touched by the judge. It needs to be only the merest touch, too, for the dog to be able to distinguish the object.

Many dogs have exceptional hearing; most can hear better than their human friends. A dog can hear higher tones than we can, and fainter sounds. A dog's hearing is at its most acute at 4,000 cycles per second, and he can hear at least up to 50,000 cycles, possibly more. The human equivalents are 2,000 and 20,000 cycles.

The eyesight of the dog and human are different in some ways. The type of dog that has eyes set on either side of his head can see above and behind to a certain extent without moving his head and eyes. Dogs with eyes frontally placed, have a "visual field" — how far around they can see — more like the limited human one. Most dogs, and particularly the sight hunting breeds like the Greyhound, have a highly developed sensitivity to movement. They can detect the slightest movement at remarkable distances, as much as 900 yards. Dogs do not have any color vision, but they can detect differences in brightness.

What the dog does in response to the stimuli received through his senses is known as his behavior. He receives the information through sight, sound, taste, smell, and feel, then interprets the messages, and responds accordingly. The response can be based on *automatic reflex*, on *instinct*, or on *learning*.

Reflexes and instinct are born in the animal, part of the hereditary pattern. Learning is acquired, and the dog's skill in his ability to learn depends on his previous personal experiences and how far he is able to use them to solve problems.

Most dogs learn rapidly and eagerly, and will even willingly learn to overcome many things, which, were they in the wild, would threaten their survival.

In obedience trials, the dog is required to lie quietly for several minutes in the open, surrounded by other dogs and strange people, while his owner goes out of sight and sound. This kind of behavior is something quite unnatural to the dog, and in the wild would be tantamount to committing suicide; but the dog can and will learn this and other tricks at the bidding of his human master.

One kind of behavior is a result of *automatic reflex* action. The dog puts his nose to an inviting looking object; it is prickly, or hot, or icy cold; his nose hurts; he withdraws it quickly. That is a reflex action. The stimulus for it was the pain the dog felt in his nose, the withdrawal of his nose is automatic, and he doesn't have to think about it. He just does it.

Possibly the dog will approach the same object another time. This time his behavior will probably be different. He'll extend his nose, but this time he won't put his nose right to the object, but will draw back before he touches it. This time his behavior is not reflex. Perhaps some faint smell, or something about the looks of the thing, has stimulated his brain; the stimuli have sparked his memory — he remembers his previous painful experience. He does not need to think. His reflexes cause him to withdraw from it. This is thoughtful behavior; he has *learned.*

Instinct governs much dog behavior, and is often confused with intelligence. Instinct is born in the animal; the dog reacts to a situation or happening without ever having to think about it or compare it with previous experience.

A female dog having puppies knows by instinct what to do, and most breeding and maternal behavior is governed by instinct. So are some of the special qualities of various breeds, such as herding in sheepdogs, chasing in sight hounds, and so on. These qualities are there and merely need encouraging by man to bring them to perfection. Possession of instinct is one of the basic needs for survival.`

A strong instinct in most animals, including the dog (and some people!) is flight when faced with danger. Another important instinct in the dog is the one connected with territory — dogs have a strong sense of territory and will guard their patch to the death if necessary. On this instinct the development of the guard and housedog is based. When living with people, the dog tends to regard his master's patch and belongings as the same as his own for defensive purposes.

Ethologists (students of animal behavior) tell us that many species of animals and birds stake out certain areas which they regard as their own territory. Among certain species this might be an individually possessed and defended piece of property, but social animals like the dog defend this territory as a pack member. Interestingly enough, there seems to be a psychological advantage to the defender operating on his own territory. We are all familiar with the small dog who fiercely barks at strangers approaching his gate, but cowers timidly when taken into a strange environment.

The "pack" instinct is another that has helped to put the dog where it is — into the human community. Dogs by instinct are pack animals (so are people!). They find security of mind and body when they live in numbers, according to a strict social code, with a leader or "pack boss," and everybody else in their allotted order of precedence. They fiercely resent intruders, and will usually accept only those who find their place in the social order quickly and without fuss.

The family dog doesn't need training to become a member of your family "pack," he does that by instinct. He recognizes the social order of the family unit, and accepts the pack boss (that's you!). The training you give him when he first comes to live with you is to teach him the rules of the pack (which may be different from canine rules), such as not relieving himself on the dining-room rug, attacking all your friends and callers, chewing and climbing all over the French antique sofa. These are the same rules you would, in your capacity as head of the family, teach the junior members of your household, or human pack.

Dogs, you see, are quite willing to regard members of species other than their own as part of the same pack. This includes not only humans, but other animals too.

Terrier Joe lived in a house in suburbia. The family had a couple of children, and the household also included a cat who did as he pleased, unbothered by anyone, including Joe. A family moved in next door, and they had a terrier, too—Spot. Joe and Spot, true to their instincts of territorial defense, paraded up and down the boundary line between their respective homes, making a great show, alert for any breaking of the rules on either part, and soon settled down to a mutual respected neighborly existence.

Until one day the cat decided to cross Spot's yard when he was taking the morning sun. Spot shot out of his doorway to drive off the intruder. Like a flash, Joe was through the fence and mixing it fiercely with his friend and neighbor, Spot.

Each dog was acting according to instinct; Spot was defending his property, and Joe, without thought of the consequent dangers, was defending his fellow pack member.

Some dogs are highly excitable, and some are placid in disposition. Some are very affectionate, while others get angry very easily. Sometimes extreme jealousy or other forms of neurotic behavior show up. This is the *temperament*, the emotional *behavior*, of the dog.

These qualities are passed on from parent to offspring — in other words, temperament is hereditary. These inherited qualities follow the basic laws of inheritance as outlined by Mendel just as do physical characteristics.

It is true that the conditions in which a dog lives and the treatment it receives, can affect its emotional behavior. A dog which is permanently chained up will develop viciousness through sheer frustration. But very often two dogs will respond quite differently to exactly the same kind of treatment and conditions. The key to temperament is in the hormones, in the glandular make-up of the individual—and this is the inherited factor. A dog may be the victim of his grandfather's hormones!

It is interesting that a particular pattern of temperament seems to be linked in particular breeds, and this may have some bearing on the special characteristics of each breed. Terriers, generally, and some of the sight hunting and shepherding dogs, are sensitive, emotional types, while the scent hounds and bull types appear to be more placidly disposed.

The basis of the dog's close ties with human beings is linked with temperament. There is in the dog an emotional dependence on its owner. Some dogs will refuse to eat when parted from their master, or indulge in other forms of highly emotional behavior which could be classed as neurotic.

The reason for the dog's need for close association with people has never been deeply analyzed. It is quite unique among animals, for although an occasional individual cat, monkey, or bird, which formed a really close attachment to a person has been noted, there is no other species in the same class as the dog. It is thought that it might be linked with the pack instinct, and yet other pack animals do not behave in the same way. The dog seems to satisfy a deep emotional need in its attachment to the human race. It could be that the feeling is mutual.

All this talk of hormones, reflexes, instincts, might seem to suggest that dog lovers for centuries have been mistaken in their contention that the dog has a good head on him, and that the canine species doesn't after all show any signs of real intelligent thought or reasoning ability.

Many scientific observers, who conduct carefully controlled experiments in animal behavior under laboratory conditions will maintain that on the results they get it appears that the dog doesn't think too deeply.

They will say that along with other animals, or rats, apes, monkeys, hamsters, and so on, the dog shows no more, nor any less intelligence, and that, in fact, apes and monkeys often show more.

On their results they may be right. But their experiments are carried out in conditions quite foreign to the everyday lives of the majority of dogs. Under controlled laboratory conditions, often using scientifically bred animals, there is little opportunity for a dog to develop the initiative and natural adaptability that it needs in the everyday world. The lab dog must lead a rather dull life.

The dog bred and reared in the wild has less of the unpredictability and illogicality of human society to contend with, too. It is the dog that lives close to people that seems to develop a greater ability to understand, to learn, and to adapt.

Even the scientists admit the outstanding learning ability of the dog. Every observant dog owner, and particularly anyone who has taken a dog into complex training routines, will endorse this. Most skills, even among people, are acquired by trial and error. In learning tricks and doing tests the dog tries at random until it hits on the right method to achieve its purpose, often failing when called on to try another time, but eventually it learns the right way and subsequently never makes a mistake.

Often, though, the individual dog will show distinct signs of initiative, as is seen in the carefully selected guide dogs used by the blind. Part of their training is aimed toward the use of their own judgment in situations unknown to their sightless owners. Once on the job there is no room for mistakes.

Going back to the bitch who housebroke her puppies — can this be put down exclusively to instinct? Could there not be a logical train of thought involved? Dogs like to please their human masters; their lives are the more secure and satisfactory when they do. A well-behaved dog knows from experience that displeasure and scolding is the result of housebreaking error. Perhaps this canine mother, combining her natural instincts to teach her puppies, put a little thought into her behavior, too.

We cannot tell for certain, because we cannot ask a dog *why* it does certain things and get an answer. The mutual understanding between our dog and ourselves must be limited because the dog does not have the power of human speech and is able to interpret only a few of the words we say to it.

An Englishman who acquired a dog from France was convinced that the animal was quite stupid—until he suddenly realized that the words of command to the dog had always been in a different language. It took some weeks for it to understand the completely new sounds and attach them to certain actions, but learn it eventually did.

One clue to the dog's intelligence is its marvelous powers of observation. A dog concentrating on its master reacts not only to the word of command, but also his tone of voice and often a tiny unconscious manner or action which precedes the actual command. For example, if you frown at your dog he cringes and if you smile he is happy. Dogs as a rule do neither, but your dog learned to recognize this strange behavior in his master and associates it properly with your state of mind.

One dog was advertised as a canine mathematical genius by his trainer. Given a simple arithmetical problem the dog would answer by barking the correct number of times. Intensive study convinced people that his master was completely honest and was not signalling the dog. However, continued study brought out the fact that when the master did not know the answer the dog, too, could not answer. Finally, when a screen was placed between the dog and his owner the dog lost all his problem solving ability.

From this it was simple to deduce what had been happening; the master waiting anxiously for the dog to answer was tense, this tension increasing as the dog's barks neared the number of the answer. As the dog gave the final correct bark, the master relaxed. The dog, by himself, had noticed this and used it as a key to pleasing his master. Perhaps this is not as astounding as a dog doing sums, but in my opinion it is every bit as clever.

Every dog in every succeeding generation has to learn for itself. There are no books it can read to fill in the gaps in its knowledge, or learn the quick way what progress its ancestors have already made. Nor can it write down useful hints and information to pass on to the dogs yet to be born.

Who can tell how far the intelligence of the dog could develop if it had the powers of communication that we humans have?